Oliver St John Gogarty

A POET AND HIS TIMES

'The only book I've stayed up
all night to read'
John Ford, film director

ULICK O'CONNOR was born in Dublin in 1929 and was educated at University College, Dublin, and Loyola University, New Orleans. He was called to the bar at the King's Inns, Dublin, in 1951. A biographer, poet and playwright, his work has achieved international acclaim. As a poet he is best known for his verse-plays in the Noh form and for *Poems of the Damned: A Translation of Baudelaire*. As a playwright, his plays have included *The Dark Lovers* (Jonathan Swift and Stella), *The Dream Box, Execution* and *A Trinity of Two* (Wilde and Edward Carson). He has acted his own one-man shows on Oliver Gogarty and Brendan Behan throughout Europe and America. In 1989, his one-man play on James Joyce, *Joyicity*, based on mime, music and words, was hailed as a success of the Dublin International Theatre Festival. O'Connor is the author of the definitive biography of his fellow Dubliner, Brendan Behan, of a highly acclaimed account of the Irish 'Troubles' 1912-1922, *The Troubles, Michael Collins and the Struggle for Irish Freedom 1912-1922*, and of *Biographies and the Art of Biography*. Alongside his prodigious literary achievements, he is also a distinguished athlete: he has played first-class rugby, was British University's welterweight boxing champion in 1950, and was Irish record holder in the pole vault. Ulick O'Connor lives in Dublin. His diaries are to be published by John Murray in spring 2001.

Oliver St John
GOGARTY

A POET AND HIS TIMES

Ulick O'Connor

THE O'BRIEN PRESS
DUBLIN

First published 1964 by Jonathan Cape Ltd.
Reprinted in 1981 by Granada Publishing Ltd.

This edition first published in 2000 by The O'Brien Press Ltd.
20 Victoria Road, Rathgar, Dublin 6, Ireland
Tel. +353 1 4923333; Fax. +353 1 4922777
email: books@obrien.ie
website: www.obrien.ie

ISBN: 0-86278-597-9

British Library Cataloguing-in-publication Data
O'Connor, Ulick, 1929-
Oliver St. John Gogarty
1.Gogarty, Oliver St. John, 1878-1957 - Biography 2.Dublin (Ireland) - Intellectual life -
20th century 3.Dublin (Ireland) - Social life and customs - 20th century
I.Title
821.9'12

1 2 3 4 5 6 7 8 9 10

00 01 02 03 04 05 06 07

The O'Brien Press receives
assistance from

The Arts Council
An Chomhairle Ealaíon

Layout and design: The O'Brien Press Ltd.
Colour separations: C&A Print Ltd.
Printing: MPG Books Ltd.

ACKNOWLEDGMENTS

The author's thanks are due to the following for permission to publish from copyright material in this book:

Oliver D. Gogarty, Senior Counsel: *Collected Poems; Tumbling in the Hay; As I Was Going Down Sackville Street; An Offering of Swans; It Isn't This Time of Year at All; Hyperthuleana; Blight; A Serious Thing; I Follow St Patrick;* 'Threnody on the Death of Diogenes the Doctor's Dog'; 'Ode'; 'To His Friends When His Prostate Shall Have Become Enlarged'; 'Ode for the Bi-Centenary of the Trinity Medical School'; 'Dunsany Castle'; 'At the Abbaye La Trappe'; prose re Tom Kettle; poems from Dunsany; 'The Rebels'; article re Arthur Griffith; poem re Michael Collins; article in the *Irish Statesman* re flying; poem to Terence MacSwiney; 'The Hay Hotel'.

Constable and Co. Ltd: *Collected Poems* of Oliver St John Gogarty; A.E.'s Preface to *Collected Poems*; *Tumbling in the Hay* by Oliver St John Gogarty.

Macmillan and Co. Ltd and Mrs W. B. Yeats: 'The Celtic Twilight' from *Mythologies* by W. B. Yeats; *Collected Poems* of W. B. Yeats; *Collected Letters* of W. B. Yeats; *Ireland After the Revolution* by W. B. Yeats.

Macmillan and Co. Ltd and Mrs Iris Wise: *Collected Poems* of James Stephens.

The Bodley Head and the Executors of the James Joyce Estate: *Ulysses* by James Joyce.

Jonathan Cape and the Executors of the James Joyce Estate: *Chamber Music* by James Joyce.

Jonathan Cape and the Executors of the T. E. Lawrence Estate: *Seven Pillars of Wisdom* by T. E. Lawrence.

Clarendon Press: W. B. Yeats's Foreword to *The Oxford Book of Modern Verse*.

MacGibbon and Kee: *It Isn't This Time of Year at All* by Oliver St John Gogarty.

William Heinemann Ltd and the Executors of C. D. Medley: *Hail and Farewell* by George Moore.

Faber and Faber Ltd: *Collected Letters* of James Joyce, edited by Stuart Gilbert.

Faber and Faber Ltd and Sir John Rothenstein: *Men and Memoirs* by William Rothenstein.

The Society of Authors: *Collected Letters* of James Stephens.

Hutchinson and Co. Ltd: *As I Was Going Down Sackville Street* by Oliver St John Gogarty; *My Ireland* by Lord Dunsany.

Ernest Benn Ltd: *Stories of Old Ireland and Myself* by Sir William Orpen.

Cornell University Library: James Joyce's letter of August 4th, 1909 to his brother Stanislaus.

A. M. Heath and Co. Ltd: an article written by A.E. on the back of a brochure for a Gogarty Lecture Tour sponsored by the Pond Bureau, New York.

Edward Colman: 'The Dead Poet' by Lord Alfred Douglas.

Field Roscoe and Co.: a letter from George Moore to Gogarty.

Messrs R. A. French: *Life of George Moore* by Susan Mitchell.

Dr Mario Rossi: *Pilgrimage in the West* by Dr Mario Rossi.

Donal O'Sullivan: 'Irish Free State and Its Senate' by Donal O'Sullivan.

Mrs Tom Kettle: Tom Kettle's Epitaph.

Padraic Colum: prose re Gogarty by Padraic Colum.

G. K. A. Bell: letter to the author from G. K. A. Bell.

General Beaslai: article by General Beaslai.

Sir Compton Mackenzie: a broadcast by Sir Compton Mackenzie.

Frank Duff: 'Eight Woman' from a report by Frank Duff.

The late Violet Clifton: letters to the author from Violet Clifton.

The late Lynn Doyle: letter to the author from Lynn Doyle.

The author is also indebted to Generals Mulcahy and Dalton for permission to quote from conversations they had with him.

* * *

I am especially grateful to my father for many things. To Oliver Duane Gogarty, s.c., and to Mrs Desmond Williams I owe thanks for generous access to family documents and permission to quote published material.

I am particularly grateful to Dr Monk Gibbon for his encouragement and help and for his work on the manuscript; I am grateful also to Mr Stuart Gilbert and Mr Gerard O'Flaherty for help in correcting the proofs, and to Mr Montgomery Hyde.

All publishers and individuals listed above are thanked for their kindness and co-operation.

I should also like to thank the following people and organizations who have assisted me in my work: Mary Adams; Richard Ahern; Florence Petry Amiel; Madame Amiel; Miss Aungier and the Smithson Agency; Agnes Bane; Donal Barrington; Piaras Beaslai; Lord Beaverbrook; the late Dr Richard Best; Earnan de Blaghdad; Colonel Eamon Broy; the late Monsignor Patrick Browne, D.D.; Seamus de Burgo; Mr Michael Burke; the late Jonathan Cape; John Chichester; Violet Clifton; Padraic Colum; the Marquess Conyngham; W. T. Cosgrave; the late Tim Costello; Mervyn Crofton; T. S. C. Dagg; Emmett Dalton; James P. Digby; Professor Myles Dillon; William Dinan; Charles Dixon; Miss Donovan; William Doolin; the late Lynn Doyle; Mrs Denise Drew; Mrs Vincent Ellis; Alfonso Farrelly; the late Professor W. R. Fearon; David Fitzgerald and the La Touche Hotel, Greystones; Frank Flanagan; Lionel T. Fleming; John Flusk; Major Dermot Freyer; M. Gannon; Lord and Lady Glenavy; Mrs Jua Golden; Charles Graves; the Guinness Brewery; Felix Hackett; the Reverend Kenneth Harper; Lady Hanson; George H. Healey, Department of Rare Books, Cornell University; James Augustus Healy; Patrick Henchy; the late Joseph Hone and Vera Hone; John S. Horgan; the late R. M. N. Jeffries; Dr W. R. Jessop; the late Augustus John, O.M.; Madge Johnson; F. W. Johnston; John Joyce; Ronan Keane; Harry Kernoff; Mrs Tom Kettle; Mr T. J. Lane; Martin Lavan; Dora Lawson; Dr John Leather; Seymour Leslie; Sir Shane Leslie; Miss Nora Lenihan; the late Marchioness of Londonderry; Miss Rita Lorigan; Judge Fionan Lynch; Sir Compton Mackenzie; Captain Dermot MacManus; Brinsley MacNamara; the late Michael MacWhite; Frank Martin; Joseph McGrath; Edward McLysaght; Miss McMenamin, Librarian of the King's Inns; Matt McQuaid; Dr J. H. Mellotte; Christopher Micks, s.c., and the Honourable Society of the Benchers of the King's Inns, Dublin; Andrew Millar-Jones; General Richard Mulcahy; Mrs May Monahan; Niall Montgomery; the National Library; Miss Betty Newson; Michael Noyk; the late Joseph O'Connor, K.C.; Robert O'Doherty; Padraic O'Keeffe; Tim O'Neill; Frank Owen;

Professor W. R. Parke, F.T.C.D., Vice-Provost of Dublin University, for permission to use University Library; William Pearson, F.R.C.S.I.; Jack Plant; Dr J. H. Pollock; Ashley Powell; Arthur Power; Mr James Quinn; F. H. Reynell; Robert Reynods; Mayflo Roden-Ryan; Professor Mario Rossi; David Ryan; Anders Sandstrom; Philip Sayers; Michael Scott; the late Judge Eugene Sheehy; W. S. Smart; Seamus Sorahan; Professor Walter Starkey; Pierce Synott; the Earl of Wicklow; Professor J. D. H. Widdess; Desmond Williams; Dr T. G. Wilson; Ernest Wood; Mr and Mrs Robert Woods.

PREFACE

W. B. Yeats in his preface to the *Oxford Book of Modern Verse*, refers to Oliver St John Gogarty as 'one of the great lyric poets of the age'. Asquith called Gogarty the wittiest man in London. Edward Shanks thought his conversation had the flavour of Wilde's. Gogarty was also a skilful surgeon, an aviator, a senator, a playwright, a champion athlete and swimmer. When Professor Mario Rossi, an Italian authority on Swift and Berkeley, met Gogarty in the 'thirties he felt he was in the presence of a figure out of the Renaissance, *L'uomo universale*, the 'all-sided man'.

> This region is animated by the presence of a man who recalls the great Italians of the Quattrocento. For me at least, to know Gogarty was to realize the enthusiasm of the man who lives with full consciousness for that admirable phenomenon which is called life.

Gogarty lived in an era when the racial elements were unifying in Ireland. The image of the new nation was naked before the eye. The mind was on fire. He was one of the first modern Irishmen combining in his make-up elements of both the Anglo-Irish and Gaelic traditions. He formed part of Europe's last renaissance, the Irish Literary Revival, – and with the exception of Padraic Colum was the only one of its important figures alive in the late 'fifties.

He was on terms of close friendship with some of those who played an important part in the evolution of modern Ireland. His tutor in the art of conversation at Trinity College, Dublin, J. P. Mahaffy, epitomized the high point of Anglo-Irish humanism. Yeats, the high priest of the Irish Renaissance, was Gogarty's friend and ally until his death at Roquebrune in 1939. Arthur Griffith, the founder of the Irish Free State, was another close friend. James Joyce was a friend of Gogarty's during their student years together.

As he had the highest admiration for Griffith, Gogarty developed a strong animosity towards Mr de Valera, the first

President of Dáil Eireann, and later President of the Irish Free State. To understand what ultimately became almost an obsessional dislike on Gogarty's part for Mr de Valera, it has been necessary to examine the political events of the 'twenties and 'thirties in Ireland in which Mr de Valera took a leading part.

In the late 'thirties the political atmosphere in Ireland began to embitter Gogarty. But when he found it difficult to adjust himself to the conditions of the De Valera regime, with the instinct of an artist, he flitted butterfly-like to another clime – to America. There he could keep intact the memory of the Golden Age, while remaining highly critical of the political regime under the new Government at home. Away from Ireland, his dream kept him afloat, and his life in the new world was crammed with activity – lecturing, journalism, talking – which preserved him as an active and alert personality until his death in New York in 1957. He was one of a small group who created the literature of modern Ireland in a brief period at the turn of the century when Europe's last island made her contribution to the civilization of the West.

ONE

OLIVER ST JOHN GOGARTY has described his maternal ancestry in a letter to Shane Leslie. Referring to an uncle of his mother's grandfather, Fitzdominick Oliver, a Galway merchant, who smuggled as a sideline, he wrote: 'These Fitzdominicks were of the De Burgo family, who came into Galway in the middle of the 14th century. Oliver Og de Burgo was a relative of that De Burgo who married Granuaile (Grace O'Malley the female sea pirate) and made it possible for her to hold the western ocean. Here is an interesting incident. One of the Lynches calling one day on my aunt, Mother Joseph who founded the convent of Oranmore, fell on his knees, and taking her hand, kissed it "for the sake of the crooked knives". This was the euphemism for pirates in the town of Galway. It shows how he identified her family with those who were in need of prayer, but who had a Reverend Mother for intercession's sake, as those barons who harried the Swiss valleys had a Pope to brother. This explains why Aunt Imelda who was her sister, and who though a hundred years old is still living at Taylors Hill Convent, would never tell me how to reach from my grandfather to'Oliver Og.'

When Oliver Gogarty's mother, Margaret Oliver, married Henry Gogarty in 1876, the Olivers were prosperous Galway millers. The merchant class were an exception to the general rule in Ireland that Protestants were wealthy and Catholics were not. The Penal Code which had deprived Catholics of advancement had little influence on commerce and even at the height of the laws against Catholics there were wealthy Catholic merchants.

On the other hand, it was extremely rare in Ireland to find a Catholic family with three generations of doctors behind it as the Gogartys could claim. Oliver Gogarty's great-grandfather had been a doctor, his grandfather was a physician to the Gormanston family in Meath, and his father was a successful Dublin physician. The reason that such a background was rare is that under the Penal Law Catholics were debarred from entering the professions. This pattern appears to have maintained itself even after the abolition of the Penal Laws (probably due to the lack of facilities for higher education for Catholics) and the leadership of the profession in Ireland was principally in the hands of Protestants until about fifty years ago.

The Olivers were of Norman stock, but the Gogartys were an old Gaelic clan. The name is a version of MacFogarty; this family were at one time a ruling sept in Tipperary and had their own chief and castle. Some of them moved to Meath where the name became first O'Gogarty, and then Gogarty. Thus Gogarty was of Norman-Gaelic stock. Though the Celt predominated in his personality he always liked to stress the Norman element in the Irish character (it has been estimated that one-sixth of Irish names are of Norman origin), the iron-visored invaders who:

> Brought rigid law, the long spear and the horsemen,
> Riding in steel; and the rhymed romantic high line,
> Built those square keeps on the forts of the Norsemen,
> Still on our skyline.

The fact that on both sides of his family Gogarty's forebears had for generations held some authority in the community is of importance. It freed him from that sense of inferiority and insecurity that often affected Catholics of his generation.

His father appears to have had rapid success as a physician. He qualified in 1867 at Trinity College, Dublin. Two years later he moved to a Georgian town house in Rutland Square. Rutland Square lies at the end of Dublin's principal street, and at one time held more dukes and grandees than any other square in the city. On the north side of it lies Charlemont House built by Sir William Chambers. Facing Charlemont House is Cassell's Rotunda Hospital. The residences in the square are tall, over sixty feet in height, faced with red-rose or wine-coloured brick. The wide sweep of the streets blending with the tall houses lends a pleasant air of proportion to the whole square.

From Rutland Square Henry Gogarty built up a large practice. A successful doctor could live well in the Dublin of those days. The professional class were the elite of the city. After the act of Union in 1800, most of the aristocracy sold their town houses, and these were taken over by the doctors and lawyers. There was no industrial revolution to give position in society to the new rich. Thus the professional classes had the field to themselves. They were eligible for peerages and knighthoods, entertained lavishly, enjoyed the pastimes of country gentlemen and secretly hoped to marry their daughters to the gentry who came up to Dublin for the Castle season, but who stayed in the Shelbourne Hotel or hired houses in Harcourt Street, instead of using their town houses as of old. Besides 5 Rutland Square, Henry Gogarty kept up a Queen Anne manor, which stood in its own grounds at Glasnevin about a mile from the centre of the city. It was named Fairfield. Dean Swift was said to have stayed there and cut an epigram in praise of a servant-girl on the window of the closet: this legend forms the basis for W. B. Yeats's play *The Words upon the Window Pane*. He had shooting grounds on the Nore: in the back of Rutland Square he kept a hunter which he rode through the streets to the Phoenix Park in the evenings. There are Dublin people who can still recall him, a blond Viking of a man with blue eyes and golden beard, seated upright in his gig as he went his rounds, accompanied by his 'tiger', a little boy in livery who stood on the step of the gig, and held the horse while his master was in with patients.

In 1876 he married Margaret Oliver. Two years later, on August 17th, 1878, their first son was born. He was christened Oliver Joseph St John Gogarty. A year later another son, Henry, was born. A daughter, Mary ('Mayflo'), and a son, Richard, completed the family.

After eleven years of marriage Henry Gogarty died of a burst appendix. It was apparently a hereditary weakness, for both his son and grandson were to fall seriously ill from the same cause, but in their cases medical science had advanced sufficiently to ensure recovery. He left his wife and children comfortably provided for. Mrs Gogarty continued to keep up 5 Rutland Square and Fairfield; but the butler and some of the servants had to be dispensed with.

Margaret Gogarty was a woman of strong character. Her complexion was so perfect that only on the word of O'Duffy the Castle dentist across the square would Dublin accept it as genuine. Her son Oliver considered he inherited his gift of the gab and inexhaustible energy from his mother. She had a sense of humour. Her daughter Mayflo recalls that when the two boys, Henry and Oliver, were out of favour, they would stand back to back, with their heads touching, behind their mother's chair before she came down to breakfast. When she had seated herself, they would read aloud from a dedication to her by a pious author in a book called

Letters of an Irish Catholic Layman, each boy reciting alternate phrases:

> To Mrs Margaret Gogarty, a lady who to all the graces and attractions of her sex, adds virile force of intellect and judgment, this little book is respectfully dedicated by the author.

This always made her smile and peace would be restored. Mayflo remembers also that Mrs Gogarty exercised strict supervision over her son's religious duties:

> 'Come back here, sir, and say your Rosary,' Mother would say, as Oliver was making for the door to go on the town. He would kneel down, running his fingers through his thick hair with impatience. Once he hit on the stratagem of putting whiskey in the cats' milk so that for weeks the two cats used to run up and down the five flights of stairs, making a frightful noise during the Rosary.

It is curious that one with Oliver Gogarty's charm and gift for friendship should have been unhappy at school. Yet he attended Stonyhurst, Lancashire, for five years and detested the place. Fifty years later he would still speak of it to a fellow old-boy as 'the accursed Stonyhurst on the Pendelhurst Range'. He considered it a 'religious jail'. It seems that attempts were made to influence him by hell-fire sermons. In a Jesuit school conformity is all-important, and Gogarty resented this.

Stonyhurst in those years probably had a trace of Jansenism in its tradition. For a period during the Penal days, it had functioned in exile at St Omer. The boys in Gogarty's day still wore French shoes with long flanges made by the College cobbler. A number of the regulations sound strange in English ears. If a boy were found with his hands in his pockets he was sent to the tailor to have his pockets sewn up. When they went to meals the boys filed along the walls in silence, as Gogarty observed, 'like criminals'.

The records show he did well at games and debates. But someone or other seems to have made his life a hell there, because for years he cherished the most inclement feelings about the place.

He had one interesting experience at Stonyhurst and that occurred during vacation. His mother left him at school one Christmas, as she could not afford to have him home. Gogarty, then a boy of sixteen, contacted the Preston soccer club and turned out for their Reserve, at thirty shillings a week. At a time when professionals came out by a different gate from amateurs at cricket matches, and professional soccer players were in a lower category still, this took some doing. Gogarty claimed that this professional interlude was the reason the Scroopes later kept him off the Trinity soccer side. After leaving Stonyhurst he had a year to spare before entering university. His mother sent him to Clongowes Wood, a Jesuit school in Kildare. This was the leading Catholic school in Ireland; a large proportion of its old boys entered the Colonial Service or the army or navy. The commander-in-chief of the British army, when Gogarty was at school, Sir William Butler, was an old Clongownian.

Gogarty was happy at Clongowes. There we begin to get a picture of the boy. His legend, though he was only there one year, outlasted generations of Clongownians. He was one of the top players on the football and cricket elevens. He played in the Irish Cup for Bohemians while at Clongowes and won a gold medal. Bohemians were a senior side and as far as I can discover only one other Irish boy has won an Irish senior cup medal while still at school. When the biographer was in Hollywood in the summer of 1962, J. M. Kerrigan, the veteran actor, recalled a vivid memory of Gogarty running down the wing for Bohemians, missing a shot at goal, and then going through the motions of knocking his head against the goal-post.

Gogarty saved a Clongownian from drowning at Clane, and another from choking in the rectory by ramming his finger down the youth's gullet, and pulling a fish-bone out, while priests and boys stood gaping.

A classmate of his at Clongowes, J. J. Horgan, now the Cork City coroner, recalls him as 'the most popular boy in the school with his soft voice, witty tongue and pallid handsome face'. Already he had begun to develop a talent for writing Rabelaisian verse. 'I remember,' Horgan writes, 'a rhymed account of his about a cricket match between Heaven and Hell which was distinctly blasphemous, and would have certainly merited dire punishment for its author had he been found out.'

After leaving Clongowes his mother entered him at the Royal University to study medicine. She chose the Royal rather than Trinity College, because the Church did not approve of the latter.

15

Yet Gogarty's father had been there, and the Royal was really rather a ramshackle institution, the remains of Newman's University, with a few colleges which prepared students for examinations before a Board whose tests were open to anyone who wished to present himself for them. Gogarty remained two years at the Royal which he spent for the most part cycling with the champion of Ireland, Charles Pease, in the afternoons, and drinking and gallivanting with medical students at night. The result was that in six terms he passed two out of ten examinations. This lack of progress may have overcome his mother's scruples about Trinity College. She entered him as a pupil in the medical school there, in September 1898. Her son's version of the affair is that the registrar at Cecilia Street failed to offer his mother a chair, while the Trinity registrar to whom she flounced off in high dudgeon, not only offered her a chair but recollected her late husband as well. Whatever the reason, in autumn 1898 Oliver Gogarty changed varsities, and made his way to where Trinity's fine Georgian portico faces, across College Green, what used to be in the eighteenth century the Irish House of Parliament right in the very centre of Dublin. One passes under the portico and emerges to see the tall pillars of Chambers's examination hall, and the chapel, confronting each other from opposite sides of a cobbled square, flanked by the stern façade of Cassel's dining-hall and the splendid bulk of Burgh's library. Here one glimpses the spirit of the place, classical, pragmatical, austere.

TWO

To James Joyce, Trinity was a 'dull stone set in the ring of the city's ignorance'. But then Joyce was prejudiced. He had become a student at the Royal which Gogarty had just left. Trinity (or the University of Dublin to give it its official title) when Gogarty entered it had reached its intellectual peak. The fame of its dons shone with a glow in the world of scholarship. Palmer was the leading Latinist of his time according to A. E. Housman, while Tyrrell was his equal in scholarship and peer as a translator. J. P. Mahaffy had a European reputation as a classicist, and was the greatest Egyptologist of his era. Dowden was the leading academic critic in the literary world of his day. H. S. Macran was the foremost living authority on Hegel. J. B. Bury was professor of ancient history; he had been appointed when he was twenty-four. George Francis Fitzgerald, the Trinity physicist, contributed to Einstein's theory of relativity, and names like Salmon in mathematics and theology, Joly in science, and Cunningham in medicine show how high the general standard was at that time.

The fellowship examination was ferocious. It included what was said to be the hardest mathematics test in Europe. These dons were tough. They liked the open air. They fished, shot or played cricket; others went on marathon walks in the hills to clear the fug of scholarship from their brain. Mahaffy and Salmon, were the prototype, big-boned, loose-jointed, with loose-hanging clothes. They looked more like squires than dons. Mahaffy was a great lover of royalty. He would refer to 'my friend the King of Greece'. But Queen Victoria was a little too bourgeois for him, 'having the manners of a badly-educated washerwoman'.

Trinity was a Protestant university. Unlike Oxford or Cambridge it had no pre-Reformation tradition. There were no Gothic windows for a Newman to dream under of the chant of priests or the swing of censers. It looked not to the Rome of the Popes, but to Greece of the Golden Age. In a sense Trinity was more Hellenic in spirit than either Oxford or Cambridge. Oscar Wilde has said that it was at Trinity he first learned of 'the aesthetic standpoint to life, and how to love Greek things'. While Pater was teaching 'art for art's sake' to a few neophytes in the woods at Oxford,

17

Mahaffy was trumpeting it through the halls of Trinity. A clergyman himself, Mahaffy used to say he was not one 'in any offensive sense of the word'. He could criticize St Paul for not attending the university at Antioch, and disturbing the proconsul Gallio with hysterical Hebrew brawls, while praising Stearne, another Trinity divine who founded T.C.D.'s medical school, because in his works though he says nothing of Jesus Christ 'he says nothing against Him'. There was a strong High Church set in Trinity, as well as the broad churchmen, and when Mahaffy proposed giving a sermon in chapel on the Unknown God he was vetoed by the authorities.

Trinity was the show-place of the Anglo-Irish. From it had come Swift (the prototype of the breed), Congreve, Goldsmith, Berkeley, Burke, Rowan Hamilton, Oscar Wilde, J. M. Synge; 'no petty people' as W. B. Yeats said later of them, 'one of the great stocks of Europe' perhaps, including himself by a remove, as his father had been a Trinity barrister. The Anglo-Irish mind combined qualities of both races. Mahaffy considered it superior to the pure English intellect as being 'more flexible in character' and felt that Anglo-Irish scholarship had a special mission 'to make scholarship more human than the English have, to be as curious as the Germans, but loathing their inelegance'.

In certain ways Trinity was unrepresentative of the Ascendancy. It was not on close terms with Dublin Castle, the seat of the Government in Ireland, which was largely under the thumb of the landed gentry. Trinity dons did not, as a rule, attend Castle levees as Anglophile Dublin Society did. Some gentry sent their sons to Trinity. But the class from which it drew its strong stock were the middle and upper-middle classes, sons of doctors, lawyers, clergy, teachers. They were too individual to conform to a rigid social caste. Thus though the university was Unionist in politics, it had had over the years a revolutionary undercurrent among its students. Robert Emmet, Wolfe Tone, Thomas Clarke Luby, the Fenian, and Smith O'Brien, were at Trinity; and as late as 1913 the first meeting of the Citizen Army, an armed working-class force, was held in the rooms of a Fellow, R. M. Gwynn, under the chairmanship of Charles Oldham.

This was the university which was to be Gogarty's 'quick forge and working house of thought' for eight years. What sort of student is it who enters under the main gate in autumn 1898? He is a

Catholic in a university that is largely Protestant; but his social origins are no different from the bulk of the students, a professional background and a public-school upbringing. He loves talking, athletics, and poetry. He will have plenty of encouragement for the exercise of his tongue during his eight years at Trinity. He can practise his cycling on the College Park racing track. For a while he will speak little of his interest in poetry. But for verse he has an astonishing memory. He has only to hear a poem read over once to him, and it remains in his memory, no matter what length the poem may be. He has memorized a good deal of Elizabethan verse, and the works of Scottish poets, anonymous and well known, Burns, Ramsay, Ferguson, and a host of ballads of which he is especially fond. At present any verse of a serious kind he writes is for his own pleasure. Only his limericks, and ballades modelled on Villon and Rabelais, he circulates for the amusement of his friends. Or if he leaves a note for them, it is likely to be in verse form.

> But Bob old cock, get here by four.
> The second room above the door
> Is where I sit and idly pore
> O'er books and papers.
> I want to send you where need is sore,
> I do be japers.

In appearance he is of average height, five feet nine, but appears taller because of his athletic figure. There is a slight effect of broadness about the face, but this is an illusion, as a sculptor's callipers have shown that it is a long narrow head of the northern type. The eyes are striking, vivid blue, so deep in colour that his daughter actually remembers their being a shade of violet at times. His hair is brown, but sometimes streaked with gold from the bleaching of the sun, and inclined to stand upright when brushed sideways. There is a fine sweep to the forehead, broad without being over-intellectual; his features are regular, but the nose is slightly large, a characteristic of the Irish face. It is a serene countenance. But there is a suggestion of concealed mobility, that has its motor point perhaps in the elfin arch of the left eyebrow, a feature brought out by both Augustus John and Sir William Orpen, when they painted Gogarty's portrait. There is the air of a dandy about him. He wears a primrose waistcoat and a silk tie in a bow; but it is his alert bearing, his trim confident walk, that suggests the man of fashion as much as the sartorial display.

Gogarty left a legend behind him in Trinity that was only equalled by one other student before him – Charles Lever, another doctor-author. He excelled at everything except medicine, and even in that demanding subject, which later formed the basis of his career, when he did buckle down to it in his final year his results were creditable. He was welcome in any group. His exuberance and vitality would have livened up a meeting of Plymouth Brethren. There was a light in those bright blue eyes, a quality in his mobile active face, that it was impossible to resist, and bred a sense of well-being and joy of living in those in whose company he talked. There was always a ready audience for his latest limerick or parody:

> There was a young man from St Johns
> Who wanted to Roger the swans.
> 'Oh no,' said the porter,
> 'Oblige with my daughter,
> But the birds are reserved for the dons.'

(The last line of this limerick, as we shall see later was to be the subject of an amusing debate between George Moore and the poet Yeats.)

Or it might be a variant of an established classic.

> Then out spoke the King of Siam,
> 'For women I don't give a damn.
> You may think it odd of me;
> I prefer Sodomy.
> They say I'm a bugger, I am.'

This limerick was a special favourite of the late Monsignor Patrick Browne of Galway, who insisted on attributing its authorship to Gogarty.

Sometimes Gogarty could be induced to recite his parody of Keats's 'On First Looking Into Chapman's Homer' – 'On First Looking Into Krafft-Ebing's Psychopathosexualis'.

> Much have I travelled in those realms of old
> Where many a whore in hall-doors could be seen
> Of many a bonnie brothel and sheebeen
> Which bawds connived at by policemen hold.

I too have listened while the Quay was coaled,
But never did I taste the Pure obscene –
Much less imagine that my past was clean –
Till this Krafft-Ebing out his story told.
Then felt I rather taken by surprise
As on the evening when I met Macran,
And retrospective thoughts and doubts did rise,
Was I quite normal when my life began
With love that leans towards rural sympathies,
Potent behind a cart with Mary Ann?

He had analysed the love cry of the tom-cat with its curious
paradox of pleasure expressed in a series of agonizing howls.

But never heard I such a roar
From painter or from paramour

As yours, Cassandra, to our coast,
As if all lunar towns were lost,
As if Isaiah's brood surprised
Were all together circumcised.

Truly it seems to me absurd,
O round-eyed as Athena's bird,
O undelighted in the Dark,
Love's martyr and Heresiarch,

To sound the converse of all joys
By turning feeling into noise,
To mock the screech-owl thus and prove
The long calamity of love.

He was a gifted mimic and his recitation of verses sniping at
Mahaffy's lisp and love of royalty was much in demand. These
verses had appeared in the Dublin University magazine under the
title 'Threnody on the Death of Diogenes the Doctor's Dog', and
were a parody on Swinburne's 'Atalanta in Calydon'.

When I wambled awound
In the gwound that was Gweece
I was given that hound
By the King's little niece
And had rather be fined e'er I found him,
        to gaze on his saddest surcease.

> He was given that hound
> By the seed of a King
> For the wisdom profound
> Of his wide wandering.
> But was it the owner, or donor, or dog
> that was led by the string?

He was a natural jester. His feats were the talk of Commons in College at night. Once he appeared at the door of the examination hall in a cab with the blinds down. The vehicle made an appalling racket over the cobble-stones, and a crowd gathered to see Gogarty emerge. He did so with a hood over his head, and was led by the cabby into the examination hall. The reason Gogarty explained later, was that he had developed a fetish about seeing a red-haired student, who always seemed to presage failure for him on the day of an examination.

On another occasion he and others sold a paralytically drunk medical student to the Royal College of Surgeons as a corpse. They had him in a sack, and since there was no outward indications of a pulse, the caretaker paid out the stipend, and placed the 'body' among other cadavers some of whom already had been the object of student research. The 'boys' waited outside for some hours, till the unfortunate student, now fully sober, came running into the street in a state of nature, shouting 'It's the last time I'll die to pay for your drink.'

One of his jokes had Dublin laughing for months. During the Boer War Gogarty contributed articles to Arthur Griffith's paper *Sinn Fein*, opposing the recruitment of Irishmen for the British Army in South Africa. When the Irish regiments returned in June 1900, after a series of victorious campaigns, the Viceroy's Court, the Lord Mayor and Castle Society generally gave them an enthusiastic welcome. The leading social magazine *Irish Society*, renowned for its snobbish outlook, printed a special 'Ode of Welcome' to the returning troops. An hour after the magazine was on the bookstalls it sold out. But it was not the social minutiae of its columns that lent it this unusual popularity, but the 'Ode' which appeared on page 14.

The Gallant Irish yeoman
  Home from the war has come,
Each victory gained o'er foeman,
  Why should our bards be dumb?

How shall we sing their praises
  Or glory in their deeds,
Renowned their worth amazes,
  Empire their prowess needs.

So to Old Ireland's hearts and homes
  We welcome now our own brave boys
In cot and hall; 'neath lordly domes
  Love's heroes share once more our joys.

Love is the Lord of all just now,
  Be he the husband, lover, son,
Each dauntless soul recalls the vow
  By which not fame, but love was won.

United now in fond embrace
  Salute with joy each well-loved face.
  Yeoman, in women's hearts you hold the place.

Knocklong   J.R.S.

When read down vertically, along the first letter of each line, a sentence appears, which implied that the street-women will enjoy greatly increased custom, as a result of the presence in the city of the newly-returned regiments. It was known soon afterwards that the poem was Gogarty's work, and Padraic Colum remembers that the joke remained a sensation in the city for many months.

Literary agility was appreciated, but it was sport which was really king in Trinity in those days. In the College Park lay the path to student fame. This park was Trinity's hidden gem. In the heart of a capital city there were acres of level playing-fields. The traffic rolled by in the streets outside. But shielded by high railings and giant elms, a cricket match or athletic competition in progress might be taking place on a village green, for all the effect the noise outside had on it. Most of the Fellows took a keen interest in college sport. During the cricket season, as 'the run-stealers flickered to and fro' Mahaffy could be seen on the pavilion steps demonstrating with his umbrella how the batsmen should have played their strokes. Tyrrell wrote in *Kottabos*, T.C.D.'s light-hearted academic periodical, descriptions of current cricket victories in the style of Thucydides.

This was a result of the Romantic Hellenism, which Thomas Arnold's teaching had revived at Rugby; many Trinity students were old Rugbeians or from schools where Arnold's doctrines had been adopted. A victor in the College Park might feel like Pindar's athlete at Delphi.

> When God-given splendour visits him
> A bright radiance plays on him
> And how sweet is life.

In 1899 Gogarty won nearly all the cycling events in the college races; he was first in the mile, the mile handicap and the three miles, and according to the college paper, would have won the five miles had his tyre not burst at the beginning of the race.

The college races were the most important outdoor social event of the year in Dublin. The Viceroy and his Court attended, and it was the occasion of the first showing of summer fashions. The College Park was usually jammed for the 'Races'. Once 30,000 people attended for the two days. In Gogarty's time bookies shouted the odds from the back of the crowds.

The same year Gogarty won the twenty-mile championship of Ireland in 53 minutes 35 seconds, a record that stood for many years. The *Irish Wheelman* of the period noted this as a remarkable performance for an athlete 'who is really a sprinter, but who by assiduous training has learned to stay'.

In addition that season he won eleven firsts in open competition. In London he beat the English champion, Isidore MacBurke, over ten miles and Larry Oswald, an Irish champion, at shorter distances. At Ballsbridge, the centre of Irish athletics, the *Freeman's Journal* notes Gogarty as having a day out, winning the double, the half-mile and two-mile handicap.

'Oliver Gogarty,' recalls Robert Reynolds, 'was a first-rate cyclist. You had to watch him like a hawk in a race. If you took your eyes off him for a second he was past in a flash, with his cry of "Up, up Balrothery". You see we trained on Balrothery Straight.' Reynolds was third in the world mile championship at Copenhagen. In 1900 Gogarty won the scratch mile in the college

24

races and the mile and five-mile double at the R.I.C. sports at Ballsbridge. In the latter race there was a crash in which five men were badly injured. Gogarty often had to come down to breakfast with gloves on to hide his lacerated hands from his aunt, who disapproved of cycling on social grounds. It was exceptional, actually, for a Trinity student to compete in open competition as Gogarty did, and he was often embarrassed to read his name on the hoardings, for fear his aunt might spot it and come down on him. This was his last year cycling. The following year, 1901, he was suspended for bad language. Three cyclists tried to ram him, and he let go with a volley of oaths which were heard by the judges. Though Bob Reynolds offered to appeal for him, Gogarty wouldn't hear of it and never raced again. His suspension in his own opinion may have done him a favour. It made him wake up to the fact that there was a Literary Renaissance going on around him.

He was fastidious about his clothes on the track as he was off it. He had his cycling singlet, with full-length sleeves which were compulsory in those days, made to order by a tailor and it fitted him like a glove. He raced at eleven stone. His racing shoes were scarlet in colour to match the pedal blocks on which the shoes were fitted. When he raced in Trinity colours his singlet was black, with an elaborate gold crest in the middle. Occasionally he competed for the Al Fresco Club, when he wore a tasselled cap and singlet of assorted colours.

His progress meanwhile in his medical studies was slow. It took him three years to pass his second-year anatomy examination. But in Trinity students of all kinds have to take out a degree in arts, and in these subjects he had more success. Dowden taught English and he awarded Gogarty the Vice-Chancellor's Prize for verse on three successive occasions. This was a record for Trinity; Gogarty received three gold medals, and each time he won a medal, there was an additional prize of twenty pounds with it. In 1901, the first year he competed, the subject was R. L. Stevenson's centenary, in 1902 'The Death of Byron', in 1903 'The Centenary of Cervantes'. The prize-winning pieces are no more distinguished than Oscar Wilde's 'Ravenna' with which he won the Newdigate at Oxford. Prize poems seldom have much intrinsic value.

Dowden, who was a poet himself of some vogue, had a high opinion of Gogarty's poetry. He helped generously with magazine editors in getting it published. As he was fond of the Caroline poets, Herrick in particular, he must have been pleased at the note of wanton whimsy in Gogarty's poem 'To Maids Not to Walk in The Wind' which appeared in print in 1904:

> When the wind blows walk not abroad,
> For, Maids, you may not know
> The mad, quaint thoughts that incommode
> Me when the winds do blow.
>
> What though the tresses of the treen
> In doubled beauty move,
> With silver added to their green,
> They were not made for Love.
>
> But when your clothes reveal your thighs
> And surge around your knees,
> Until from foam you seem to rise,
> As Venus from the seas ...
>
> Though ye are fair, it is not fair!
> Unless you will be kind
> Till I am dead and changed to AIR,
> O walk not in the wind!

Dowden had written definitive lives of Goethe and Shelley. He held a salon on Sunday afternoons, in his house at Temple Road, which Gogarty sometimes attended. It was at Dowden's house that the young Yeats had made his first acquaintance with the literary world. But Yeats considered that Dowden was 'withering on the barren soil of Unionism' and they broke with each other. Of 'Chaucerian head and ambassadorial carriage' Dowden very much represented the majesty of the academic world to the public and when he entered a tram-car slightly bewildered, clutching his parcel of books tied with string, a place was always quickly made for him. Did he even suspect that his pupil Gogarty was to be, with Oscar Wilde, the only genuine poet to come out of this great classical period in Trinity's history?

Gogarty was taken up by the Fellows in a way that no other student had been since Oscar Wilde was at Trinity. Tyrrell, Mahaffy and Macran invited him to dinner at their houses, and to parties which they gave in rooms at Trinity. They filled his capacious memory with classical poetry, Virgil, Ovid, Catullus, Horace, Pindar, Aeschylus, Homer, Theocritus, Martial, Moschus, Bion. His quick brain enabled him to rival them in apt quotation, a pastime at which they excelled. He was, of course, more subdued in their company than he would have been with his fellow students. Sometimes in their presence he felt like a 'goldfish surrounded in the crystal sphere of knowledge, in which all I could do was go round and round'. But they valued him for his personality, his wit and charm, his gaiety, which bubbled out of him when some humorous thought or fancy entered his mind.

The dominant influence upon him was probably Mahaffy. There is no biography of the latter, though as R. M. N. Jeffares has observed in the Chatterton Lecture to the British Academy, 1960, he richly deserves one. His influence on Gogarty, as on Oscar Wilde, is important, so it is necessary to go into some detail about his background and accomplishments here. Henry Jackson the Cambridge scholar has said that Mahaffy's misfortune was that his versatility in scholarship sometimes prevented him from getting the recognition he should, as people felt so much knowledge could not reside in one man, whereas 'he had done so much work in four branches of learning as would earn him a European reputation in any one of them'. Besides his distinction in classics and Egyptology, he was also a Doctor of Music, and had written the music for the Grace in chapel. As a young man his commentaries on Kant had been praised by Mill. His versatility was not confined to learning. He had shot for Ireland at Wimbledon, and played cricket for Ireland. Shane Leslie remembers seeing him take down a snipe at ninety yards. He knew the pedigree of every racehorse in Ulster, and had written a book on fly fishing, at which he was an expert.

His social talents were outstanding, and he was a famous conversationalist. The Kaiser used to invite Mahaffy to stay with him, to enjoy the benefit of his brilliant chatter. The Queen of Spain was another close friend. Oscar Wilde who was Mahaffy's pupil in the 'seventies, referred to him 'as my first and last teacher'. Mahaffy was for him 'a really great talker, an artist in vivid words and eloquent phrases'. When Wilde was a student he and Mahaffy went on a tour of Greece together and Wilde had an opportunity of observing Mahaffy's flair for turning ideas spontaneously into arresting images. Mahaffy's repartee and epigrams delighted Wilde. Certain Mahaffyisms were it not for their local allusions might be Wilde's own.

'In Ireland the inevitable never happens, but the unexpected often occurs.'

'An Irish atheist is one who wishes to God he could believe in God.'

In reply to a question as to what constituted the nature of an 'Irish Bull' he answered: 'An Irish Bull, madam, is always pregnant.'*

Mahaffy's wit has a lightning quality reminiscent of Wilde. When an over-persistent advocate of women's rights asked him: 'What is the difference between a man and a woman?' Mahaffy replied, 'I can't conceive.' In moments of danger his humour did not desert him. When one of the Leslies removed some of Mahaffy's auburn side-locks, with a misdirected shot, during a shoot at Castle Leslie, Mahaffy's comment was: 'A little more to the left and you'd have blown half the Greek out of Ireland.' Once when someone informed him that Traill, against whom he bore a grudge for snaffling the provostship from him in 1904, was sick, he remarked, 'Nothing trivial I hope.'

Traill may have recovered on that occasion, but Mahaffy was eventually to be his successor.

Mahaffy's conversation was by all accounts unique. Since his technique influenced Oscar Wilde, and Edward Shanks has observed that Gogarty 'exemplified the rich Dublin talk, that astonished London when it was first heard on the lips of Wilde', it is probable that Gogarty and Wilde both shared a common conversational heritage from Mahaffy.

There seems to have been something of the mesmeric quality of the Irish seanachaidhe or story-teller, in Mahaffy's talk; he knew the country-side well, and was aware of the plastic use of language that is to be found among Irish peasant folk. Shane Leslie says,

Until you heard Mahaffy talk, you hadn't realised how language could be used to charm and hypnotise. With this

* The originator of the Irish Bull was Sir Boyle Roche, the last Speaker of the Irish House of Commons, who was quite unaware of the merriment he occasioned by his choice remarks. He observed once:

Why should we put ourselves out of the way to do anything for posterity, for what has posterity done for us.

Another remark which stopped the business of the House for half an hour was:

The best way to avoid danger is to meet it plump.

gift, there were no doors which could not be opened, no Society which was proof against its astonishing effect. Kings and Queens, famous men and beautiful women, all must come under its powerful and compelling spell.

Mahaffy considered he had brought conversation to the level of an art form, and wrote a book on the subject. Gogarty read and re-read his *Art of Conversation* many times. It was among the few books which he kept to his death. He conceived an evening's conversation as a German might view going to a symphony concert, or a Frenchman visiting an art gallery; the same sort of pleasure might be obtained if the evening were manipulated by an artist in words. All present must be induced to take part in the talk; conversation was an 'eranos', a contributory feast, not the show-place of a monologuist. Tactfully, Mahaffy would get on terms of what he called 'fictional' equality with his company so that there would be give and take among the flow of ideas. If the thread of the talk was being worn thin by an indifferent talker he employed what he called the art of 'graceful interruption'. No one was to be offended but the talk was gently restored by the master to its proper level. He disliked what he called the 'tyranny of truth' in conversation, the pedant who is always demanding precise facts and figures. It is typical of his approach that, in other matters a person with a scholar's passion for exactitude, to the conversationalist he allowed the plastic licence of the artist. For Mahaffy conversation was a stream along which the mind flowed, enlivening facts as it encountered them with the bright light of the imagination.

Mahaffy's friendship with Gogarty continued after his pupil had gone down from Trinity. In later years he used to come to fish at Gogarty's place in the west of Ireland. Augustus John recalls with a gleam, that Mahaffy was the only one who could keep Gogarty quiet. 'Silence Gogarty' he would say if he was concentrating on his fishing, and Gogarty's fountain flow of talk would dry up instantly.

'If he had known less' said Oscar Wilde of Robert Yelverton Tyrrell, 'he would have been a poet.' But Tyrrell put his poetic instinct only into translations, and into stimulating those with whom he came in contact by his love of Roman and Greek literature. Gogarty was open-mouthed at Tyrrell's marvellous

29

display at lectures, and he longed to meet the Master, who was a handsome man with the profile of a Caesar. One day a message came to drink a glass of wine with Tyrrell in his rooms. The drink was served by a splendid butler in velvet livery, with gold edgings, Gogarty taking wine and Tyrrell whiskey. Tyrrell had noted a daring claim of Gogarty's that Tennyson's ear had failed him on only one occasion, in the diaeresis after the fifth foot in a couplet of 'Locksley Hall'. Such a sensitive ear could not be left untutored.

After this they became firm friends. Tyrrell used to visit his pupil at Fairfield, where they would sit after tea, drinking and talking under the yew trees. In such pleasant fashion was Gogarty introduced to the delights of classical literature. At Stonyhurst he had learnt to compose Latin verses 'like jigsaw puzzles irrespective of ear. We used a gradus to check the quantities of the vowels. The result of our work was futility. Hexameters meant nothing to the teacher for he was deaf to the stateliest measure ever moulded by the lips of man.'

But Tyrrell initiated him into the subtle beauty of Roman rhythm, so that he came to love the classics, as he loved Villon and the Elizabethan and Scottish poets.

Tyrrell's sarcastic wit had, I think, some influence on the development of Gogarty's sense of humour and examples of it are worth quoting. He was anything but a teetotaller, and furious when he encountered Temperance Hotels. 'There is no such thing,' he used to tell outraged proprietors, 'you might as well talk of a celibate brothel.' When a bore at table grew overpowering Tyrrell pushed a plate towards him saying, 'Have some tongue, like cures like.' Once he was interrupted when launched on a conversational flight by someone who inquired the way to the lavatory; Tyrrell said without turning, 'The first door on the right marked "gentlemen" – but don't let that deter you.' He used to remark ironically to his students how much the original Greek was of use in elucidating Browning's translation of the *Agamemnon*, and refer in terms of praise to the Irish Channel, because by drowning Edward King it raised up Lycidas.

It was probably through Tyrrell that Gogarty met H. S. Macran. Macran was a man of the sweetest possible nature and he and Gogarty became really close friends. 'You know I always loved you, Oliver,' Augustus John remembers Macran saying to Gogarty years afterwards, when they had made up some difference in Jammet's bar. Macran came out to Fairfield with the same end in view as Tyrrell, the moulding of a youthful inquiring mind in appropriate sylvan surroundings. He guided Gogarty at an important time of his life through the difficult sea of metaphysics. He took him through Hegel, Kant, and the English empiricists, and gave him a firm grounding in the principles of abstract thought. This was of the greatest importance in Gogarty's subsequent literary career. It saved him from the great danger of the modern poet surrounded by scientific tags and social slogans, who becomes a pseudo-metaphysician, incorporating into his verse ideas that are beyond his comprehension as an artist. Gogarty never brought his philosophy directly into his verse. He disapproved of the

> English curse
> Of mixing philosophy up with verse.
> I can imagine a poet teaching,
> But who can imagine a poet preaching?

He always wrote with the poet's pen, the pen of fire. An excellent example is 'The Image Maker' which Sir Arthur Quiller-Couch has included in the *Oxford Book of English Verse*. It is unnecessary for the reader to know that the poem is based on Aristotle's Hylomorphic theory. In the forge of his imagination, the poet has tempered the metaphysic with the glow of art.

> Hard is the stone, but harder still
> The delicate preforming will
> That, guided by a dream alone,
> Subdues and moulds the hardest stone,
> Making the stubborn jade release
> The emblem of eternal peace.
>
> If but the will be firmly bent
> No stuff resists the mind's intent;
> The adamant abets his skill
> And sternly aids the artist's will,
> To clothe in perdurable pride
> Beauty his transient eyes descried.

Or in his poem 'The Phoenix' when he writes of the soul's instinctive yearning for perfection the reader can take the meaning, without knowing of Plato's theory of the origin of beauty:

31

But where would be this seeking for,
   This wistful straining after things:
Islands surmised from lines of shore,
   Unless within me there were wings,
Wings that can fly in and belong
Only to realms revealed by song,
That bring those realms about their nest
Merging the Seeker and the Quest?

Above all Trinity cast Gogarty in the mould of the classical poet. Tyrrell brought him in touch with Greek and Roman literature: Mahaffy brought him into the world of Greeks and Romans. With his powerful imagination Mahaffy could draw modern parallels with ancient disputes, that brought them vividly before the eye of the listener. He re-created the ancient world and re-populated its Parliaments and streets with figures of flesh and blood. Handsome, athletic, brimming with poetry, Gogarty was ideal material for these dons to work on. They drew him into their twilight world of Athenian culture, created behind the curtain of Trinity's seclusion, and formed his personality according to their image of a Greek of the Golden Age.

We can see in a tiny poem, 'To Death', how he has achieved the true Sophoclean standpoint, a feeling for human grandeur in facing calm-browed the process of decay, 'realising', as he wrote in a letter in 1905, 'that behind life is the sadness of death, yet sanely and largely making the best of it, Divine beneath the Fates'.

But for your Terror
Where would be Valour?
What is Love for
   But to stand in your way?
Taker and giver
For all your endeavour
You leave us with more
   Than you touch with decay!

Even in the new democracy of the Free State when he served as a senator, Gogarty still retained his admiration for the aristocratic spirit of the Golden Age, his disdain for the mouthings of the mob, what Mahaffy would have called well-bred arrogance.

Tall unpopular men,
Slim proud women who move
As women walked in the Islands when
Temples were built to Love.
I sing to you. With you
Beauty at best can live
Beauty that dwells with the rare and few,
Cold and imperative.
He who had Caesar's ear
Sang to the lovely and strong.
Virgil made an austere
Venus, Muse of his song.

The Stoicism of the Roman Seneca speaks through his poem
'Non Dolet':

Our friends go with us as we go
    Down the long path where Beauty wends,
Where all we love forgathers, so
    Why should we fear to join our friends?

Who would survive them to outlast
    His children: to outwear his fame –
Left when the Triumph has gone past –
    To win from Age, not Time a name?

Then do not shudder at the knife
    That Death's indifferent hand drives home,
But with the Strivers leave the Strife
    Nor, after Caesar, skulk in Rome.

Nowhere does Gogarty show himself more classical than in his
resistance to the lure of iambic ease. Classical poets as a rule did
not use iambic metres for lyric verse. Instead Gogarty has bent the
English tongue to difficult classical metres, anapaests ('To Death'),
choriambics, sapphics. His superb metrical ear and command of
language enable him to achieve a felicity with these rhythms that
is equalled in English only perhaps by Swinburne. Three verses
from 'Portrait with Background' show how perfectly he can
marry words and rhythm under the difficult discipline of Sapphic
measures.

Here your long limbs and your golden hair affright men,
Slaves are their souls, and instinctively they hate them,
Knowing full well that such charms can but invite men,
     Heroes to mate them.

Eyes of the green of the woods that maddened Tristram!
Fair skin and smooth as the rosy-footed dove's wing!
Who would not fight, if he saw you, against this tram-
     melling of Love's wing?

Aye; and bow down if he saw but half the vision,
I dare not call to the mind's eye, to adore you;
And be, if that great light shone with precision,
     Awe-struck before you.

Violet Clifton, poetess and authoress, and a friend of Gogarty, wrote to the biographer in 1958:

> Beyond the rest of Gogarty's personality there was always present, the classical, the Greek more than the Roman, and, darkling in his mind, an atrocious Jerusalem, the early Christians a band of communists threatening the intellectual life of the West.

This might have been a description of the sceptical disposition and classical standpoint of that exceptional divine, John Pentland Mahaffy, or of Tyrrell's for that matter. Violet Clifton knew neither Mahaffy nor Tyrrell. That she should have discerned in Gogarty a similar disposition to theirs, shows how powerful an influence they had on the formation of his character during his student years at the college of the 'Holy and undivided Trinity'.

THREE

JAMES JOYCE, it seems, thought that the Dublin he had grown up in had certain distinctive qualities not enjoyed by more famous metropolitan centres. 'Dublin has been a capital of Europe for thousands of years,' he wrote to Grant Richards. 'It is supposed to be the second city of the British Empire. Moreover, for reasons which I cannot detail here, the expression Dubliner seems to me to bear some meaning, and the same cannot be said for such words as Londoner or Parisian.'

One quality which would have struck a visitor to Edwardian Dublin was the air of indolence about the place. There were no factory chimneys to blacken the landscape. The atmosphere was leisurely, divorced from the pace of an industrial city. There was an almost Latin disregard for time, which may have had its origin in the strong Catholic element among the people. The sea air, too, induced alternate moods of lethargy and elation, typical of maritime climates. The presence of the university and the garrison contributed to the leisurely mood; the gowned students sauntering out for a talk and coffee into the centre of the city, the colourful cavalry strolling through the streets with jingling spurs in the early afternoon suggested a life that was not tied to the routine of the counting-house, or the tyranny of the clock.

The pace of life left plenty of time for tongue-wagging. A facet common to all citizens was the feeling for words. The poor had the Gaelic flair for language as 'fully flavoured as a nut or apple' that their forebears from the country had before they came to live in the city. O'Casey's dialogue has shown how the imagery of Synge's peasant folk survived among the Dublin poor, but transmuted in the crucible of tenement life with overtones of sarcasm and derision. The story-telling techniques that Lady Gregory found round the Connacht firesides were alive in the city too; only the Dubliners did not talk of men carried away on eagles' backs or princes turned into swans, but used their narrative gifts in weaving episodes from occurrences in their daily lives, and around the activities of local 'characters' who provided admirable material for the employment of a story-teller's gifts. In fact any event of note in the city was sure to unleash its chains of anecdotes and

35

embroidered commentary among the wits and raconteurs as soon as it reached their eager ears.

This passion for conversation obtained at all levels. The Chief Secretary's Lodge, the Viceregal Lodge, the tables of judges and doctors in Fitzwilliam and Merrion Squares, the houses of the dons, were meeting-places for the best talkers in the town. The middle classes had their musical evenings with songs, monologues, instrumental performances, dramatic recitals, and talk in between, the last item taking up more than a fair proportion of the time.

The Countess of Fingall, who introduced Edward VII to Father Healy of Little Bray, a famous talker of his day, has recalled the almost compulsive talking habits of the Dublin of that time: 'I cannot count the wits and story-tellers of those days; you used to see men buttonholing one another at street corners in Dublin, to tell stories and roaring with laughter over them.'

The natural surroundings and architectural layout of Dublin also had their influence on the personality of the people. Dublin is a city as George Moore said pleasantly about it, 'Wandering between hill and sea'. In the Dubliner's mind is the knowledge that he can always get to sandy beaches, or goat-paths in lonely hills, in less than a half-hour. Dublin Bay with its long beaches stretches for almost forty miles, and behind it lies a crescent of hills each merging into one another, with soft names like Kilmashogue, The Feather Bed, The Sally Gap, The Silver Spears. The architects who laid the city out in the eighteenth century were always conscious of the natural beauty surrounding it. They crowned their public buildings with green domes to merge with the sky, and the tidal waters of the Liffey. Between the tall houses and wide streets they framed panoramas of the hills, so that on clear days vistas of green and gold strike the eye at the end of street or square. They bent stone until it accommodated the clouds and knew exactly how to use hill and sky against an urban background. Always in Gogarty there was a pastoral awareness of nature, exceptional in one so deeply involved in the stream of city life. The hills and beaches of the city were his escape hatches to beauty, when his professional career and social activities began to limit his free time. He would roar up the hills in his Rolls at lunch-hour, or gallop on the beach before breakfast in order to nourish the persistent demand in him for the prospect of nature.

The situation of the city helped satisfy this craving in his being. As a young man after he had given up cycling, he spent many hours roaming the silent hills, the silence broken, as Padraic Colum remembers, by the chant of Gogarty reciting ode after ode of Pindar; or swimming in the sea along Dublin Bay. Hardy as Vikings, he and his poet friends gave the weak northern sun the same adulation as the sun-kissed Greeks, defying the cold winds and stinging salt water, to feel on their bodies as young pagans might, the caress of its life-giving rays.

> Lords of the morning, since you set
> Within this ancient heart
> The flame that burnt my youth away
> And set my life apart,
> I bring you in this urn of truth
> The dust-white ashes of my youth

wrote one of Gogarty's swimming companions, the poet Seamus O'Sullivan, who felt the forces of nature shaping his manhood, though he like Gogarty had been born and bred in the heart of the city.

Armoured in eccentricity Endymion strode unconcernedly through Edwardian Dublin. He was 'a character' who dressed in a deerstalker hat, lace jabot, knee breeches, buckled shoes, two spare swords, a fishing rod and an umbrella. There may have been method in his madness, for he had a cocked hat for Trafalgar Day, and military tabs for Mafeking anniversary, as if he indulged in sly satire of the establishment. There was Alabaster, the Museum Keeper, who had invented a piano which played colours instead of chords; William Travers Humphreys Lyttleton Cox, the barrister, who could be seen on week-ends with his camera photographing the meaty folk-lore inscribed anonymously on the walls of public lavatories; 'Bird' Flanagan, an elaborate practical joker, with a rich father who could afford to pay for the results of his son's exploits, who rode a horse into the Gresham Hotel through the swing-doors; he also purloined a piccaninny from a Zulu village transplanted to Dublin for the Exhibition of 1907, and returned it to the French pavilion, as a gesture against the decline in the French birth-rate. A rival jester, hoping to defeat Flanagan at a fancy-dress ball, appeared dressed as the Holy Ghost at the Earlsfort Terrace Skating Rink, March 1909, and, assisted by two disciples, laid an egg the size of a Rugby football, before the mob fell upon him and chased him, wings askew, from the arena.

This was the picaresque flavour of Dublin. The city had an appetite for the eccentric; as many acted a part they did not resent it if occasionally one went too far and let his dreams overflow into life.

Another element in the environment of Dublin had its influence on the formation of Gogarty's character. This was a tradition which had survived in the popular imagination from the eighteenth century: the tradition of the 'Bucks', 'Fireaters' and 'Shams' who flourished side by side with the passionate oratory and patriotic spirit of the Anglo-Irish Parliament in College Green. The legend lived on in the novels of Charles Lever, and in the street ballads which recorded their feats and escapades. Among them was 'Buck' Whaley who walked to Jerusalem for a bet of £10,000 and played handball against the Weeping Wall amidst the wails of indignant rabbis. Another was 'Tiger' Roche who even in the days when travel was difficult was 'wanted' in places as far apart as London, Canada and Australia for duelling activities. 'Buck' English once shot a dilatory waiter, and then had him charged on the bill. There was 'Fighting' Jack Fitzgerald who used the Dublin mob to stave off arrest by the police, on his frequent visits to the metropolis, where despite the fact that he was of the landed class, he was a wanted man.

A duel in those days could start at the drop of a hat. Though duelling was illegal judges occasionally issued challenges to impertinent barristers, and since the Four Courts was beside the duelling grounds in the Phoenix Park, their lordships could get back to hearing quickly, if their aim was in.

The Bucks' Castle (the Hell-fire Club) can still be seen on a hill-top near Dublin. Here they galloped in the evening dressed in red and black, the devil's livery, not so much to show their sympathy with Satanism, as their contempt of superstition. Their leader was Jack Parsons, the Earl of Rosse.

As Stephen Gwynn says, Dublin never quite left the eighteenth century, and there were vestiges of this tradition extant in the city in the Edwardian age.

When Joyce came to write *Ulysses* he saw Gogarty as a descendant of the Bucks, a primrose-vested gallant against the

38

picaresque society of lower middle class Dublin. Gogarty is Buck Mulligan in the book.

There is an elegance and panache about Gogarty as a young man that is reminiscent of the Bucks. Like them he seemed to relish danger for its own sake. This is evident in his passion for speed. First he sought it in cycle-racing, then in powerful motor-cars, finally in aeroplanes, anything that would fulfil his bodily urge 'for swift movement and direct it towards the All-Mover ... for movement is the ritual recognition of the divine nature of our substance.'

His bravery was instinctive. He simply didn't feel fear in the ordinary way. Two airmen, who flew in the days when flying was a lethal pastime, have assured me that Gogarty was quite fearless in aeroplanes. He accomplished courageous acts with casual indifference. J. F. Byrne, Joyce's friend – Cranly in *A Portrait of the Artist as a Young Man* – once saw Gogarty pull a man out of the Liffey, climb dripping over the river wall and slip away without giving his name. On another occasion, talking to Robert Reynolds, Gogarty was showing him a new suit he had on, when word went up that a man 'had done the Liffey'. Gogarty hopped over the wall like a sparrow, retrieved the drowing man, and the next day Reynolds received a postcard with a figure of a youth drawn on it, his trousers shrunken half-way up his legs. On July 27th, 1901, he rescued a would-be suicide named Max Harris, after a desperate struggle in which he had to knock out the drowning person before bringing him ashore. For these two rescues and an attempted rescue at Balbriggan on August 4th, 1899, Gogarty received a bronze medal and two testimonials inscribed on vellum from the Royal Humane Society. The bronze medal was awarded on July 15th, 1898, and the testimonials on October 19th, 1899, and July 15th, 1901. This medal and the testimonials are in the possession of Oliver D. Gogarty, Gogarty's eldest son. He never talked or wrote about these events afterwards, and it is only from his family's newspaper reports and reminiscences of contemporaries that it has been possible to compile a record of them.

Cycle-racing in Gogarty's day had some of the physical danger of a duelling contest about it. Bookies gave odds on the competitors, and crashes in which men were killed or badly injured were often engineered by unscrupulous cyclists. Gogarty hadn't a scintilla of fear in his make-up once he mounted his machine. Up North, once, at Ballinafeigh Sports, he was told that attempts were to be made to involve him in a crash, as he looked a likely winner, but that didn't deter him from competing. Since he was the sole competitor from Southern Ireland he had a ticklish job. Ulstermen are loyal – to one another.

> The tall fellow closed in on me. He had the advantage of half a length. As I was about to be killed his handlebar hit my elbow and he changed his mind as suddenly as his direction. He went like a human projectile into a sea of heads, for he left the track where the side was banked up to the spectators' chins. I heard a roar that nearly distracted me for I was open to the least stimulus. I am clear at last and alone in the straight and goodbye to the mounting pyramid of flesh and steel far behind.

When he was cheated by underhand methods at sports he never lacked the courage to speak his mind. Once at Jones Road, Dublin, he was forced out of a race; later on a codfish appeared among the prizes, with the note attached: 'Dedicated to the Sharks of Jones Road from Oliver Gogarty.'

Gogarty himself felt an affinity with the flamboyant atmosphere of eighteenth-century Dublin, when the austere architecture of the city first began to show itself against the skyline. He knew its legends and ballads and was constantly searching for new material that would add to his picture of the age, just as a Londoner might pore over the age of Falstaff, or a Parisian over the Paris of Villon, to imbibe the ancestral spirit of their cities. When he wrote his first prose work he called it after a ballad of the Bucks, *As I Was Going Down Sackville Street* – a street 'which is paved with the cobblestones of the 18th century, and in it a braver Dublin rings, than we will ever see again.'

FOUR

OUTSIDE the walls of Trinity exciting events were shaping the future of Ireland. There was the Literary Renaissance which was to produce among others, in a short period, W. B. Yeats, J. M. Synge, Padraic Colum, Lady Gregory, A.E. (George Russell), James Stephens, James Joyce and Sean O'Casey. But Trinity had set its face against the creation of a distinctive Irish literature. One of the Fellows stated in print that there was no literature in Gaelic which was not either stupid or obscene. Dowden entered the field of public controversy and became a bitter opponent of Home Rule and the Literary Revival. Perhaps that is why when the figures of Trinity's great age died, much of their fame died with them. Posterity passed them by, because they missed the opportunity of establishing contact with the revival of native culture that was taking place in Ireland, and from which the Anglo-Irish writers drew their inspiration. Yeats's phrase that Dowden 'withered on the barren soil of Unionism' applied to others besides Dowden.

During the first decade of this century Ireland was in a state of intellectual and political ferment. The Abbey Theatre brought before popular audiences the works of Yeats, Synge, A.E., Lady Gregory, Padraic Colum, George Moore and others. In painting and music there were names like Orpen, Hugh Lane, John McCormack, Hamilton Harty and Herbert Hughes. Arthur Griffith founded Sinn Fein, a political group devoted to national self-determination, which was to sweep the country at the elections thirteen years later. The Irish Republican Brotherhood had reorganized secretly, and was preparing for armed revolution. Irish Socialism had established itself among the working classes, under the leadership of James Connolly. The Irish Agricultural Co-operative Society was revolutionizing farming techniques in the country-side. The Gaelic League had formed branches throughout Ireland, where Nationalist and Unionist met together on common ground to learn the Irish language.

The prospects of Home Rule seemed bright, with the return of the Liberals in 1905; the Irish Party at Westminster seemed about to succeed where Parnell had failed. Through these activities ran a common thread: they were different manifestations of the same theme. Whether their origins were political or cultural, Unionist or Nationalist, they represented the struggle towards a unified personality that was taking place in the national being irrespective of class or creed. 'There was an eagerness in the air not solely political,' James Stephens noted about this vigorous decade in Irish history. 'Dublin functioned in a state of verbal excitement and used prose instead of grammar. There was an athletic delight in being alive, a complete non-recognition of poverty in its meaner modes. The mind was up. What it was up to, no one knew or cared.' The alchemy which makes a nation was at work. A new Irishman was coming into existence, neither Anglo-Irish nor Gaelic, but a blend of both races. This welding of racial elements unleashed an elation in the national being productive of exceptional energy in those who lived at that time. What John Addington Symonds has written of the Elizabethan and Florentine man can be usefully applied to Ireland in the first decade of this century:

> There is a heritage of power prepared for them at birth. The atmosphere in which they breathe is so charged with mental energy that the least stirring of their special energy brings them into contact with forces mightier than the forces of single natures.

The Anglo-Irish were descended from English settlers. They had become the established ruling class in Ireland at the end of the seventeenth century. Their great names included Swift, Berkeley, Grattan, Burke, Sheridan, Goldsmith, Congreve, Hamilton, Shaw, Wilde. Government policy had been designed to prevent their mingling with the native population whose culture had not yet made itself articulate in the European sense. But by the nineteenth century the barriers between the two races had begun to weaken. Official edicts proved impotent against the influence of climate and personality. Both races began to share common characteristics of temperament and outlook. A wave of enthusiasm for the ignored culture of the Gael swept the Anglo-Irish in this century. It pertained to all levels. Scholars began scrutiny of ancient Gaelic texts. Successful professional men devoted their leisure time to antiquarian and archeological studies connected with Gaelic culture. Sir William Wilde, father of Oscar Wilde and one of the leading oculists in Europe, wrote in 1853

42

what is still a standard work on Irish archaeology. Oscar's mother, Speranza, the poetess, published Gaelic folk-tales, which she noted down from the lips of the peasantry. A Dublin barrister, Sir Samuel Ferguson, was the first to translate the Gaelic epics into English poetry. Standish O'Grady, a Protestant landlord, re-wrote the Irish heroic cycle in stirring prose that influenced the leading poets and playwrights of the literary period. The founder of the Gaelic League, Douglas Hyde, was the son of a Roscommon parson.

Yeats and A.E. were to be the effective prophets of the period. With the artist's eye they discerned the metamorphosis that was taking place in the national being. A.E. prepared to hail 'the first born of the coming race', the new Irishman, a composite of Gael and Gall (foreigner),

> One river born from many streams
> Roll in one blaze of blinding light,

while Yeats sought the principle of unity that would 'bind the peasant visionaries that are, the landlord duellists that were, in one Celtic phantasmagoria.' Both practised occult rites, believing that there were no material barriers which could not be overcome by the resources of the imagination.

Since, Yeats thought, all people had their first unity from a mythology that married them to rock and hill, might not the myths that were known and sung among the uneducated classes, if they were brought before the educated classes, hasten the progress of the unity he desired? Later he was to wonder if the myths that were known and sung among the uneducated classes, taken on some turbulent life of their own, like the painted horses of Japan he had once read of, who escaped from their picture frames and trampled the rice fields before returning to their prison frames, wet from the fields but 'trembling in stillness'. Some of the insurgents in the Insurrection of 1916 had been influenced by Yeats's poems.

> Did that play of mine send out
> Certain men the English shot?

A.E. had been associated with the Dublin Theosophical Society from its beginning and was one of the originators of occult study in Dublin. Presently he became interested in the Celtic movement,

43

discovering that the gods of the Gael were close relatives of the Eastern deities, who belonged to his own cult. His doctrine was aristocratic, heroic ... all men, he believed, bore within them their own divinity, and it needed some adventure of the spirit, some gesture against materialism for each man to recover his inheritance in the Age of Gold. Ireland's function in the modern age was to preserve the imagination from corruption by the machine.

Many were attracted by A.E.'s ideas; his personal influence was immense. Young men whose highest ambition should have been the distillery desk or the banking counter abandoned their dream of a watch-chain on an ample waistcoat, and met on three nights a week at the rooms of the Theosophical Society at Adelaide Road. What more staid household can be conceived than that of the Orange member from Portadown? Yet Charles Johnson, the eldest son of this family, threw aside Trinity scholarships and a promising career in one night, after he had come in contact with A.E.'s theosophists; afterwards he left Ireland for Russia and married Madame Blatavsky's niece, in the meantime translating the Upanishads. On week-ends these young theosophists went to the hills and discussed matters far removed from the atmosphere of the suburbs they had left behind. Lying on their backs on the heather gazing over Dublin Bay, they let their imagination wing over Howth, beyond the continent behind, till they had drawn from their subconscious images what they believed were visions of Hindu or Celtic gods.

'We had caught' – writes Charles Johnson – 'the word handed down through the ages with secret laughter, that we ourselves are the inventors of the Game of Life: the Kings of this most excellent Universe, that we need not knock to be admitted for we already are and always were, though we had forgotten it, within the doors of life. There was a gaiety and lightness in the air then, a delight of new discovery that I do not think we shall find again.'

They too were part of the pattern of awakening Ireland, of the excitement of those times, though they did not know that the elixir that filled them was from the nation's font, believing it to be an exaltation of their own making.

Gogarty had become a friend of Yeats before he met either Moore or A.E. His first glimpse of the poet was at a play-reading

44

given by Lady Gregory at the Nassau Hotel in 1901, which he attended with James Joyce. He was immediately struck by Yeats's aristocratic presence and chanting incantatory voice. Later Mrs Gogarty secured the poet for one of her 'evenings' in Rutland Square, and here Yeats and her son had their first meeting. He became a fairly frequent visitor at the Gogartys. Oliver regarded him with awe. For him Yeats was the ideal of the poet, beautiful in mind and feature, the aristocratic ideal that Athens admired. For a while he was timid of Yeats, as he would have been with few others. Then one night at his mother's house after the rest of the visitors had left, Yeats remained behind to transcribe at Gogarty's request the lyric 'Shy one of my Heart', which he did by the light of a candle balanced on the piano. Gogarty knew he was making some impression on Yeats's somewhat aloof personality. Soon Yeats began to consult him on classical sources. It is generally thought that Yeats didn't begin his first attempt at Sophocles' *Oedipus* until 1908, owing to Gilbert Murray's refusal to make a literal translation for him in 1904. But a note from Gogarty to an Oxford acquaintance shows that the poet turned to his young friend instead and asked him to give him a version which he could turn into English verse. To G. K. A. Bell Gogarty wrote in February 1904, 'I am preparing a trans. (verse) of Oedipus Rex for Yeats.' *Oedipus* in fact was to be Yeats's finest dramatic work. Later, as he completed the play in the 'twenties, he made Gogarty chant passages to him in Greek so that he could capture in English some of the assonances of the original. There is a charming picture of Yeats at George Moore's salon, in another letter to Bell, written by Gogarty the same year:

> Yeats was at Moore's the other Saturday, and drank whiskeys and sodas, and recited a passage from a play he is composing, 'Deirdre.' The effects of his reciting this are not to be transmitted to you. He forgot himself and his face seemed tremulous as if in an image of impalpable fire. His lips are dark cherry red, and his cheeks too, take colour, and his eyes actually glow black and then the voice sets all vibrating as he sways like a Druid with his whole soul chanting. No wonder the mechanics in America are mesmerized. I know no more beautiful face than Yeats', when lit with song. Moore of course talked Bawdy. The conversation was very interesting

to me. At Moore's everyone becomes inspired to talk without any affectation. Moore is the most sincerely affected man I know. His mannerisms have become real Moore.

The Yeats that Gogarty met was quite different from the Pre-Raphaelite poseur of the 'nineties, with flowing cape and wide hat, whom George Moore had described as resembling 'a huge umbrella left behind at a picnic party'. The well-known Augustus John portrait painted in 1907 has caught perfectly the metamorphosis in Yeats's character: the dreamer of the Celtic Twilight has gone, to be replaced by the public man, the fighter at the Abbey, the I.R.B. member of O'Leary's Fenian Faith, with only a hint in the slant eyes and faun nostrils of the Communer with the Land under the Wave. John O'Leary returned from banishment in Paris, a falcon-faced ancient, had turned Yeats's eyes towards his own country. 'I need but two followers' – he said once – 'Yeats and Rolleston.' This contact with the stream of Irish nationalism gave Yeats's work a new purpose. It cut him off from an aimless society which could have corrupted him. Evenings which he might have spent in an artificial atmosphere, he occupied with lecturing on the revived Irish literature and the necessity for the creation of a national culture. Conscientiously he and Maud Gonne rolled up the carpets that had been laid out to welcome visiting royalty, and wrote letters to the newspapers protesting against the impropriety of royal visits while Ireland was denied its freedom. Yeats, the poet, could hardly have failed to appeal to Gogarty; the man of action enthralled him.

It is in a sentence written many years later that Yeats revealed what most attracted him to Gogarty. When the *Oxford Book of Modern Verse*, edited by Yeats, appeared in the 'thirties, he wrote in the preface after praising Gogarty's bravery in defending himself against gunmen:

> Irish by tradition and many ancestors, I love though I have nothing to offer but the philosophy they deride, swashbucklers, horsemen, swift indifferent men. That is the reason, though perhaps not the only one, why I have given Gogarty such space, and think him one of the great lyric poets of our age.

Here is Yeats seeking again for his link between the two Irelands.

46

Out of old Gaelic stock has come a figure with the qualities of the 'swift indifferent men', the legendary figures of the hunting-fields who were the heroes of Yeats's youth; another sign that a fusion of racial qualities was taking place. This was Yeats's favourite tack. In Gogarty he discerned characteristics of the Anglo-Irish squires, just as in Kevin O'Higgins, the brilliant young statesman of the new Irish State, he was to see the iron quality of the great names in Anglo-Irish history.

> We have as good blood as there is in Europe; Swift, Berkeley, Burke, Grattan, Parnell, Augusta Gregory, Synge, Kevin O'Higgins are the true Irish people and there is nothing too hard for such as these. If the Catholic names are few, history will fill the gap.

Here was the 'coming race' that A.E. wrote about in *The Inner and the Outer Ireland* 'made out of a union of Saxon, Dane, Norman and Gael, dominated by the last, and looking back to it as to an ancestral self.'

George Moore's return to Dublin to take part in the Literary Revival caused a sensation. He was the leading English novelist of his time. He had already written *A Modern Lover, A Mummer's Wife, Drama in Muslin, Confessions and Opinions, Esther Waters*, and *Evelyn Innes*. As a stylist he had inherited Pater's mantle. He had introduced realism to the English novel, doing for the English language 'what Zola had done for the French'. He had been a leading aesthete in the 'nineties, one of the few to survive Wilde's debacle. It was largely through his perceptive critical writing that French impressionism gained recognition in England.

At the turn of the century his popularity was at its height. He had conquered two cities. In Paris in the 'eighties he had been part of the famous group of writers and artists who used to meet at the Nouvelle Athènes. In *Confessions of a Young Man* he has left delightful vignettes of Degas, Manet, Zola, Villiers de l'Isle Adam, Verlaine, Copée and others. Manet who painted a famous portrait of Moore said to him: 'No Frenchman occupies in London the position you do in Paris.' Later in his trilogy *Ave, Salve* and *Vale*, he was to set down his impressions of the Literary Revival, anticipating Joyce and Proust with his technique of

47

'romantic autobiography', depicting his environment with the microscopic eye of a Monet, and including himself in the pageant he had created.

Moore was a landlord and a Catholic, who had abandoned religion, class and race for his art. What brought him back to Ireland? He has told us in *Ave* how he heard, like St Patrick, a voice in his ear telling him to return, as he was walking down Bouverie Street. Then there was the telegram from his friend, Edward Martyn: 'The sceptre of the intellect has passed from London to Dublin.' England had begun to dissatisfy him. The Boer war infuriated him. At least in Dublin he wouldn't have a boisterous middle class shouting imperialism in his ear. He was filled with enthusiasm for the Gaelic language revival in Ireland. Literature needed a new language to express itself. English had worn itself out with use. It would soon be 'a dry shank-bone on the dust heap of empire'. Half ironically he occupied himself with dreams of argosies sailing up the Liffey, and poets singing in the Bowers of Merrion Square. One uses the phrase 'half ironically' because most of the reasons given above probably arose from Moore's chameleon-like changes of mood, and his natural petulance. The main reason for his return to Dublin was that he had a nose like a bloodhound for art. He scented a renaissance just as he discovered a centre of artistic activity in Paris in the 'eighties. London without Wilde, Whistler, Sargent, Beardsley no longer interested him. He was seeking fresh fields and in Dublin he found them. He set up home in a large Georgian house in Ely Place, a cul-de-sac near the centre of the city. Here he soon gathered round him at dinner-parties and evening gatherings the leading figures of the movement. Moore disliked reading books, but liked wearing an idea to a thread in talk, and Dublin was ideal for this purpose.

'A.E.,' John Eglinton says, 'pullulated ideas. Yeats walked with his head in a cloud of ideas. In Moore's room where he wrangled over abstractions, the air towards midnight would grow dim and overcharged with ideas.' It was at one of these gatherings that Moore was introduced to Gogarty. He was immediately fascinated by the young man.

'Gogarty,' he wrote, 'is the Arch Mocker, the youngest of my friends, the author of all the jokes that enable us to live in Dublin, of the Limericks of the Golden Age, full in the face with a smile in his eyes, and always a witticism on his lips overflowing with quotations.'

Quite a mead of praise from the leading English novelist for a young student. Yeats has observed that the artist must be shaped by nature and art to some one out of half a dozen traditional poses, be he lover, saint, sage and sensualist, or mocker of life. Gogarty and Moore were 'Mockers of Life'. Padraic Colum has noted of Gogarty that he could not observe a person for long without becoming aware of some defect or inadequacy in him. Moore had the same piercing eye, and like Gogarty had no scruples in later turning the results of his observation into a witty remark or epigram. His attitude was, and Gogarty probably followed him in this, that wit was a creative artifice and therefore exempt from moral stricture as a work of art is. Irishmen delight in derisive mockery when it is sheathed in the anodyne of wit. Moore used to ask himself was he capable of sacrificing brother, sister, mother, fortune, friend for a work of art. Before he left Ireland he was to provide the answer. The Trilogy resolved his scruples for him. John Freeman said of it:

Never have the privileges of friendship and the accidents of acquaintance been more widely misused.

Later, when Gogarty wrote *As I Was Going Down Sackville Street* he treated his friends with a similar Goncourt detachment, sparing neither their virtues nor their vices, an approach that obviously derived from Moore.

Moore used to make a fetish out of his aesthetic licence to pillory his friends as well as his enemies in print. When Edward Martyn failed to give in to clerical pressure and insisted on proceeding with the production of *The Countess Cathleen*, Moore was bitterly disappointed. 'What a chance it would have been,' he said. He had wanted to write a pamphlet to be entitled *Edward Martyn and his Soul*. 'No one in literature has ever written that way about a friend, it would have been a sensation.'

Moore, who had a poor memory, was fascinated by Gogarty's ability to quote at will from various sources. Often the young man recited whole ballads to Moore as they went on walks, perhaps the fifty-three verses of 'Kinmont Willie', or the forty-seven verses of 'Tam Lin', or shorter ones like Drayton's 'Agincourt', the 'Bonny Earl of Moray', or 'Sir Patrick Spens'. Moore began

49

to wait outside the National Library in the evenings for Gogarty to finish reading, and then bring him back to Ely Place for drinks and cigars to enjoy his talk. The two were sometimes seen together in the streets taking the air, the young man's finger raised at Moore's ear beating out the time of a ballad, or emphasizing a witty point, while Moore listened with a slight look of astonishment in his porcelain-blue eyes. Moore's dress at this time was very un-Dublin. He still dressed like a boulevardier with peg-top trousers, a malacca cane, and a straw hat over his flimsy yellowish hair. Gogarty with his high Edwardian jacket, primrose waistcoat, and silk tie tied in a thick bow, must have made quite a contrast to Moore's conscious Bohemianism. A.E. has recalled Gogarty's success at Moore's evenings:

I had long hoped to meet the author of the witty verses and scandalous sayings that circulated the city. Then one night I met Gogarty at George Moore's, before the war. He was then an undergraduate at Trinity, and when he came into the room, Moore had the rare experience of being brilliantly out-talked in his own house. There was no subject his wit would not illuminate: We had been questioning about the round Towers, whether they were Christian or pre-Christian, and Gogarty ended our controversy by a sentence, 'Of course they were pre-Christian; no parish priest could get through the doorways.' No, this was not born out of irreligion. It was only the exercise of his God-given wit and irony which angels, not surely irreligious beings, might feel, seeing some too earthly minister of their Great King.

Gogarty frequently had a new ballade or limerick with him when he arrived at Moore's. These were given to Yeats, A.E., and Moore with the injunction that they were to be locked away, though A.E. thought the precaution unnecessary as the verses were so ingenious even the victims must laugh at them.

These Rabelaisian verses were not shallow jestings but the work of a scholar and artist in words. How we exulted in that dazzling conversation, which spared neither the maker of the Universe or His creatures. He would remember verses which preserved the character or perversities of his friends in poem, whose art was such it was a compliment to have one's defects preserved in them.

50

'Who is that astonishing young man?' William Archer asked Richard Best, after he had heard Gogarty in action at Moore's, although Best thought Gogarty sometimes spoiled Moore's evenings by talking too much.

Gogarty's success was remarkable for one so young. He became almost a cult. In his absence they quoted and discussed his limericks. There were arguments as to what were correct versions, as clerics might have quarrelled over the interpretation of ancient manuscripts. One evening Moore recited his favourite, 'There was a young man from St John's,' but found Yeats in disagreement with him about the last line. ' "The birds are reserved for the dons," Moore; not "The swans are reserved for the dons." '

Finally, the poet retired to a corner, and began to compare the two versions chanting the lines alternately beating his hand up and down in rhythm as he did so. In a few minutes he returned, 'Birds, Moore, birds,' he announced decisively.

Moore has left us a portrait of Gogarty in *Salve* which is valuable because it depicts in some detail his conversational style. He noted Gogarty's power of perceiving distant analogies, piling imagination upon imagination, spinning his speech out as a butterfly spins from a chrysalis; his habit of becoming grave like a dog that licks his lips after a savoury morsel, whenever an amusing remark was made; how he became restless if kept out of the conversation too long, like an athlete waiting to get into the arena. One night Moore is discussing his proposed departure from Dublin with some friends. The wicket clangs, Gogarty enters, lowering his voice when complimented on a famous limerick, as Yeats does when 'Innisfree' is praised. Before anyone can speak he has spotted an analogy and is comparing Moore to Ovid banished to the Pontic Sea, sitting with his friends the night before his departure. This gives him an opening to bring in Sir Thornley Stoker, Moore's rival as a connoisseur, an affluent surgeon, who has equipped his house, Gogarty suggests, from the proceeds of specific operations.

> The Aubusson carpet in the drawing-room represents a hernia, the Ming Cloisonné a floating kidney, the Buhl cabinet his opinion of an enlarged liver, the Renaissance bronze on the landing, a set of gall-stones.

When Moore, to change the flow of the conversation, announced that he had a capon for dinner weighing over five pounds, Gogarty cried:

What beneficent Providence let it into such excesses of fat. It delved not nor span, nor wasted its tissues in vain flirtation; a little operation released it from all feminine trouble and allowed it to spend its days in attaining a glory, which Moore with all his literature will never attain, the glory of fat capon. 'The unlabouring brood of the coop'; you know Yeats' line. For a long time I thought Yeats was referring to priests, but he must have been thinking of capons; he knows nothing of capons, he must have been thinking of the stars.
O Songless bird far sweeter than the rose
And virgin as a parish priest God knows.

Later, A.E. talks of Gogarty's reckless imagination, as the young man is off again describing the race between nuns, who are turning fashionable residences in the suburbs into convents ('with money out of purgatory's bank, nothing succeeds in Ireland like a convent, a public house and a race meeting') and the monks who are eagerly searching for monastery sites; comparing the nuns to tiercels and the monks to hawks, and maintaining that the nuns must win as the hen bird is the fiercer of the two.

From this record of Moore's, it is possible to savour something of the flavour of Gogarty's conversational style. In Moore's circle Gogarty was among famous talkers. Sir Desmond McCarthy has written of Yeats that he was the only talker he ever heard 'who will launch the high poetic phrase in conversation'. Ernest Boyd's phrase about A.E.'s talk, 'a great rhythmic torrent which carries away the hearer', conjures up a picture of the effect he had on his listeners. Moore was himself a superb talker. But Gogarty had an asset which his literary friends had not, a conscious style acquired from his master at Trinity, under whose tutelage Oscar Wilde had learned to use that golden voice

And conjure wonder out of emptiness,
Till mean things put on beauty like a dress,
And all the world was an enchanted place.

(Lord Alfred Douglas)

FIVE

F OR a while Gogarty became the arch-poet of a group of medical students who frequented the lawless purlieus of the city. They repeated his limericks and ballades of the brothels with gusto round the town, as he produced them. Sir Walter Raleigh as a young man liked to have round him 'boisterous blades and those that had wit'. From such 'gracieux gallants' did Villon form his friendships, and Shakespeare found relief from his pen's toil in the company of those whom he used for his portraits of tavern life in London.

Gogarty's friends had alert minds and an abundance of wit. An allusion or pun among them was caught at once, and rewarded with a swift glance of acknowledgment before another capped it. Their language, laced with medical or classical argot, was often incomprehensible to outsiders; and their double entendre and allusion were too swift for less rapid minds to follow. Vincent Cosgrave, John Elwood, Simon Broderick, with James Joyce tacked on as a 'medical student's pal', were his chief companions about this time. Cosgrave is Lynch in James Joyce's *Portrait of the Artist as a Young Man*, the student who argues the aesthetic question with Stephen Dedalus. He was a youth of curious contrasts, a cynic and unbeliever but with a deep love of medieval church music. Sometimes as he and Joyce passed through the decaying streets, they would intone Gregorian chants, chaste music that was written to echo past Gothic arches in the sweep of golden chasubles and the rising of perfumed incense. Gogarty and the others followed behind, delighted and amused. Gogarty had a real liking for Elwood, whom he remembered for his dancing eyes, beautiful mouth, and lightning, somewhat oblique wit. He may have romanticized his looks, because others who knew Elwood have not the same recollection of his physical appearance.

Elwood professed Socialism, was a member of the I.R.B., the secret physical force organization, and was known as 'Citizen' from his habit of addressing people in that mode.

Though of inexhaustible resource in argument, or in the organization of escapades, neither Elwood nor Cosgrave seem to have had a flair for the practical business of life. Elwood became an obscure country doctor, and Cosgrave jumped to his death off

London Bridge in 1908, when his mother died and his source of income gave out. Elwood had a term, 'artist', which he used to describe one who created his personality for the diversion of his friends. Perhaps he and Cosgrave put too much of their energy into their personalities, and didn't reserve enough for the battle of life. Perhaps they were victims of the frustration underlying Irish life where talent often aborted through lack of opportunity for men of their religion and class.

A favourite drinking place for Gogarty and his friends was Nighttown, the abode of the Dublin lights-o'-love. Medical students enjoying a special licence in these regions by reason of their healing function were as Gogarty wrote 'safe in every shee-been from the Gloucester Diamond to Hell's Gates, when the Kips were in full blast'. You could drink all night in the Kips without having to absent yourself on felicity upstairs. This was one of the advantages of the place for medical students whose duties involved their being abroad at hours when it was difficult to obtain refreshment elsewhere. Gogarty was fascinated by the un-trammelled personalities he came across in his visits to the Kips. He revelled in the frothing eloquence and corrosive balaclavas of the brothel owners, a language uncloyed by the cliché-sodden conversation of the suburbs. 'Here', wrote Gogarty, 'reigned the Shakespearean London of Jack Greene. Here nothing but the English language was undefiled. The names of its bullies, brothel owners and frequenters were typical of a city which like Vienna had forged for itself a distinct identity.'

The word 'Kips' is probably from the old Danish Dublin 'Keep' or 'area cordon'. The place was unique in the British Isles in that it was licensed by the police. Vol. 10 of the *Encyclopaedia Britannica* says: 'Dublin seems to form an exception to the usual practice in the United Kingdom. In that city the police permit open brothels confined to one area, but carried on more openly than in the South of Europe or even Algiers.'

Gogarty was at his ease in this atmosphere. The Kip queens deferred to him. Joyce, with a touch of the bourgeois in him, could not quite bring off Gogarty's air of nonchalance. So he became quaint instead. Astonished madams were lectured on points of Greek drama, or he would intone hotly in a whore's ear a chaste Gregorian psalm. Gogarty celebrated Joyce's unorthodox approach to drabbing in a limerick:

54

There was a young fellow called Joyce
Who possesseth a sweet tenor voice.
He goes to the Kips
With a psalm on his lips
And biddeth the harlots rejoice.

The madams were often women of intelligence. Meg Arnott, one of the most successful, lived in a mansion in Mount Merrion, and had a daughter at an expensive English convent school. On Saturdays, to increase custom, she drove her girls up Grafton Street in a landau, while they nodded plumed hats to customers, with discreet smiles. Mrs Mack, a more cruel specimen, was fond of confiding in Gogarty her sardonic reactions to her customers. 'Them incorporated accountants make me sick. Never come here decent and honest; but always with excuses.' She had, he recalled, 'a brick red face, on which avarice was written like a hieroglyphic, and a laugh like a guffaw in hell.' (See Gogarty's Rabelaisian ballad, Appendix, p. 305.)

The smartest part of Nighttown was Tyrone Street, where the old Georgian houses were more or less in good repair. The ladies wore evening dress, and each month a special costumier visited the street to make sure they were in fashion. Railway Street, Mabbot Street and Faithful Place were the cheap spots. Here the girls wore only raincoats which they opened occasionally as a lure to hesitant clients. It was in one of these streets that a courageous reformer, Mr Frank Duff, encountered a scene reminiscent of a jungle orgy:

Eight women ranged themselves in a circle and silence reigned. The carrier of the methylated spirit stood in the centre of the circle. To each woman she gave *two* glasses one large and one small. The small glass was filled with methylated and the large with water. Then immediately down went the glass of methylated spirit followed by the glass of water to prevent the spirits actually burning her. There they were rigid except for trembling hands, their eyes staring out of their heads all riveted on the methylated and following its circulatory procession. This procedure was repeated until all got their share. Then a regular witches' dance began round and round till the little breath they had gave out.

This was the sordid side to the Kips. Sometimes the bullies handed out fearful beatings to the girls: bodies were found floating down the Liffey after a night's shennannigan there. Gogarty didn't close his eyes to this aspect of the life. His medical experience brought home to him the horrors of whoredom. He saw too many lives shudder to a screaming end in the 'Lock' Hospitals of Dublin to over-romanticize the Kips. But he discovered here a survival of a life that had passed out of the fabric of Europe years before. The artist in him reached out to the effervescence of spirit that he encountered amid the squalor and vice, and he found, as Wilde did, that between artist and criminal there is often a common link:

> Laughter is the primeval attitude towards life, a mode of living that survives only in artists and criminals.

Even in the polluted air of those reckless nights, his eye for beauty never left him.

> In the east down Summerhill a shaft of sunlight lit the great tenements of crumbling rose.

Late-night revellers from the Kips usually stopped at the Hay Hotel in Cavendish Row for coffee and crubeens. 'The Hay' was run by Maria, the Gogarty's cook, who had married their butler, Stephen, and set up her own establishment. It got its name from the fact that hay was kept in one of the windows so that the cabbies' horses could have an appetizer while their masters were inside with their customers. The Hay survived the downfall of the Kips which were wiped out in 1924, and in a ballad Gogarty has commemorated the weird underworld of his youth and the fantastic characters who inhabited it.

THE HAY HOTEL

> There is a window stuffed with hay
> Like herbage in an oven cast;
> And there we came at break of day
> To soothe ourselves with light repast:
> And men who worked before the mast
> And drunken girls delectable:
> A future symbol of our past
> You'll, maybe, find the Hay Hotel.

Where are the great Kip Bullies gone,
The Bookies and outrageous Whores
Whom we so gaily rode upon
When youth was mine and youth was yours:
Tyrone Street of the crowded doors
And Faithful Place so infidel?
It matters little who explores
He'll only find the Hay Hotel.

Dick Lynam was a likely lad,
His back was straight; has he gone down?
And for a pal Jem Plant he had
Whose navel was like half a crown.
They were the talk of all Meck town;
And Norah Seymour loved them well;
Of all their haunts of lost renown
There's only left the Hay Hotel.

Fresh Nellie's gone and Mrs Mack,
May Oblong's gone and Number Five,
When you could get so good a back
And drinks were so superlative;
Of all their nights, O Man Alive!
There is not left an oyster shell
Where greens are gone the greys will thrive;
There's only left the Hay Hotel.

There's nothing left but ruin now
Where once the crazy cabfuls roared;
Where new-come sailors turned the prow
And Love-logged cattle-dealers snored:
The room where old Luke Irwin whored,
The stairs on which John Elwood fell:
Some things are better unencored:
There's only left the Hay Hotel.

Where is Piano Mary, say,
Who dwelt where Hell's Gates leave the street,
And all the tunes she used to play

57

Along your spine beneath the sheet?
She was a morsel passing sweet
And warmer than the gates of hell.
Who tunes her now between the feet?
Go ask them at the Hay Hotel.

L'ENVOI

Nay; never ask this week, fair Lord,
If, where they are now, all goes well,
So much depends on bed and board
They give them in the Hay Hotel.

SIX

WHEN Oliver Gogarty went to America in 1939 on a lecture tour he was to find that part of his fame for Americans lay in the fact that he figured as Buck Mulligan in James Joyce's novel *Ulysses*.

There is now no doubt that the original of Buck Mulligan was Gogarty. Gogarty admitted the fact in public on many occasions. He lived in the Martello Tower with Joyce, as Mulligan does with Stephen Dedalus in the novel. Oliver Gogarty saved three men from drowning in the Liffey. Mulligan saves seven. The name Malachi Mulligan has the same metrical arrangement as Oliver Gogarty.

'Two dactyls tripping and sunny like the buck himself', says Mulligan referring to his Christian and surnames. Twenty years before Joyce wrote this, George Moore had discerned the dactyls in the name Oliver Gogarty. He had given Gogarty's name to a character in his novel *The Lake*, a renegade priest called Oliver Gogarty. When Mrs Gogarty, Oliver's mother, complained, Moore chirruped back 'Madam, supply me with two such joyous dactyls and I will gladly change the name.' Joyce would have heard about Moore's remark from Gogarty and it almost certainly gave him the inspiration for Malachi Mulligan's name in *Ulysses*.

Padraic Colum tells me that Buck Mulligan's dialogue is a pretty accurate description of Gogartian conversation in the period during which Joyce knew Gogarty.

> The talk of the 'Buck' in the opening of *Ulysses*, the interjections from him in the library and the hospital are as right as could be – not only the words but the pace of the words.

Passages from *Ulysses* suggest the conversational techniques which Moore, Colum and A.E. noted in Gogarty. Colum remembers his conversation as an astonishing verbal display with

> its sudden shifts and inexplicable transitions, its copious quotations of poetry, along with frequent plain statements of practical issues

while Moore, as noted in a previous chapter, has commented on Gogarty's power of perceiving distant analogies as he talked and

59

relating them to the subject on hand. These qualities are suggested in Mulligan's conversation as he talks with Stephen on the parapet of the Martello Tower in the opening chapter of *Ulysses*.

[Mulligan] came over to the gunrest and, thrusting a hand into Stephen's upper pocket, said, 'Lend us a loan of your noserag to wipe my razor.' Stephen suffered him to pull out and hold up on show by its corner a dirty crumpled handkerchief. Buck Mulligan wiped the razorblade neatly. Then, gazing over the handkerchief, he said: 'The bard's noserag. A new art colour for our Irish poets: snot-green. You can almost taste it, can't you?'

He mounted to the parapet again and gazed out over Dublin Bay, his fair oakpale hair stirring slightly.

'God,' he said quietly. 'Isn't the sea what Algy calls it: a grey sweet mother? The snotgreen sea. The scrotum-tightening sea. Epi oinopa ponton. Ah, Dedalus, the Greeks. I must teach you. You must read them in the original. Thalatta! Thalatta! She is our great sweet mother. Come and look.'

Stephen stood up and went over to the parapet. Leaning on it he looked down on the water and on the mailboat clearing the harbour mouth of Kingstown.

'Our mighty mother,' Buck Mulligan said. He turned abruptly his great searching eyes from the sea to Stephen's face.

The 'Algy' referred to is the poet Algernon Swinburne. Quotations from Swinburne abound in Gogartian epistles. In a letter written in June 1904, he actually quotes the Swinburne phrase which Joyce puts on Mulligan's lips: 'our grey sweet mother'.

When *Ulysses* appeared in 1922 and Gogarty saw himself depicted as Mulligan, he was furious. It seemed to him in the nature of a betrayal that Joyce should have written about him as he did.

That bloody Joyce whom I kept in my youth has written a book you can read on all the lavatory walls of Dublin,

he snarled to a friend who questioned him about the book shortly after it appeared. When Norah Hoult, wishing to place Gogarty as a character in one of her novels, gave him smoke-blue eyes because, as she said, Joyce was always right about such things,

Gogarty replied indignantly that this was not so. Augustus John, who was a close friend of Gogarty's, could never draw him out on the subject of Joyce. Likewise, when John went to sketch Joyce in Paris, he could get no response from his sitter when he brought up Gogarty's name. Another artist, Sean O'Sullivan, did elicit a comment from Joyce while he was engaged in painting him; he happened to mention that Gogarty was a successful surgeon in Dublin. 'God help anyone who gets into the hands of that fellow,' is how Joyce received the information.

As late as 1938, when Philip Toynbee was visiting Gogarty in Ely Place, Dublin, he mentioned Joyce's name, and the only reply he got from his host was: 'James Joyce was not a gentleman.' When he went to America in 1939, Gogarty created a sensation in literary circles by attacking aspects of Joyce's work which he looked on as confused and lacking in artistic merit. Those critics who praised the obscurities in Joyce's work, he regarded with contempt. On a brochure sent to me from New York in 1954, Gogarty had noted down his reactions to this type of criticism. The brochure dealt with a forthcoming 'study' of *Ulysses* and was heavily studded with neo-Freudian jargon.

'Bloom lived in No. 3 Clare St., Dublin,' Gogarty wrote. 'Yet the Jews have made him a symbol of the blossoming earth. Can Joyce adulation go further than this?'

Why should Gogarty have taken umbrage at the portrait of himself that appeared in *Ulysses*? At first glance it may seem paradoxical that he should have complained at a depiction of himself which showed him as a handsome Greco-Celt, with the wit and brilliance of a Regency gallant. But when *Ulysses* appeared in 1922, Gogarty had become a considerable public figure in his own country: he was by then one of the leading surgeons in Dublin and was about to become a senator of the new Irish state. If he became associated with the wild, carefree, Rabelaisian character of the Buck, it could have done him harm in public life. Remember that Joyce had obtained much of the material out of which he had created Mulligan from Gogarty's own lips and from letters which he had received from him when they were on terms of intimate friendship. To use such material later on, careless of whether it might injure the person concerned or not, was an act which could be construed as treacherous, and Gogarty regarded it as such. There are, as well, secret little gibes in *Ulysses* which must have galled Gogarty when he read them. There is, for instance, a sneering reference to Gogarty's father, a brilliant and fashionable doctor, held in high repute before his death at the age of fifty-three. Mr Richard Ellman, incidentally, repeats Joyce's slander in his biography of Joyce, relying on no other authority than the reference in *Ulysses*.

The irony of the matter is that while Gogarty with some reason regarded Mulligan's portrait as a betrayal, Joyce nurtured a paranoid belief that he would be betrayed by Gogarty at some stage. In the novel, Buck Mulligan is shown as abandoning Stephen when trouble starts in Westland Row. Mulligan is the Judas on that night. Joyce undoubtedly had a fixation on this subject. He saw betrayal in situations where none existed. He wrote to Stanislaus in 1906 expressing his confidence that Gogarty would betray his friend Arthur Griffith and the Sinn Fein movement: 'No doubt whatsoever exists in my mind about this. It is my final view of his character, a native Irish growth.' How wrong Joyce was in his prognostication can be seen from the fact that Gogarty remained Griffith's intimate friend until Griffith died in 1922, after being elected President of the Dail Eireann.

In fact, Gogarty's acts towards Joyce were those of a generous and faithful friend. He rejoiced in Joyce's creative gifts, and for this reason he gave him money and lent him clothes so that the artist might practise his craft undisturbed. One of the reasons he had conceived the idea of living in the Martello Tower in Sandy-cove was that Joyce had told him he wanted a year to write his novel, and the Tower seemed to Gogarty the best place in which to house his friend for the task. Gogarty states this in a letter to an Oxford friend written in 1904. In these circumstances, to find an implication of betrayal laid against him in *Ulysses* must have been a bitter pill to Gogarty.

The relationship between Joyce and Gogarty was a complex one. They shared many common interests, and a certain compatibility of temperament attracted one to the other. But it would have required a more equable temperament than either possessed to reconcile the divergencies in their backgrounds and outlook on life.

They met for the first time in the summer of 1901. Gogarty was then twenty-two years of age; Joyce, nineteen. Gogarty, who had met Joyce casually on another occasion, went up boldly to him in

a tram and asked him if he wrote poetry. Joyce repli€
'Yes.' This didn't deter Gogarty from asking Joyce to
following Thursday. Joyce arrived, as he had promised
field, which was quite near the centre of the city. He fou.
astonishment, that he and Gogarty had much in common. He had
known Gogarty's reputation in the city as a cyclist, swimmer, and
fashionable man-about-town, but he hadn't suspected that he was
a poet as well. Gogarty's extraordinary memory for Greek and
Latin verse fascinated Joyce.

Himself a shy visitor at the feast of the world's learning, he was
charmed to find a friend who could quote Virgil, Homer, and
Catullus as easily as another might Shelley or Wordsworth. In
return, he would sing for Gogarty airs from the psalm-books of the
lutanists or some old forgotten song of the Elizabethans that he
had salvaged from an obscure music sheet. His favourite airs were
Dowland's 'Weep You No More, Sad Fountains' and a piece
which began,

> Farewell and adieu to you, sweet Spanish Ladies,
> Farewell and adieu to you, ladies of Spain,
> For we have received orders to sail for old England,
> And we hope that one day we may meet you again.

Gogarty induced Joyce to adopt his method of writing verses on
a sheet of vellum, one verse to a single sheet. After a while Joyce
began to come out regularly to Fairfield to show his new work to
Gogarty and discuss it with him. They used to go together to the
garden behind the house and sit on a pair of old green seats that
stood under a great semicircle of yews, the same bower of beauty
to which Gogarty took Tyrrell and Macran. Mulberry bushes grew
on the lawn, protected from the north wind by the trees, and
behind lay the kitchen garden and a large orchard. 'On the east
a stone wall, topped with foxgloves red and white, self-sown from
the herbarium beneath, let the level sun flood in over the bay, and
stipple the dark yew hedge with points of moving gold. The beds
were marked with boxwood margins and contained foxglove,
mullein, digitalis, lily of the valley, bryony and thyme.' Here the
pair composed exquisite, fragile verses, whose mood indicates how
their imaginations were influenced by the prospect of nature about
them :

My love is in a light attire
Among the apple-trees,
Where the gay winds do most desire
To run in companies.

. . . .

And where the sky's a pale blue cup
Over the laughing land,
My love goes lightly, holding up
Her dress with dainty hand.

(James Joyce)

My Love is dark, but she is fair,
As dark as damask roses are,
As dark as woodland lake water
That mirrors every star.

But, as the moon who shines by night,
She wins the darker air
To blend its beauty with her light,
Till dark is doubly fair.

(Oliver Gogarty)

Another factor which bound them together was that both young men were in loquacious revolt against what they regarded as the smug conventional outlook of the Dublin middle classes. Padraic Colum remembers that the two seemed to be engaged in some enterprise – an apostolate of irreverence. 'The rationalism of Catholicism and the nonrationalism of Protestantism, the nonsensicalism of Irish nationalism, the stupidity of British imperialism were satirised by them in verse or anecdote.' Gogarty's Rabelaisian ballads, which Joyce circulated enthusiastically round the city, are one example of their joyous rejection of the attitudes of bourgeois belief. Also they flouted convention by their open visits to the Nighttown area in Dublin.

Another way in which their iconoclasm exhibited itself was in the perpetration of practical jokes. On one occasion Joyce decided to run Gogarty for the Vice-Chancellor's poetry prize in the Royal University. Gogarty had not known, until Joyce told him, that, as a former student, he was eligible for the Gold Medal. He had already won two of his three Vice-Chancellor medals for poetry in Trinity. Gogarty hurriedly composed a poem on the set theme, which was, in 1903, the Death of Shelley, and allowed Joyce to write in the last line for him: 'Shines on thee soldier of song Leonidas'. He duly won the Gold Medal. Joyce and he proceeded to the main door of the Conferring Hall of the Royal to obtain a dispensation which would enable Gogarty to absent himself from the presentation of the medal. To have been present at the ceremony would have meant hiring a special gown. The porter answered them.

'Is this the Royal University?' Gogarty said.

'You know bloody well it is,' the porter replied.

'It was a flower show last time I was here,' said Gogarty, which was literally true, as the hall had been used for a flower exhibition. Since the Royal University was only an examining body, its premises were often used for other purposes. Permission was refused for him to absent himself. So he and Joyce bought a gown out of a rag-man's sack, and amid cheers he went up for his medal, looking as if he had been through a cyclone. That night, from a sanctuary in the Kips, Joyce dispatched a pawn ticket to Sir James Meredith, the Vice-Chancellor of the University, for the value of the medal, which was twenty-five pounds.

Just how much Joyce and Gogarty were in revolt against the popular mind can be gathered from the fact that neither of them was sympathetic to the Celtic aspects of the Literary Revival which was taking place around them. Gogarty feared the 'Celtic chloroform', which he maintained 'would freeze the Sapphic current of his soul', and declared his opposition to what he termed 'the epidemic of the disinterred', a reference to the vogue of writing about the Celtic heroes, which was popular at the time. Joyce considered that the Celt had contributed nothing 'but a whine to Europe'. This was their outlook in a period which was throwing up 'Celtic' poets of the calibre of Yeats, A.E., James Stephens, Synge and Colum. But with the exception of Colum, all these writers were of Protestant, Anglo-Irish stock. Gogarty and Joyce, on the other hand, came from an older stock of Irishmen whose connections with the cultural inheritance of Europe had been minimized since the bulk of the Catholic aristocracy and upper class had left Ireland for Europe after the siege of Limerick in 1693. Young intellectuals of Joyce's and Gogarty's class tended to turn outwards towards Europe for a renewal of the inspiration their ancestors had shared when they were part of the Western tradition.

Tom Kettle, a contemporary of Joyce and Gogarty, spoke the mind of his generation when he wrote, 'If Ireland is to become truly Irish, she must first become European.' If they turned to an ancestral image at all, it was the Scandinavian strain in the Irish stock that attracted them rather than the Celtic one. Tom Kettle whose name was of Norse origin used to talk of his ancestors 'who came out of the sea'. Joyce's works are laced with references to the Viking adventurers who built Dublin in the ninth century.

Here Dane-Vikings . . . ran to beach, their blood beaked prows riding low on a molten pewter surf.

(Ulysses, page 67)

It pleased Gogarty to note in Dublin street-children survivals of Scandinavian traits: 'snub-nosed and hawser-haired like their roving ancestors'. In his poem 'Fog-Horns' he recalls the era when the blond-beards settled the east coast of Ireland and founded his native city:

> The fog horns sound
> With a note so prolonged
> That the whole air is thronged,
> And the sound is to me,
> In spite of its crying,
> The most satisfying,
> The bravest of all the brave
>   sounds of the sea.
>
> From the fjords of the North
> The fogs belly forth
> Like sails of the long ships
> That trouble the earth.
> They stand with loose sail
> In the fords of the Gael:
> From Dark Pool to White Ford
>   the surf-light is pale.
>
> The chronicles say
> That the Danes in their day
> Took a very great prey
> Of women from Howth.
> They seem to imply

That the women were shy,
That the women were loath
To be taken from Howth.
From bushy and thrushy,
    sequestering Howth.
No mists of the Druid
Could halt or undo it
When long ships besetted
The warm sands wave-netted.
In vain might men pray
To be spared the invader
To that kind eye of gray,
To the Saint who regretted
Sea-purple Ben Edar.
They sailed to the town
That is sprung from the sea
Where the Liffey comes down
Down to roll on the Lea.

.   .   .   .   .   .

Where the long ships had grounded.
You hear them again
As they called to the Dane,
And the glens were astounded.
War horns sounded,
And strong men abounded
When Dublin was founded ...

Only a few months after their first meeting, Joyce and Gogarty
had already become a familiar pair in the city streets. For a year
or so they were seldom out of each other's company. There are
people still in Dublin who can recall seeing them striding along
arm in arm, a handsome pair of mockers whispering irreverences
in each other's ears. Whenever a remark of Gogarty's particularly
pleased Joyce, he would stop deliberately, throw back his head,
and guffaw loudly.

There were certain similarities in their appearance. Both had
long Celtic faces and pale complexions. They had blue eyes of
such a singular kind that people meeting them for the first time
were immediately struck by their quality. Joyce's eyes were steel
blue: Gogarty's were darker in shade. Their hair was brown,

though, as has been pointed out, Gogarty's was often streaked with gold from the bleaching of the sun. Joyce could not afford to dress with much taste, but Gogarty was known round the city for his elegant bearing and primrose waistcoats. One student remembers Gogarty's superb aplomb as he emerged from Trinity, and greeted two plumed whores with a sweeping regal bow.

Joyce, before Gogarty met him, had already become a character in the city. He was aloof in bearing and demeanour; but he had a caustic tongue and a sense of showmanship that enabled him to keep apart from the herd and at the same time to impress his personality upon the public mind. He always managed somehow to create an air about himself and have his exploits talked about around the town. Too poor to dress elegantly, he nevertheless, from his meagre sartorial resources, managed to assemble a number of items which gave him a distinctive appearance. He was usually to be seen in grey flannels, yachting cap, and tennis shoes, with a blackthorn stick under his arm. This led Gogarty to say to him one day, 'Where's she moored, Commander?' This was typical of Gogarty. He liked to elaborate on Joyce's character and present him to the public in as interesting a fashion as possible. Colum recalls that it was solely as a character and partly a Gogartian creation that Joyce was known to Dubliners at that time. Gogarty had different names for Joyce. At one time he used to refer to him as 'Kinch'. This was in imitation of the cutting sound of a knife. 'Kinch says' was an opening gambit for a Gogartian monologue. At another time his name for Joyce was 'Dante'. He had achieved his ambition by getting Joyce to shave – and he had done so by showing him Dante's profile and suggesting that without the down on his chin, Joyce would bear a resemblance to the Florentine. After Joyce came back from Paris he had taken to lilting a new ballad called 'Cadet Roussel': this gave Gogarty an idea for a new Joycean title. 'Have you seen Cadet Roussel?' became his greeting for a while.

In December 1903 Joyce went off to Paris with the intention of studying medicine. In January Gogarty went to England to spend two terms at Oxford University. One happy result of their separation was that they communicated with each other by letter and as Joyce hung on to his Gogartiana like a leech, there is in existence today at Cornell University a formidable body of correspondence which passed from Gogarty to Joyce during the period they were apart from each other. With a few exceptions Joyce's letters to Gogarty were destroyed in the fire at Gogarty's country home in 1923, when his house was burnt down by the anti-Treaty forces.

Gogarty's purpose in going to Oxford was to have a shot at winning the Newdigate Prize for English verse. Dowden felt that his favourite pupil, having won the Vice-Chancellor's prize three times running in Trinity, stood a chance of bringing off the double by winning the Oxford award as well. The matter was arranged through Macran, who saw to it that Gogarty should meet F. W. Lee, a Fellow of Worcester College, for tea while he was in Dublin. Lee was so impressed that he arranged that Gogarty should go up for two terms to Worcester and work under W. H. Hadow, the philosopher, who was also a friend of Macran's.

Gogarty arrived in Oxford on January 25th, 1904, including in his baggage, T. S. C. Dagg remembers, a barrel of Guinness stout – an example of the Dubliner's contempt for that beverage if brewed on any but Liffey water.

At Bletchley Station he noticed a star falling. Was it to be a good or bad omen for his Newdigate?

Oxford was many times larger than Trinity. Each college has a separate life of its own. Yet Gogarty appears to have made an instant impression. An Oxford friend told J. M. Flood that after a week people were asking, 'Did you hear Gogarty's latest?' One particular mot he perpetrated against William Temple, the archbishop's son, set him on the road to conversational fame.

He made a friend at Worcester College of George Bell, who has recalled the impression that Gogarty made on him at that time:

> Oliver was filled with poetry and a fascinating and inspiring companion. He was fond of the Gardens at Worcester, and he and I in the summer of 1904 often met on the Lawns there. We used to walk by the river past the locks and admire the laburnums.

George Kennedy Alexander Bell was destined to be Bishop of Chichester from 1929 to 1958. He was a prominent figure in English public life, one of the leaders of the Ecumenical movement in the 'twenties, a patron of the drama and an enlightened humanist.

The rumour of the entertaining Irishman spread in Oxford, and Gogarty was in constant demand. When the punting parties began they proved ideal for Mahaffy's pupil. Propped up with cushions, he would lie back and talk, his mind stimulated by the pleasant natural surroundings while his companions attended to the movement of the boat. When they tied up for lunch his talk flowed on, continued through the meal, till they departed, when Gogarty would settle himself comfortably in the cushions again, words bubbling from his lips, in what seemed to his English friends an inexhaustible fountain of wit, erudition and improvisation.

As at Trinity his flair for the picaresque made him the subject of student tales. He drank the sconce at Worcester. This entailed drinking five pints of beer from a silver cup in one go, without letting the cup down from the lips. The performance nearly froze Gogarty's tonsils off, but he went through with it.

'I was weaned on pints,' he explained.

He joined the Oxford Gaelic Society which was an offshoot of the new enthusiasm for the language in Ireland. The Oxford students took weekly classes in Irish. One of them was Dermot Trench, son of Archbishop Trench. Another was an aristocratic and wealthy Spaniard of Irish descent, Señor O'Neill. O'Neill possessed a magnificent motor-car and a chauffeur. He was rather pretentious about his rare chariot, and not inclined to allow his fellow students to share a seat with him in it. One day while he was out of town Gogarty succeeded in convincing O'Neill's chauffeur that he had permission to use the car. He then drove round Oxford dressed in a fur coat (also O'Neill's) visiting the different tradesmen to whom he owed money, and they were numerous. The tradesmen were summoned to the window of the car as it stopped at each shop, and peremptorily asked why they had been plying the occupant with bills. Mesmerized by his magnificence, they muttered apologies, some of them offering to send up additional goods immediately, offers of which Gogarty at once availed himself. When someone with him in the car reminded him that a wine-dealer from whom he had just ordered a cask of wine was already owed four pounds Gogarty replied loftily, 'Well now I owe him eight.' They then drove to Blenheim, Gogarty directing the chauffeur from the back seat with taps of his stick on the shoulder. Later he and his guests enjoyed wine and foodstuffs which had been sent post-haste to Gogarty's rooms, by shop-owners terrified of losing the patronage of so magnificent a customer. O'Neill was furious when he found out the trick that had been played on him. Apparently his sense of humour was more Iberian than Irish. I am indebted for this anecdote to Mr William Dinan who was up at Oxford at the same time as Gogarty.

Gogarty worked hard at his Newdigate poem. But when the results were posted up he found he was only proxime accessit. His friend Bell had won the Prize. With typical modesty Gogarty maintained that Bell had written a better poem. Dowden when Gogarty showed him Bell's poem agreed that this was so, and Gogarty wrote at once to Bell telling him of Dowden's opinion. One reason for Gogarty's lack of success may have been that the form prescribed was heroic couplets, which he regarded as the metre 'of Alexander Pope and all the bores of the eighteenth century, Goldsmith excepted'.

In the meantime he and Joyce had been corresponding constantly. These letters are studded with archaic turns of speech which Gogarty, Joyce, Elwood and Co. often used among themselves as if in recognition of the fact that they belonged to a more gracious and elated age than the one they were living in. Phrases such as Gogarty's:

> Inform me how thou liltest; at present I wind the pastoral pipe.
> By the Christ's crust I am sorry I cannot make haste to help you.
> Let me know if thou wouldst fain travel.
> I am travailing. Verily verily I say unto thee in answer to thy urging, I am living in College. Neither in town or on the town.

or Joyce's:

> You will not have me faithfully. Adieu then inconsequent.

Gogarty in his letters often breaks into Biblical parody:

> This epistle pleaseth me. Thou art yet in London, but a little while and thou shalt see me. Thy remarks concerning chastity pained me, but not so much as chastity. Most marvellous foul sin in chiding sin, when thou thyself hast been a libertine.

In another epistle of this kind, Joyce is felicitated on having been the recipient of the 'stigmata' after an over-ardent but incautious pursuit of Venus among the drabs of dockland.

In a letter written from Dublin to Joyce in France, Gogarty parodies the Kiltartan dialect of English words and Irish idiom, which Lady Gregory used in her plays and which had become a popular mode of expression with the Celtic Twilight writers.

Dear Joyce,
It is myself that write to answer the letter you kindly sent me and I writing for it in Ireland. For a long time I have been wanting to speak to you and tell you what I was thinking about you. Yourself it is that must have had the strange thoughts about me not writing to you, and you so long gone from the old place where you were born and reared. There are fine poets in your country who have been making songs in the tounge [*sic*] in which the sons of Usna were betrayed.

By the time that Gogarty was established at Worcester, Joyce had given up medicine and gone back to Dublin, to be near his mother, who was dying. Gogarty wrote to him describing the delights of the Towery city and asking Joyce to come over and spend some weeks with him, the travelling expenses to be undertaken by Gogarty. The letter is addressed 'from the Bard Gogarty to the wandering Aengus', a pet name Gogarty had for Joyce, borrowed from a figure in a Yeats poem, and one which Joyce later makes Mulligan confer on Stephen Dedalus in *Ulysses*. From the opening sentences it will be seen that Gogarty had undertaken the task of subsidizing from his meagre resources Joyce's living expenses:

The only explanation of my tardiness in forwarding funds to you is my difficulty in obtaining them. The 10/– I hope reached you. Fairview is not an office for changing postal orders into cash. However I guessed you would be directed to the General Post Office from Fairview P.O. Chamber Music immediately springs into my mind from the appearance of the above abbreviation. Go and see the holy women – disguised if you like it as the gardiner [*sic*] – then send me a detailed account of the position of my lady of love. I fear she has no money and is unwilling to ask for it. Poor Jennie is a good soul. This cunning Druid, O Wandering Aengus, obtained but a 2nd place in the Newdigate, further cause for impecuniosity. My Alexandrines I think are traditional – hence these tears – damn tradition and the impenetrability of professors' souls, but perhaps to damn tradition is to reject Rome and England, and we must have the one as we must have lingerie on ladies and we require the other as the ladies. However good luck – O Aengus of the Birds. Sing sweetly so that the stones may move and build a causeway [*sic*] to Oxford. Yesterday I was under the poplars green on the blue waters. I wish you would seriously think of coming over here for a week. I have two new suits, one for you; and everything you need – the credence of shopkeepers without which faith we cannot be healed. Good luck old man.

Another letter is more specific in its demand that Joyce should pay a visit to Oxford.

Be Jaysus Joyce
You must come over here for a day or two next fortnight, I want your advice. The single from Dublin to Oxford is twenty-seven shillings; I shall send you travelling expenses. (I couldn't trust you with more.) Let me know if you will come thus. I want to get dhrunk, dhrunk [*sic*].

One begging letter of Joyce's drew a poetic reply from Gogarty, in parody of A.E. Gogarty had lent so much money to Joyce that he had none left for himself to take him out of Oxford.

> I thought, beloved, to have bought for you
> A gift of quietness for ten and six,
> Cooling your brow, and your landlady too
> With ready spondulicks.
>
> Homeward I go not yet because of those
> Who will not let me leave, lest they repine
> For from the Bank the stream of quiet flows
> Through hands that are not mine.
>
> But O my Knight: I send to you the stars
> That light my very creditable gains
> And out of Oxenford though on my arse
> My scorn of all its pains.

Gogarty was always anxious to secure Joyce against his creditors by getting him to capitalize on his really exquisite tenor voice. From Oxford he wrote urging Joyce to make practical use of his musical gift and promising to get him engagements.

> When I return to Thule, I shall get you many engagements I hope, to sing at entertainments. Revenge yourself by singing for the garrison. Educated people in Ireland are the garrison – the soul is the garrison of the body. I am revenging myself on the Professors of Poetry here by Socratian corruption of youth. Have you read Aphrodite, by Pierre Louys?

Gogarty even went to the extent of copying out unpublished Elizabethan songs from the Bodleian in Oxford so that Joyce might have fresh material for his concert repertoire.

> There are a lot of unpublished Elizabethan Lyrics in the Bodleian some of which I am transcribing. One or two of the drinking songs are excellent, I shall send them to you when time allows.

One of the letters addressed to 'James Augustus Joyce, Scorner of Mediocrity and Scourge of the Rabblement', introduces those two gallant aspirants to the healing profession who later figure in *Ulysses*, 'Medical Dick and Medical Davy'. Gogarty's ballad about their activities is, unfortunately, unprintable. In another letter he reports a conversation which readers of *A Portrait of the Artist* will recognize as substantially the same as the one that takes place between the blasphemous student, Temple, and Stephen Dedalus on the steps of the National Library.

> I discovered a disciple of yours, a two year medical at the Play. He divides his rustic hair in the middle and doesn't shave his meagre beard. He with a fearful joy informed me that he was an Atheist.

> JOYCE'S PUPIL (volunteering): I am an Atheist, you know, I am an Atheist.
> GOGARTY: Yes. What does that mean?
> J'S.P: You know, I don't believe in God.
> GOG: No. And what is God?
> J'S.P: Oh! Everyone knows about God – God is – any fool could tell you what God is. I don't believe in religion. (Cleary here becomes interested.)

GOG :   Indeed. What is religion?

J's.P :   I don't go to Church or to Mass.

Gogarty's last term at Oxford came to an end in June 1904. According to William Dinan, a fellow student with Gogarty at Oxford, Gogarty's popularity suffered a slight set-back in his last few weeks there.

> At a lunch I gave in Worcester a scholar called Seton got drunk became a nuisance and bored Gogarty. Gogarty got up and made a rather irreverent remark which gave offence, as Seton was a Church student; though Gogarty didn't know that he was, when he made the remark. It got round Oxford, and a set rather gave Gogarty the cold shoulder. You see he was a typical Trinity man. In Trinity they don't give a damn about the conventions; its life is part of the life of a large city. But in Oxford where society is closer, introvert, you have to keep the conventions. You could break the Law with impunity provided you didn't contravene a convention at the same time.

On June 13th Gogarty wrote to the Bursar Mr W. Gerrant, to notify him that he had completed his term, and to convey his thanks to the Bursar for giving him 'such beautiful rooms'. Oxford did much for Gogarty. His mind flowered there like the chestnut trees he used to see between the towers of Worcester. At Trinity it had been mostly with the Fellows that he discussed poetry and philosophy. But at Oxford he found he could confess his enthusiasm for Beauty unabashed, in conversation with students like G. K. A. Bell, Christopher Stone, Compton Mackenzie and other friends there. It was not considered a pose to spread oneself on a phrase of poetry or to show enthusiasm for painting or architecture.

A lover of Arnold's poetry before he went to Oxford, many of its surroundings had magical associations for him. He spent a lot of his time walking the country-side, or riding to more distant places on an Indian motor-bicycle he bought from a dealer named William Morris, the future Lord Nuffield.

He continued to pour out his thoughts to George Bell in letters written during the two or three years following the time he went down from Oxford. In his first letter written to Bell in June, after

Gogarty had returned to Dublin, we can discern the influence of the ardour of his Oxford period. Compare this passage for instance with the hard cynical humour of his letters to Joyce quoted a few pages previously.

He describes a visit to Howth Hill in company with a girl. Howth is the long peninsula which stretches over Dublin Bay.

This was the most happy day I ever wish to spend. First of all I rose at 3.30 and saw the dawn then – a letter from you. Then a talk with a Platonic friend (John Eglinton), sphering and unsphering the spirit of Plato, and, after lunch, a visit to the beautiful Hill of Howth, 'all but island', the northern arm of our beautiful bay that takes the morning to its breast – The southern arm is the 'Golden Spears' of which I praised to you ere this. The air was Lesbian. I climbed the fields and gradually reached a woody land that looks towards Lambay island and the dim northern hills. Below the mountain's crest, I stayed in one of the beautiful brakes whose rhododendrons flush the air and the ground is soft with moss or bracken. It was like lying on a purple cloud above the dawn ('in the fields divine, and pastures blue of heaven'). You know that the mountain slopes: a little well or 'secret spring' freshened the middle of the ground which was islanded. Hazels, oaks, ashes and banks of bloom on the one side, rhododendron-covered rocks on the other – and rushes which had 'tufted heads'. I lay under a rhododendron and watched the midges dance like a fountain for joy of the sunlight. I mixed light purple rhododendron leaves in a girl's red brown hair – hair that becomes golden in the sunlight – you've heard me spout:

> When the sun shines on Mary's hair
> The splendour seems to own
> That solid rays of sunlight there
> Are blended with the brown;
> And in the golden coils of it
> A thousand little rainbows sit.
> Then neither wonder that my sight
> On her is wholly shed,
> When she can take the heaven's light
> To bind about her head;

Or that to her I captive fall
Who holds the rainbows in her thrall.

Well, this was she. Then we went up a sandy cliff road and whilst talking the foolish words more wise than all philosophies and watching the sunset on the waters and over the mainland I got an idea for an hymn or evensong, which later I must evolve – insist and spur me.

The same letter contains an amusing description of Joyce in which he records his delight in the quaint activities of his friend.

Joyce has written two pretty songs. I am disposing of 30 of his lyrics at £1 apiece or 5/– for one (Joyce's reckoning) to pay his digs bill. He was lately seen perambulating this tuneful town, with a large malay book made of palm leaves borrowed of Starkey (it looked like a Venetian blind) under his arm looking for a buyer. As he said to me, 'It aroused so much interest I think I was justified in telling the rabblement (his profane friends) that I got £7 for it.' 'How much did you really get, Joyce?' 'Two and sixpence.' Isn't Joyce delightful? As Thoreau says, 'Only with parity life is sweet, it's near the bone.' Joyce went to visit the 'Mummers', his name for Yeats' players in the Irish National Theatre, at practice. He being drunk fell 'the second time' as he said and two or three ladies passed over him lying. I called one morning about it. He was just after this escapade and woke with a black eye – the gift of an angry lover whose lady he had importuned being ignorant of her lover's presence. His handkerchief was full of blood and drawing it from his pocket at the breakfast table he said, 'This reminds me of Veronica.' The 'Shy one' of his heart is perhaps not generally considered shy. He always quotes Yeats parodied, to heal or endorse his deeds. 'And little shadows come about my eyes' – this his black eye. Yeats won't give him the address of the lute maker so he cannot tour Margate and Falmouth as he intended, singing old English songs. The Mummers have gone to the Rosses, west Sligo : Yeats country. Joyce wishes to follow and horrify them on their holiday by bringing an holy woman or blessed damozel. His last parody – of O'Sullivan this time.

The Sorrow of Love

If any told the blue ones, that
mountain-footed move,
They would bend down and with batons,
belabour my love.

The original, you may remember, is Starkey's.

The Sorrow of Love

If I could tell the bright ones that
quiet-hearted move,
They would bend down like the branches
with the sorrow of love.

When he had returned from Oxford, Gogarty and Joyce decided to remove themselves from the madding crowd and take up residence in a Martello Tower which was situated near the sea on the outskirts of Dublin. These Towers had been built round the coast of Ireland as a protection against invasions in Napoleon's time. A century later some official in Dublin Castle hit upon the idea of conditioning them and letting them out to private citizens as dwelling-places. To Gogarty and Joyce it seemed an ideal retreat in which to practise their craft.

In a letter written to Bell about the middle of July, Gogarty outlined his plans to help Joyce:

Joyce is to hold his estate at the Tower. The rent will be about £18 a year and as he won't have to pay it the scheme is feasible. He must have a year in which to finish his novel.

On the 22nd he writes to say that he and Joyce are to go into the Tower in a week's time:

I shall furnish the Tower with Chippendale sticks, no pictures. The Bard Joyce is to do the housekeeping. He is to Watts-Dunton me also.

After he had installed himself he wrote to Bell describing his new domicile:

In the tower there are four rooms. One large one above, and three below. Two of those below are only pantries, one containing a well; the other is copper-sheeted and was a maga-

78

zine when the place was used as a fort. The upper chamber in which I now write, and where the apostles assemble on occasion, is reached by a ladder stairway and is about twenty feet off the ground. The walls are nine feet thick and the door massive. The view is splendid. Howth, to the north. The mountainous arm of the Bay, changing with every cloud and affording wonderful successions of colour in pink on a hot and sunny day. Purple or cerulean on clouded days. And, on days when there is an intermittent sunshine the hill gleams yellow as if clothed with fields of corn. 'The barren steeps in ferny fields of corn.' To the south, that is behind one looking to Howth – Killiney stands; a tricipetal hill the middle head of which is cursed by an obelisk – a beauty blasting sight: conformity petrified. Some night I may blow it up. It's coming out of that when I have collected sufficient dynamite for the purpose; but it may take months as I shall have to spread my purchases over a long period to avoid the suspicion which would arise if I bought a lb. at once. This is a grand place to work in: the sea-blue air and green trees all around me, no dust, noise or cars nor civilised people to trouble.

In the same letter there is an example of how a single occurrence could trigger off in Gogarty's mind a rapid series of brilliant images.

I bought a lobster today alive, and when I put him in a little pool his marvellous colours reappeared freshly so that I resolved to restore him to the 'great sweet mother' and I took the twine off his claws and sent him seaward. I suppose they'll catch him again if he has not taken his experience to his ganglion. I am without him to supper now but perhaps it is better to have had him feed whatever little of the idea is in me with the beauty of his colouring than to supply my more transient need with the muscles inside his skeleton. Surely I'm not a Christian? No, the Galilean incidents around the lake: filling nets with fish and actually increasing other lakes prove that I have not imitated. My lobster is now wandering in the weird submarine moonlight which they say is emitted night and day by the animalcules at the sea-bottom and stretching his stiffened joints and (if he could) wondering has he been to Hades and gained a rebirth. Yesterday I saw

79

shoals of mackerel swimming waveringly in the dim green depths their backs all marked with dark waved bands as if the shadow of the ripples had fallen upon them and remained. Many people were pulling them out momentarily with lines and hooks from boats and chucking them into the bottom of the boats. They couldn't eat them all, I suppose they rotted. It's awful. Fishermen, real ones, have no poetry, nonchalant, heavy louts as a rule. The poets put the glamour on them ... the tunny fishers in Theocritos shall fish for ever, yet they would have cheated Theocritos to the last obol, or taken too many tunnies for their wants or their market if they got the chance.

One can visit this Martello Tower today. It has not changed in fifty years. You approach the metal steps which lead into the Tower through the garden of Mr Michael Scott, a Dublin architect who has built his house beside the Tower. Inside is the main room where Joyce and Gogarty used to sleep; downstairs are well-built ovens which were installed to enable the garrison of the Tower to cook their meals. Once up on the roof, the panorama of Dublin city unfolds itself. To the left, a crescent of Georgian dwelling-houses, painted in pleasant blues and yellows, fits snugly into the gentle curve of the bay. At the end of the crescent lies Dun Laoire, known in 1904 as Kingstown, with its huge Edwardian hotels and nineteenth-century Gothic church towers. The mailboat pier creeps out in a long spine from Dun Laoire sea-front.

In the Tower Joyce and Gogarty lived in remote content for a while. How long exactly they were there together it is difficult to say. While they undoubtedly quarrelled, there is no reason to believe that Joyce quitted the Tower immediately as a result of a quarrel. He left Ireland on October 12th, and between the beginning of August and that date he probably stayed intermittently at the Tower, with a constant period from the beginning of August until near the end of that month. Mr Oliver Gogarty, Gogarty's eldest son, has suggested that his father and Joyce did not enter the Tower until August 17th, his father's birthday, but the letter of July 22nd would seem to indicate that they may have been living there before that date.

Joyce taught in a near-by school in the daytime and returned

80

every evening to the Tower. The money he earned helped to pay for the food and drink of the occupants of the Tower. Foodstuffs were cheap and easily obtainable. Lobsters could be bought for twopence, and milk was a penny a pint. This left money for glasses of Guinness in Murray's bar and for the vellum paper on which they used to write their verses.

One evening Dermot Freyer, son of Peter Freyer the surgeon who invented the prostate gland operation, visited the Tower and found poems for Joyce's volume, *Chamber Music*, which Joyce had thrown behind him in a drunken fit of despair as he staggered into the night.

Gogarty used to swim two or three times daily in the forty-foot bathing-pool which was directly below the Tower. He specially liked to swim in the sunset when the water became soft and crimson-flecked. Joyce, though he hardly hints at this in *Ulysses*, was quite an adequate swimmer and sometimes accompanied Gogarty on his swimming trips. Gogarty recollects seeing Joyce one day deliberately staggering on the strand at Howth carrying a sweeping brush on his shoulder. 'Jesus wept and when he walked he waddled,' was what Joyce replied when questioned about his curious pose. It was while they were living at the Tower that Joyce and Gogarty had their first quarrel. Gogarty was to complain later of an increasing seriousness in Joyce's demeanour, of his silences, and of being unable to rally him from 'being sullen in the sweet air'. He began to notice also that his friend was adopting a conscious, artistic pose.

Joyce had collected his pose when he was in Paris. There Rimbaud became his model. Rimbaud influenced him so much that he sent Gogarty a picture of himself dressed in imitation of the master in broad-brimmed hat and flowing cape. The French poet's conception of the artist's function suited Joyce perfectly. Under the new dispensation he could become a high priest in the service of beauty instead of the priest of God he had wanted to be in the God-intoxicated periods of his youth. But Gogarty, who had no liking for priests anyway, was unwilling to accept Joyce in his new sacerdotal role. When Joyce started to adopt Rimbaud's custom of deliberately reviling those who had helped him, Gogarty found himself unable any longer to stomach his friend's Latin posturing. 'I have broken with Joyce', he writes to a friend in Oxford on Agusut 16th, 1904. 'His want of generosity became to me inexcusable. He lampooned Yeats, A.E., Colum, and others to whom he was indebted. A desert was revealed which I did not think existed amid the seeming luxuriance of his soul.'

The quarrel between the two did not, as Joyce's brother suggests, mean the end of their friendship. It might have blown over in a few weeks if Joyce hadn't left Dublin hurriedly in October with a servant-girl whom he later married. Gogarty described Joyce's flight in a letter to Dermot Freyer. The play on the place-name is a typical Gogartian touch. 'The Bard Joyce has fled to Pola, on the Adriatic. A slavey shared his flight. Considering the poet's preaching and propensity the town he has chosen for the scene of his future living is not inappropriately named.'

It is necessary to advance slightly in the narrative in order to observe the course of the friendship between the two.

A year after Gogarty's note to Freyer was written Joyce and Gogarty had made up their quarrel. A request from Joyce to Gogarty that the latter might visit him in Trieste drew an enthusiastic reply from Gogarty, whose letter was forwarded from the Waldorf Astoria in New York, where he was on holiday. He wrote that he hoped to make a world tour and would certainly visit Joyce in the course of it. He missed, he said in the letter, 'the touch of a vanished hand and the sound of a voice that is still.' America promised great financial rewards for Joyce's singing voice, he added, if only Joyce could go over and try his fortune there. Whether Gogarty did visit Joyce in 1906 is not known. But in 1907 he and Joyce were corresponding on their old familiar terms. Gogarty spent that year in Vienna on a postgraduate course in ear, nose, and throat surgery under Hajek and Chiari. Joyce was by then working as a bank clerk in Trieste. Gogarty had become so keen to have Joyce with him again that he offered to pay his expenses in Vienna for three weeks and get him some work teaching German there. He suggested a summer tour of the Mediterranean by steamer, on which they would write verses together in the old familiar fashion while Gogarty would undertake to pay the fares. Joyce agreed to Gogarty's plan for publishing in Trieste 'Ditties of No Tone', a collection of Rabelaisian verse by Gogarty and his friends which Joyce had been urging Gogarty to publish for some time. Joyce, however, must have failed to do as he said, for Gogarty wrote to Dermot Freyer, one of the contributors, that 'the Diminutive Dante', Joyce, had let him down over the publication of 'Cockcrows', which had been Joyce's suggested title for the work.

Joyce's brother, Stanislaus, has claimed that it was he who persuaded Joyce against going to Vienna on Gogarty's invitation. Stanislaus regarded Gogarty as a tempter who would wean his brother away from the cause of art. He believed that his brother's temperament necessitated his being kept free from the carefree, convivial company of his countrymen if he was to achieve an important place in literature, and he felt that a visit to Gogarty might undermine Joyce's purpose by arousing in him nostalgic memories of Dublin and making the circumstances of his exile seem unbearable. There may have been less altruistic reasons for Stanislaus's dislike of Gogarty. Gogarty had rebuffed him by telling him that there was only one freak in the Joyce family, and he had no relish for any others. Perhaps Stanislaus may have been jealous of the fascination that 'burly, bustling Gogarty' exercised over his brother. Whatever the cause, Stanislaus, as he has stated himself in print, set out deliberately to destroy the association between his brother and Gogarty.

Joyce returned to Dublin for a holiday in 1909. He had been five years absent. Gogarty, who was now established as a young surgeon, hearing that Joyce was in town, sent him a note asking him to come and see him and proposing that they have lunch at the Dolphin together.

31. VII'09   15 *Ely Place*
                                                       Dublin
Dear Joyce,
          Curiosis Cosgrave tells me you are in Dublin. Before trying to get you to come to lunch at Dolphin on Monday next at 1 O'c. I would like to have a word with you. My man will drive you across (if you are in). I leave town at 5 each evening; but there can be changes if you turn up.

He will call about 3.20. Do come if you can or will. I am looking forward to seeing you with pleasure. There are many things I would like to discuss and a plan or two to divert you. You have not yet plumbed all the depths of poetry; there is Broderick the Bard! of whom more anon.

                                                       Yours
                                                       o.g.

Joyce seems to have accepted this invitation, but before the date for lunch came around, Gogarty, finding himself involved in a surgical consultation, wrote and asked Joyce could he come on another date.

2 VIII.'09   15, *Ely Place,*
                                                      Dublin

Dear Joyce,
            I find that at 1 o'c. tomorrow there is a patient coming who cannot come at any other time. I will be glad if, in view of this, you will forgive a little postponement of the lunch. I will let you know.

                                              Yours
                                              O.G.

There are two accounts of their subsequent meeting, one Joyce's, the other Gogarty's. Gogarty has written that Joyce came along to Ely Place and, after sitting in the dining-room for some time, looked out of the window at the roses in the garden and said enigmatically, 'Is this your revenge?' After he had made this remark he rose and left the house. This was the last Gogarty saw of his contrary friend.

Joyce gives a somewhat different account of the affair in a letter to Stanislaus dated August 4th, 1909.

Gogarty met me in Merrion Sq. I passed him. He ran after me and took me by the arm and made a long speech and was very confused. He asked me to go to his house. I went. He made me go in and rambled on. To everything, I said, 'You have your life. Leave me to mine.' He invited me to go down to Enniskerry in his motor and lunch with him and wife. I declined and was very quiet and sober. He offered me grog [?] wine, coffee, tea: but I took nothing. In the end he said, blushing, 'Well do you really want me to go to hell and be damned?' I said, 'I bear you no ill will. I believe you have some points of good nature. You and I of six years ago are both dead. But, I must write as I have felt.' He said, 'I don't care a damn what you say of me so long as it is literature.' I said, 'Do you mean that?' He said, 'I do. Honest to Jaysus [*sic*]. Now will you shake hands with me at least?' I said, 'I will; on that understanding.'

Joyce's account would appear to contain at least some inaccuracies if we look at it in relation to the evidence contained in the two letters referred to above. There is no reference to the fact that Gogarty had written to him or to the fact that he had seemingly accepted the invitation to lunch. It is probable that Joyce was, as usual, on the defensive when writing to his brother about Gogarty and was anxious to impress on him his obdurate resistance to the siren-lure of Dublin life. Whichever account is true, Joyce's or Gogarty's, this was to be the last occasion on which the two writers met.

But Joyce never forgot Dublin and it is probable he never forgot Gogarty either, whose personality embodied so much of the spirit of that Norman-Norse and Celtic town. Joyce decided that the carefree convivial atmosphere of Ireland was unsuited to his purpose as an artist. But he often expressed regret at his enforced exile from the city whose conscience he had articulated into literature. 'When I die,' he told an Irish friend in 1939, 'Dublin will be written on my heart.'

Joyce sacrificed race, religion, and friends in his unswerving devotion to the cause of art. His sense of dedication acquired from the religious training of his youth stood him in good stead for his vocation as an artist. It gave him the strength of purpose to retire from life into a cell of his own making for the purpose of giving expression to his particular vision. Gogarty as much as Joyce did believe that the artist should 'pour into the mould of art' all that his heart would hold. But he felt it was by 'loving life and using it well' and not by withdrawing from it, that he would have revealed to himself the inner harmony which is the poet's vision. Influenced by Mahaffy and Tyrrell, he would have regarded asceticism whether in the cause of art or religion as a medieval degeneration from the Attic belief in the development of personality in every aspect. He had never acquired the penitential habit as Joyce had, when the hell-fire sermons of the Jesuits terrified him with visions of damnation. We can see from a remarkable letter written by Gogarty to Bell in January 1905 how repugnant the whole concept was to him and how he favoured instead a Graeco-Christian synthesis which laid its emphasis on the supreme necessity of personality.

I read Huysmans' *En Route*, the other day and read therein

his appreciation of the very plaint that made me miserable. I felt, and I suppose I did justice to, the standpoint from which he looks – the music is very impressive certainly. Perhaps the calm that asceticism brings is bought at too great a cost: it makes Man miserable. It is not 'the still, sad music of humanity' but Man's unmanfulness and whinging [sic]. Surely not the least part of the cross each man must take up and bear is the knowledge that life is at best a burden: a knowledge that makes men best who face it: a knowledge that our greatest, from Sophocles to Matthew Arnold, have not shirked?

I cannot but think that religious people who live in ostrich holes and let their reason atrophy have disobeyed the very injunction they fancy they are following – they have not taken up their cross. Abstinence from luxuries – even when it is not accompanied by abstinence from work – does not constitute a cross for anyone but licentious millionaires or brainless lordlings certainly I find it a greater trial to gaze calm-browed at the inevitable end and, standing alone, support my own soul than to look at life communing with saints, through the windows of a cathedral. They too 'stain the white radiance of eternity'. Stoic and Epicurean alike kept unenslaved by luxuries, to reach mental contentment; the monk pleads that God's pleasure is manifested to him by the peace of mind which he enjoys. They are all alike: the Stoic for fortitude denies himself and does his duty; the Epicurean for the sake of ease has a care that no passion enslaves him; and the monk in order to please God gains peace of mind. They all seek their own comfort and the monk is the least un-selfish – he lives at the expense of the community. His good deeds consist in distributing things which he does not earn. He merely transfers property and gains in charity. He succeeds most of all and at the greatest cost to others in pleasing himself.

If I were to please myself I would like to live alternately at the sea and in the country or town: to travel a little, dabbling in literature on the plea that I sought beauty in order to confer it on mankind. This scheme might work were it not that tradition is otherwise: God is more popular than uranium mines. Or I might believe in a Deity less rational than myself who would be worshipped best by my reducing myself in a convent to a condition that he would punish me for, anywhere else in the world. Ah, well! though I worship nature yet I realise the ethical necessity of Personality and for His sake think it better to knowingly serve to the best of my power than, shirking the responsibility of His godlike gift reason, sleep it out in a cell.

This letter indicates that Gogarty's insatiable appetite for so many different forms of human activity was not merely the result of an emotional urge but of a carefully worked-out philosophy of living. Motivated by a 'belief in the ethical nature of personality', he had become by middle life a champion athlete and swimmer, a surgeon, a senator of the Irish Free State, a dramatist, poet, and aviator. Could there be a bigger contrast to Joyce's policy of monk-like withdrawal from reality? This passion for living not only may not have interfered with Gogarty's progress as an artist but may actually have helped to give his verse its special character. A.E. considered that it was Gogarty's refusal to separate art from life that brought a fresh, joyous note into his work. 'Oliver Gogarty has never made a business of beauty, and because he is disinterested in his dealing with it, the Muse has gone with him on his walks and revealed to him some airs and graces she kept secret from her other lovers, who were too shy or too awed of her to be natural in her presence.' Yeats was perhaps thinking of a similar quality when he wrote: 'Gogarty never stays long at his best, but how beautiful that best is, how noble, how joyous.' When he compiled the *Oxford Book of Modern Verse*, Yeats included seventeen of Gogarty's poems, to Joyce's three.

One wonders what Joyce must have thought as he learned of the high praise accumulating around Gogarty's poetic achievement. He had once referred to Gogarty and Yeats as the 'blacklegs of literature'. But as he matured he must have realized that there was another path to Parnassus besides the Calvary-like one he had chosen for himself. Yeats he came later to recognize as one of the great poets of the twentieth century, and perhaps in middle life the intolerance of his youth may have diminished sufficiently to allow him to see Gogarty's genius in its correct perspective.

By a coincidence, when he died in Zürich in 1940, the two books found on his desk were Gogarty's recently published life of

St Patrick and a Greek Lexicon, presumably there in order to translate Gogarty's Greek quotations. Those were sad years for Joyce when the world seemed to be breaking in pieces around him. One wonders if, as he read through those pages typically Gogartian in their witty discursiveness, he recalled again the gay companion of his youth, and regretted their broken friendship – broken by his own will in his unswerving purpose 'to forge in the smithy of [his] soul the uncreated conscience of [his] race' with weapons of 'Silence, exile and cunning'.

SEVEN

On November 28th, 1905, Gogarty spoke at the first annual convention of Sinn Fein. This is an important date in Irish history. At this convention Arthur Griffith laid down the principles which were to form the basis of his policy thirteen years later when Sinn Fein ousted all the other parties in the elections for Westminster and ultimately secured self-government for Southern Ireland. At the public meeting held on November 28th in the Round Room of the Rotunda, which preceded the convention, Gogarty spoke to a motion proposed by a Co. Meath landlord, John Sweetman. The motion was:

> That the people of Ireland are a free people, and that no law made without their authority or consent, is or can ever be binding on their conscience.

Gogarty's speech is polemical in the grand manner with a Ciceronian ring about it. Padraic Colum has written that Gogarty at this time:

> saw himself as a Roman, a man of the camp and Senate, speaking a language of order and command.

An occasion like this allowed him to indulge his senatorial whim. He began:

> Now I do not rejoice to hear any man fume against England. But England assumes that most awful of responsibilities, that of governing a nation against her will, – the law of the oak is not the law of the ash, and the law of England is not the law of Ireland.
>   The British Government is a tyranny because it forces on Ireland legislation which the people of Ireland repudiate, and which the very condition of Ireland itself repudiates ... This is the sweet grace of English law by which we are to allow ourselves to be judged. This is the sweet grace of the law by which a foreigner is King over here.

He ended with a vigorous rhetorical flourish:

> From Leonidas to Emmet the best blood in the world has

been shed for the principle we are in danger of forgoing, by forgetfulness in the past, and confusion in the future ... We are governed by a force of constabularymen, picked from our own people, spied on by other fellow-countrymen of our own, disgraced in the eyes of the nations of the world by our prowess in the British Army, separated and alienated from our educated men, in a word made the victims and tools of the most disgraceful government in the world.

At the convention which was held at eleven p.m. after the public meeting concluded, Arthur Griffith proposed:

That the policy of the National Council of Sinn Fein be: National self-development through the recognition of the duties and rights of citizenship on the part of the individual and by the aid and support of all movements, originating from within Ireland, instinct with National tradition, and not looking outside Ireland for the accomplishment of their aims.

After Griffith had finished speaking the proposal was formally seconded and Gogarty rose to support it. It is noteworthy that his is the only speech reported in Griffith's paper, *The United Irishman*. The leader of Sinn Fein already had a high opinion of the young Trinity student:

Mr Gogarty in supporting the motion said they were there to discuss the present position of Ireland and ought not to consider any country but their own. He at all events would confine himself to mentioning England once. There was yet in Ireland, in spite of extraordinary, persistent, and pernicious attempts to crush it, an idea that we were in our own right entitled to be a free and separate people; and if there were even only one man present at the Convention to represent this idea instead of the numbers he saw present, it would be to him a hopeful augury. It was surprising after so many centuries of insidious denationalisation that there still remained men in Ireland undeceived, in spite of the Anglicising system of education, into thinking that they were merely the inhabitants of a province of imperial England or that her interests were their interests, or that their lives and traditions were one with hers. It was the system of education that contributed most to denationalisation and it was this system he wished to attack and expose and correct. Money was taken from the Irish people by forced taxation to supply the needs of Irish education. How was this Irish money used to educate Ireland? The language of Ireland was suppressed, the history of Ireland was ignored or mis-stated, the attention of Ireland was turned to a foreign country, the character and tradition of which was the direct contrary to the character of the Irish tradition, the focus of national life was set in London. Who were responsible for all this? Ourselves. Yes, without either ignorance or apathy so preposterous and absurd a proposition as that a foreign nation could or should rightly educate another would not be tolerated for a moment. England dare not educate us as Irishmen: she would be raising up judges to denounce her and condemn. She taught us for her own purpose and we had taste of the result – narrowness in the primary schools, grinding in the Intermediate, and the final stages of education left unprovided with a University or any means of training either efficient or adequate for national life, with the result that we were dependent on England, for we were trained to be so. Without technical schools or commercial prosperity the unskilled were forced to enlist in any of the three standing armies – Constabulary, Metropolitan or imperial. This we could stop, and we to some extent had stopped it – by supporting our own manufactures – the least that could be asked of us. As regards a remedy for the condition of primary education, he thought that, as the Christian Brothers were the most competent teachers in regard to primary and secondary education, there was sufficient national spirit to supply them with the necessary funds to extend and carry out an educational system which had not the acquisition of monetary gain as the end and purpose of both those taught and those teaching as the prevailing system conduced to, elsewhere. As regards a remedy for the University system, the first thing to understand was that the difficulty of nationality was the most important: one had to identify himself mentally several times a day, and recall to mind to whom he belonged, if he would avoid being changed into one of those nationless nonentities such as the Universities in Ireland were tending to produce. It was very sad to see young men in a University who might be something if they were anything, going unconsciously on with the hope of a snub from some officer at a British Army mess as their only ambition in life. This could be altered by the infusion of some courage and a healthy spirit of independence into the college men of today. Again we had ourselves to blame that such a thing could be. He was no enemy of England *qua* England to an Englishman it could not be better, but for an Irishman nothing could be worse. He had great dislike for England, *qua* Ireland, and so thought the anti-enlisting campaign of the utmost importance. Every individual should assist in preventing Ireland from continuing to be a farm whereon is raised meat to supply the army of Great Britain and the dinner-tables of the people. In conclusion, he urged that the Council should issue a declaration of its aims to the country so that it might continually keep in mind that it is geographically, historically and spiritually distinct from England, and that it must treat itself with consideration for these vital facts if it had a desire for anything more than a geographical existence.

Both of these speeches were hot stuff for those days. How hot can be judged from the fact that Macran wrote to G. K. A. Bell in Oxford in alarm saying that the authorities in Trinity might take action if Gogarty didn't modify his views. Gogarty was aware of this himself; as he had told Bell in a letter written some while before, his pamphlet writing and contributions to Griffith's paper were mostly anonymous, because he feared he should be 'kept out of diplomas, etc., if they were published under my name'. He wrote now to Bell, to ease his friend's mind.

> My politics are chiefly confined to articles in a weekly paper decrying the policy of sending members to Parliament to get Home Rule, which would deprive them of the livelihood they enjoy in the getting of it. We have no longer any State, no Athens now. But in order to build a city in my soul, I exercise myself in writing against the palpable abuses of my time.

Gogarty had been writing for Griffith since 1899; they had met one another in An Stad, a tobacco shop at the corner of Rutland Square, where members of the Irish-Ireland movement used to meet, Gaelic Leaguers, I.R.B. men, hurlers, footballers; Michael Cusack the founder of the Gaelic Athletic Association was a well-known figure there. Griffith respected Gogarty's athletic background. Also he saw that he belonged to a class that it would be useful to recruit into his movement. He soon had Gogarty writing for him in his paper *The United Irishman*. This was a remarkable journal. Though radical in policy, Griffith's personal influence was such that it had a more distinguished list of contributors than any Irish newspaper has had since. Yeats, A.E., James Stephens, Padraic Colum, Seamus O'Sullivan, Alice Milligan, George Birmingham, then a parson in Mayo, were some of the people who wrote in its pages. Griffith ran the paper entirely on his own. He regarded his body, Gogarty later said about him, 'merely as an indispensable engine of communication and beyond that he had little respect for it'. He never received more than thirty shillings a week for his work. Yet he was, according to James Stephens, 'the greatest journalist working in the English language, one of the important writers of English prose'. He had modelled his style on Swift. Below is a fair example of his prose, though it is impossible to convey by an extract the various moods which Griffith was capable of expressing, and which made him such a formidable controversialist.

We intend to decry the work of no Irish party nor to belittle the character or asperse the motives of any Irish publicist who may differ from us, but we feel certain that if the eyes of the Irish nation are continually focussed on England, they will inevitably acquire a squint. For in our own experience, we have known some good Irishmen who by too constant gazing on the Union Jack acquired a degree of colour blindness, which caused them to perceive in it an emerald green tinge. To be perfectly plain we believe that when Swift wrote to the whole people of Ireland 170 years ago, that by the laws of God of nature and of nations, they had a right to be as free a people as the people of England, he wrote common sense; notwithstanding that in these latter days we have been taught that by the law of God, of nature and of nations, we are rightfully entitled to the establishment in Dublin of a Legislative assembly with an expunging angel watching over its actions from the Viceregal Lodge. We do not deprecate the institution of any such body, but we do assert that the whole duty of an Irishman is not comprised in utilising all the forces of his nature to procure its inception.

Griffith's own political programme was practical, and carefully worked out. He grounded his claim on British law. His premise was that the Act of Union was illegal. Gladstone had said that he knew of no fouler or blacker transaction in the history of man than the making of this Act. Therefore, Griffith argued, the provisions of the Renunciation Act of 1782 which admitted the right claimed by Grattan's Parliament, to be bound only by laws enacted by the King and Parliament of Ireland, were still operative and binding under English law. The means by which he sought to have the provisions of the Renunciation Act adverted to, and the Act of Union set aside, was the abstention from Westminster of the Irish members, and the setting up of an assembly at home, until such times as the Imperial Parliament declared itself bound by the provisions of its own laws in relation to Ireland. Griffith maintained that there was an exact parallel between the state of affairs in Ireland and that of Hungary during the struggle for independence with Austria, in the nineteenth century. It was on the success of Deak's policy of abstention from the Austrian assembly, that Griffith based his claim to have discovered a solution for the problems of Ireland.

> We must retrace our steps, and take our stand on the compact of 1782 and the Renunciation Act as Deak took his on the Pragmatic sanction and the Laws of 1848.*

Griffith's proposal was that if the Irish members withdrew from Westminster and set up a parliament in Dublin, this parliament would function with its own civil service, judiciary, and a local government administration, established in opposition to official government institutions.

The importance of Griffith's policy rested on two factors. Firstly it had a broad practical basis, which made it applicable to the various changes of political situation which could occur in

* Last article, *United Irishman*, July 1904, of a series of twenty-seven on the Resurrection of Hungary.

Ireland. When Sinn Fein won a majority in the 1918 general election Griffith's policy of abstentionism was put into operation. Parliament assembled in Dublin, courts were established and a local government administration set up, side by side with the official British ones.

When Dublin Castle suppressed the passive resistance movement, the physical force element in Sinn Fein claimed the right to resort to arms to defend their Parliament. Without the moral force of Griffith's abstentionist administration behind it, the physical force movement could not have succeeded or received the local and international support that it did. The second factor in Griffith's Sinn Fein policy was that it envisaged a solution which would resolve the division between the two opposing forces in Ireland, Unionist and Nationalist. Griffith had included a plan for a dual monarchy in his policy. There was to be a king of Great Britain, and a king of Ireland – again on the Hungarian model. This would have provided a satisfactory imperial link for the Unionist elements. Griffith himself was by nature and conviction a separatist, that is he believed in the complete separation of Ireland from the Empire. But he recognized the existence of another class of Irishman, who did not think as he did, and it was to absorb them into the new Ireland that he devised his policy. Pragmatism was his greatest virtue. He once said, 'I am a separatist but the Irish people are not separatists. I think they can be united under this broad policy.' He was thinking of the Unionist element. It was because he devised a policy which could bring all classes of Irishmen together under a common ideal that Griffith may rank with O'Connell and Parnell as one of the three great Irish leaders in the post-Union period.

I think Griffith was Gogarty's closest friend. Certainly there was no one he admired more. A.E. said that Gogarty's tongue spared neither the Maker of the Universe nor his creatures. But Gogarty never made a witty remark against Griffith. Griffith's personality was sacred to him. At first it was the relationship of a disciple to a master, but in a short while it became that of two men united in the mutual pleasure they took in one another's company.

It was a curious friendship. Griffith was a man of a few words. Churchill described him as that 'rare phenomenon, a silent Irishman'. He could go on long walks without ever making a remark to a companion who might be a close friend. His mind was analytical, pragmatical, to some extent unaesthetic. Gogarty recognized this but maintained that Griffith had a right to be so. 'The spear must be narrow.'

But Griffith had an Irishman's capacity for enjoying himself in company. He was never happier than when sitting listening to witty and interesting conversation. His small blue eyes, set under a pale straight forehead, would twinkle when Gogarty entered a group. Most unlike himself, Griffith could roar like a bull at Gogarty's humour which he had a particular appreciation of. He respected Gogarty's association with the great minds of Trinity, whose intellects Griffith admired though he differed from them in politics. It is one of the glaring deficiencies of that age that persons like Griffith, and Mahaffy and Macran, were prevented from meeting in social intercourse because of the rigid political atmosphere which prevailed then. Griffith recognized the serious side of Gogarty's nature. He paid attention to his opinion on important matters. He saw beyond the laughing mask presented to the motley, and never regarded Gogarty merely as a gay companion with a talent for wit and poetry.

In 1905 when Gogarty was spending his summers in the Martello Tower, Griffith began to come out for week-ends to stay with him. Padraic Colum, Seamus O'Sullivan, James Stephens were others who used to lie out on the flat roof of the Tower, till they

tired the sun with talking and sent him down the sky.

For many years this brief release from the toil of the city was the only holiday Griffith took.

He was a great admirer of Gogarty's physical prowess, and on one occasion attempted to swim a mile between Sandycove and Bullock harbour in Gogarty's wake. His strength gave out some yards from the shore; yet so great was the awe that Gogarty held him in, that it was only when the bubbles were coming up that he dived in to rescue his friend. To have offered help to Arthur when he was not absolutely in need of it, would have been a liberty that would have brought a sharp reproof.

Gogarty saw Griffith as a leader in the classical mould, with his aloofness from public opinion, his disregard for self-advancement, his unswerving devotion to a single purpose. When Griffith died in 1922 something died in Gogarty too.

Before his death Griffith confided in his friend a matter which shows the high regard he held him in. He suggested to him that he might be Governor-General of the New Irish State. Griffith himself was President of the Provisional Government, and would have none of Tim Healy. 'He betrayed Parnell.' But Griffith died before the appointment was made and Healy and not Gogarty became the first Governor-General of Ireland.

EIGHT

I T was between 1904 and 1906 that Gogarty wrote to Bell the
series of letters which run to about 50,000 words in length. I
have already drawn on these letters for the narrative; but as
there are other extracts which throw a sidelight on the development of his mind, and his activities during these years, I have
formed a short chapter from passages selected from the mass of
correspondence. Sometimes the letters have a conversational
ring. It is not difficult to imagine Gogarty describing to a group
this visit to a dentist:

> I am just out from the dentist so I hasten to write to you from
> the sympathy I feel in my dear heart. The day is so much
> brighter, and quiet, such a luxury, since my visit to him, that
> I incline to think that the existence of dentists is quite justified;
> their vocation is a little misdirected – they should be used to
> comfort convicts under the death-sentence or to dissuade
> suicides. The welkin of my mind cracked; the suppliant wool
> on the instrument availed nought to allay the agony; the
> treadmill exceeded in speed of grinding the mills of God
> thereby becoming diabolic; a light flame tingled beneath my
> skin: I was like Sappho for 20 mins. but not from the same
> cause, though my ears rang and my forehead perspired –
> cold perspiration. Now it is over. I am like Swinburne's
> Marlowe – '*gold on his mouth* and morning in his eyes'.

In February of 1905 his mother had induced him to go on a
retreat in a monastery. This entailed silence for three days while
he listened to sermons and performed religious exercises. It
torpedoed Gogarty. Shut inside all day he missed 'the clouds of
Aristophanes which were not compensated for by clouds of
incense'. But he was always anxious to please his mother on such
matters, and Bob Reynolds, his cyclist friend, used to be deputed
to take him to confession. Once Gogarty emerged at speed from
the confessional. 'He says I'm going to hell,' he said. 'Come on.'

> I am sorry that I never thought of communing with the
> rafters of the Church during my punishment in such incon-
> genial surroundings. They were I remember made of pine

and must have waved their covers on some south-facing brow or rocky headland. I should have welcomed the thought then.

Having driven two Irish miles in a chill February evening when the sun could not be seen setting for the aqueous light in the West, I reached a large manor house which had lost all but the necessaries of upkeeping it. A large plain cruciform chapel stood near and from one arm of it the monastery built of grey stone extended. Everything felt cold grey and forbidding.

After kneeling in the cement coloured gloom of the chapel for some ten minutes I heard chanting and responses rising and falling in some distant part of the monastery. A little while and a pointed Gothic side-door opened and about 60 tall dusty white-clothed monks filed in. There was no sound but the cavernous echo of their feet on the empty floor. When they took their places in the choir they commenced singing vespers or compline. After a pause one walked up through the long aisle and lit two solitary candles in the darkness round the altar. Then

> 'Requiem aeternam dona eis, Domine,
> Et lux perpetua luceat eis.'

and such like in the nighttime.

I remember thinking with indignation to what a pitch the language that they chanted ... had come. Even the tenderness of the Virgilian tones that were a prophecy might not avail; but this ...

How far Macran had developed Gogarty's metaphysical bent, is reflected in a distinction he draws between the classical and romantic schools, in a letter of February 1906:

Yesterday I asked myself was there ever a classic drama composed in the modern sense i.e. austere, colourless, unromantic. This distinction between classic and romantic cannot be maintained. Gregorian music is classic: but are there not beauties forgotten by us which may have appealed to its contemporary hearers? This modern admiration for the cold and classic only exists because it is modern and the 'classics' are old. Landor is 'Greek' and 'classic' but he is more 'classic' than Aeschylus or Euripides. Surely every word in

Aeschylus must have been as full of mystery and romance as 'alien corn' or 'ancestral voices' – romance native to the Greeks? Forgetting this, or being out of touch with it we call the white marble classic. It was coloured once.

The element of the dandy in his character appears itself in another letter. He complains that Dermot Trench, the third occupant of the Tower, has left, taking with him Gogarty's cryselephantine shaving brush; Gogarty was most disturbed and sent a telegram to Balliol, Oxford, to have his precious brush returned.

'I would not mind so much if Trench had not by leaving *his* brush as a substitute suggested that they were coequal. The only personal extravagance and luxury that I indulge in are summed up in that divine brush. These things make life important.' (It was the same instinct that later made him have his plays bound in deer-skin from Lady Leconfield's herd at Petworth House.)

In April 1905 he writes to Bell to tell him how he had visited Yeats on Bell's behalf. Bell was editing a series of poetry anthologies in the Golden Age series. Unwin, Yeats's publisher, had refused permission to include some Yeats poetry in the anthology, and Gogarty was deputized to go and ask the poet for personal permission to use his poems:

The other morning I called on Yeats. The porter of his hotel said that he was in but that a lady was with him. I said that I would call in 20 mins., and that if Yeats was going out in the meantime to ask him to wait in to see me. One does not like catching Yeats amid his muses. Lady Gregory had gone to Coole Park – you read how Yeats 'stood' or walked rather, 'among the seven Woods of Coole' – but Miss Horniman had taken her place and received me when I called. In the parlour were: 'Letters to Mr Watt'; 'Yeats Plays' interlined and filled with MS. leaves; and some other books; on the mantelpiece, a bottle of sweets (black currant sweets for Yeats' cold) and a bottle of smelling salts. Many letters in a portfolio which he showed me saying: 'Miss Horniman writes all my letters now – I leave them over for a week and then we answer them all in an afternoon.' Miss Horniman said, 'Do you know, Mr Gogarty, that sometimes we have to go out to ask how to spell a word?' I made some little jocular remark about Yeats' writing saving his spelling but that with her handwriting she had to be correct.

Miss Horniman was the fairy godmother of the Abbey Theatre. The philanthropic daughter of a London tea millionaire, she had given Yeats the money to buy the public platform he desired for the dissemination of his ideas. Dublin gossips talked about the battle between her and Lady Gregory for Yeats's favour. Having elicited a promise from Yeats that he would write to Unwin on Bell's behalf, Gogarty mentions his other purpose in coming to see the poet: to show him the translation of *Oedipus* into English, which Yeats had asked him to do, in order to adapt it for the Abbey. Gilbert Murray had refused to help Yeats in the matter.

> I received a long lecture on modern literary language. Yeats forgave William Morris for his archaism for it was both original and scholarly. An archaism was only admissible when one had discovered it for oneself. There was no defence for the continuance of mere metrical conventions, 'hast' 'shalt' 'thou' 'thee' 'wert' 'art' etc. They were part of a language highly artificial and conscious, a language that would pass for poetry at a future date, in a single instance, where the rest of the literature was lost. Meanwhile I was beginning to see what Yeats wants, and to see how deliberate the use of his archaisms were. He derives them from the 'folk' language ... He calls all inversions in verse, and 'thee' and 'thou' conventions, labour saving devices and assures me he could improvise verse by the hour if he permitted himself the use of inversions and the conventional language of poetry.

Yeats used the same argument to George Moore in a slightly different form, in *Ave*. It is the search of the modern poet for purity of language, which did not begin, as some critics appear to think it did, with Mr T. S. Eliot.

> Here an argument occurred to me that one of the most beautiful elegies in any language (Moschus' Lament for Bion) and one which Shelley is largely indebted to in his 'Adonais' was written by a 'Grammarian'; and I asked Yeats might not its 'beauty' be due to the fact that it alone has preserved to us all the conventional epithets and uses of a whole period, and

by remaining the sole example received singly the praise that otherwise might have been dissipated over many writers.

I don't know how far my supposition is justified but surely you will admit the introduction of Moschus because it charmed Yeats and showed him I had been attentive ...

This verse alone would make Moschus a poet by virtue of the second person and the third person of the Blessed Trinity, Matter, Metre and Music. There is some remarkable internal chiming in Greek poetry noticeably in Moschus which has never received attention. Read the first seven or eight lines and observe the *wailing vowels*.

> Archete sikelikai to Pentheos archete Moisai
> Ai ai tai malakai, men epei kata kapon olontai.
> Ede ta chlora selina to T'euthales oulon anethon
> Husteron au zoonti kai eis etos alle phounti
> Ammes hoi megaloi kai kapteroi, hoi, sophoi, andrei.

Andrew Lang's translation, though it does not attempt to catch the chiming of the Greek, renders the mood of the poem with great beauty.

> Begin ye Sicilian Muses begin the dirge; Ah me when the mallows wither in the garden, and the green parsley, and the curled tendrils of the anise, on a later day, they live again and spring in another year; but we men, we the great and mighty or wise, when once we have died, in hollow earth we sleep, gone down into silence; a right long endless and unawakening sleep.

Both Bell and Gogarty shared a deep admiration for Robert Bridges and Swinburne. These two poets possessed superb metrical ears, and had resolved difficult classical metres into English equivalents. Often Gogarty tried to interest Yeats in Bridges, but Yeats was too taken up at the time, according to Gogarty, with 'Buddhism or some emotional philopastery in its English guise' to pay much attention.

Swinburne was Gogarty's idol. Twice he had made a pilgrimage to Wimbledon where Swinburne lived 'armed with a laurel wreath and a sonnet fit to empty a town' to pay his respects, but each time he had been foiled by Theodore Watts-Dunton, who was literally Swinburne's warder, allowing him

twopence a day for drink, and letting him out only at certain
hours. Profiting by Gogarty's experience, Bell determined to try
and nab Swinburne during the short journey that Watts-Dunton
allowed him to make in the afternoon between their house and the
'Rose and Crown' in Wimbledon. His purpose was to present
Swinburne with a copy of his Newdigate. But the 'best-laid
schemes ... gang aft agley', and when Swinburne saw Bell
coming at him from behind a tree, he mistook him for one of the
blackmailers who were continually appearing to remind him of
his unsavoury past, and fled as fast as his little legs could carry
him. Bell having given Gogarty a brief summary of the incident,
Gogarty replied in verse clamouring for more details of the
encounter.

> Before you say a long farewell
> Or sound for me a parting Bell,
> From London's crowded town,
> I pray you tell what things are done
> Within the blooming 'Rose and Crown'
> Of wayward Wimbledon.
> And tell me all you left unsaid
> About the Bard with nose as red
> As cochineal enclareted.
> For you must make him doff his hat
> With meteoric sashes that
> Are fashioned like a great cravat
> As pendant and preposterous
> As his would be, could Aeschylus
> Rise from his grave by Gela lent,
> Where Aitna stands a monument,
> To advertise in Rotten Row
> Himself with poet-Yeats-like bow,
> (If we've agreed about the bow, it
> Reveals the greatness of the poet).
> And shows the hair 'to ashes turned',
> That hair that Balliol almost burned
> For knowing naught of Genesis
> And, ah, too much of Guinnesses.
> A head within so strange a hat
> Must surely be worth looking at.

You know the beverage each bard chooses
Bespeaks his favour with the Muses.
Homer, as Horace presupposes,
Arguitur laudibus vinosus –
And wine-dark was his song:
As wine-dark as those isles that be
Amid the sunned space of the sea
Where summer clouds do throng.
Whatever Pindar's barmaid brewed her
We know it mixed ἄριστον ὕδωρ
So it was, therefore, strong.

He confesses to Bell in June 1905 that he is 'really sick of his medical studies'.

Life is so short and art so long there is not time to lose. Inspiration comes to him who keeps the roomiest apartments for leisure in his mind. One cannot bind the two hands of Apollo. It is an awful nuisance having to distract oneself so much in making money, when one may never put money making as an end in itself. After all – the great difference between our lives and the lives of the Greeks as represented in their literature is this: the Greek was free from care as regards money matters; Plato considers philosophy possible only for those whose leisure was assured; we, without our leisure being assured, are struggling for the fruits of calmness and contemplation while all the time our ears are beset and deafened with the babel of the market.

How can we catch those unheard melodies? And confusion of thought ensues: we forget that all those things over which we vex ourselves in ethical dispute and puzzle on, were postulated and taken for granted by the men of old. Not until Christianity with its 'glad tidings' to all men rose and with it rose all men, did the old aristocracy of intellect and power end and disappear. We must consider the weakest link in the chain nowadays, and this consideration leaves me room for other considerations. Athens built on slavery could enjoy liberty. The common people were treated according to their kind, the nobles according to their position: so all the fruits were *the few*; the many leaves produced them. We try to be fruit and leaf together and – it can't be done. Our greatest men were those who either spared no-one – Cromwell, or so conducted their lives that the people have not been able to disentangle themselves from the confusion of opinions.

His prejudice against Celtic aspects of the revival is apparent in Gogarty's letters. I have already shown how he and Joyce reacted to the movement – Gogarty fearing that 'the Celtic chloroform would freeze the Sapphic current of his soul' – and given the reasons for their dislike of it. In a letter to Bell dated December 1905, Gogarty justifies his rejection of a Yeats play by clever classical analogies, but ingenious though the argument is, as a dramatic criticism it fails. The fact is Gogarty had little critical sense when it came to the judgment of a dramatic work. The play he is probably referring to in the passage below is Yeats's *On Baile's Strand* which dealt with Cuchullain, the central figure of the Irish heroic cycle; in an article in the *Evening Mail* a few months before, Gogarty had referred to Yeats's Cuchullain as 'a trivial peckish wavering old man'.

You will only think the plays good when you have forgotten great drama and remembered only contemporary revivals. I intend soon to denounce this lilliputianism in Art: this making ordinary common people protagonists, sending Apollo not even to earth but to the swineherd's hamlet; investing the peasant with divinity, reducing God to the ancestral ape. Of old the protagonists were better than ourselves and capable of intense and grander suffering; and by contemplating these we became ennobled ourselves—

Nowadays, the passions fit for gods are grafted on to non-representative and ignoble peasants, incapable of feeling greatly, even if they were not incapable of inspiring their audience with sentiments noble, awful and divine. And the peasant protagonist cannot be ennobled to the dignity of drama without making drama more undignified by not painting the peasant true. This is what Aristophanes probably kicked Euripides for – Dressing His Kings in rags: appealing to sentiment. It was indecorous in a dramatist, and indecent in Art. Awful Aeschylus, glorious Sophocles, how we are fallen. And that Aristophanes foresaw it all. Shakespeare's natural intuition forbade him to dethrone his Kings – though Lear wandered crownless. Ibsen is indecent beyond the expression of my disgust, though I grant him all genius. And then the little theatre disgracing us in England. Go, but when returning write down endorsing this – you will then avoid discomforting disappointments.

There are constant references in these letters to George Moore. 'When Moore wishes to pity himself before an audience and joke at Dublin' – Gogarty writes in August 1904 – 'one of his mots is: Huysmans is in a monastery, Zola's dead and I'm in Dublin.' As he prolonged his stay in Dublin, Moore's antics became notorious. In May 1906, Gogarty wrote to Bell:

Moore has gone away, with the wife of some fellow who is shooting in Scotland. He has gone away for a week or two. His last cruise, as he calls it. He calls the husband Bang Bang. 'Bang Bang will send us grouse.'

Moore has recorded how as a child he threw off his clothes and ran naked in front of his nurse, screaming with delight at the embarrassment he caused her. This instinct remained with him. He loved to shock. Yeats remembers him coming into a room after an assignment with his latest mistress, flopping down in a chair with a remark – 'I do wish that woman would wash.' His conversation in mixed company in Dublin was often inexcusable; but when reproved for it, he would gaze out of his wide blue eyes with a bland expression in his face as if surprised that anything he said could possibly have given offence. Gliding around his dressing-room with shoulders dropped like a champagne bottle and impeccable taste in food and art, he seemed the embodiment of French licence, when he was actually a lineal descendant of the Irish satirists, with a huge appetite for mockery. He knew of Dublin's acoustic qualities. His latest antic would be round the city in a day. He had his cook arrested for serving an omelet under false pretences. He disagreed with the colour of his neighbours' door, and complained that it clashed with his own. When he began a law action, they encouraged tom-cats to intone love-calls outside his window at night. Moore replied by hiring a pipe band to play outside theirs.

It is hard to conceive that the change of religion which he underwent in Dublin was done with any other motive than that of creating mischief of the sort in which he delighted. Moore knew perfectly well that the manœuvre most likely to cause a sensation in Dublin would be for a Catholic to leave the Church, so he scheduled his 'conversion' with care, and announced the change-over to Protestantism with a flourish of trumpets in the *Irish Times*.

His tongue caused even more havoc than his play-acting. Douglas Hyde had irritated him by not calling him to speak at a meeting, so Moore spoke of 'the droop of Hyde's moustaches through which the Irish frothed like porter'. This finished him with the Gaelic League. Hyde bred a Gandhi-like reverence among his followers.

Moore had always had an uneasy collaboration with Yeats. Presently he began to refer to Yeats's 'middle class background'. The poet was livid; he knew Moore was a landed gentleman, and in a position to make such remarks with telling force. When A.E. pointed out that the Yeatses' spoons had Butler crests on them, and if Yeats had his rights he would be an Ormonde, Moore replied with a gibe, and said passages in *The Countess Cathleen* were clearly derivative from the spoons.

Gogarty found that his friendship with Moore did not prevent him from becoming a target for Moore's mockery. When *The Lake* appeared in March 1906, he discovered his own name in one of the opening chapters. Moore had used the name Oliver Gogarty for a renegade priest in the book, whose prototype, a Father Connellan, was well known in the Irish country-side.

> I am sending you a copy of Moore's 'The Lake' [he wrote to Bell in May]. It is such a risk for me to keep it, lest being forgetful I leave it under my mother's eye, that I send it on to you. One cannot long be offended with Moore any more than one could fall out with March. I am reconciled: and to hold me to it he tried me with the book. In a few days he produces his pamphlet against the clergy. I made him nearly weep with vexation when I pointed out how he had thrown away through flippancy chances of greatly impressing his country-men. When he became a protestant he did so avowedly because the priests had the King's racing colours on their vest-ments. The joking made him appear too futile. Had he pro-tested, as he could easily have done and with sufficient reason, that inasmuch as the Catholic clergy had always insisted on the fact that no one could be a true Irishman who was not a

Catholic, and vice versa; and, as the King had condemned Catholicism, those who received him in Maynooth could be neither true Catholics nor Irishmen, he (G.M.) would be forced to abrogate them and their creed. It would have been a splendid hit. The clergy here are rather sorry that they were so prominent when the King came to Ireland. But Moore turned the thing into a light joke and so lost ground.

Mrs Gogarty was not impressed by her son's friendship with Moore whom she regarded as theologically unsafe. When Moore called at the Gogarty home for Oliver, Mrs Gogarty would refuse to come to the door to see him if her son was not in. Mayflo, Gogarty's sister, who with her brother's flair for phrase, remembers Moore as looking like 'an aborted egg', used to be dispatched to the hall to tell the novelist that Oliver was not at home. Moore used to revenge himself on Mrs Gogarty by criticizing her stained-glass window on the front landing, gesturing with his stick and uttering his condemnations in a loud, piercing voice.

Gogarty perceived what Yeats's dislike of Moore blinded him to, Moore's deep-seated devotion to the single thing that counted in his life, his art. Yeats thought Moore an 'artless man' and later attacked him viciously in his autobiography. There were many different Moores; Moore the gentleman who rode at Chester race-course, and spent the first pounds of his inheritance on an expensive shooting case; Moore the novelist living in cheap London lodgings, examining the lower classes with the microscopic eye of the realist writer. There was Moore the boulevardier whom Dublin knew. Edward Martyn said a marvellous thing about Moore when he observed: 'Moore's a bit of a bank holiday sort of fellow ye know.' He meant it as a deprecating remark. But Moore would have been quite at home with a bank holiday crowd, moving and jogging in and out of them, observing and noting with his clinical eye. He might play the jester in the Dublin salons, but Moore the artist was always at his elbow recording the reactions of his audience, and always including himself faithfully in the pageant. Thus in his Trilogy (*Ave*, *Salve*, and *Vale*) he 'built up' as Virginia Woolf says 'the airy chambers of a lifetime, the habitation of his own soul, in a cadence that will give him a place among the lesser immortals of our tongue'.

Gogarty never fell out with Moore. He accepted the fact that he could never rely on him. You might treat him as a friend and be rebuffed. He knew Moore was incapable of gratitude. But between the two there was some bond which is perhaps best defined in a note Gogarty wrote just after Moore's death.

For all his unaccountableness and petulance, to me at least, Moore was as transparent as a child, else why this sudden gush behind the eyes, when I think of how far I shall have to journey for help before I find another to whom the Muses are as dear or who served them more or longer. His life is written out by himself where he lived it, where few men have lived more courageously or consistently, in the world of art.

In the summer of 1906 Gogarty went on a short holiday to America with an old friend of his father's, Dick Burke of Fethard, Tipperary. In a letter he gives an early impression of a world which was for him strange and novel, and it is worth quoting in full.

Saturday June 1 1906   *The Waldorf Astoria,*
                                                      New York

'Out of the golden remote wild West where the sea without shore is' I send you word. I have been here since the arrival of the 'Caronia' – a palace pushed into the sea – on Wednesday last; and I could not get time before this to answer your letter.

I am amazed at America; particularly at New York, city of saloons, offices, hotels. The last few days have been a continuous rush – characteristic of this people sans composure; 'sans taste', too. Millionaires who are paupers in enjoyment of anything save the table, have fed and fondled me. Verily it is not a city of poor relations: but I could not endure this place for more than a week even were the 'heat waves' to keep off. As I write now it is 5 a.m. and I sit on the 12th floor of probably the world's largest hotel. A breeze much warmer than the temperature of my body supplies me with Aeolian Turkish baths – everything is possible in America. There are not a few advantages here: one can stare at the strangely dressed, care-worn, childish people with the sure and certain knowledge that you will not know one of them. Their clothes to my English eye are too big – pretentious. They are cut so that they may convey a notion of strength and bulk – they succeed in making their owners truly American – 'The pale, windy people', to quote Yeats.

This city is, I must admit, more *magnificent* than London. The hotels here would make the Carltons, Cecils, Victorias etc., mere pot houses. Two-thousand people may be accommodated here for instance, and 16 lifts are in constant use. Roof-gardens where plays and bands are played ease the pallid ones o' nights. Needless to add the bands are redolent of America – cake-walks and the intermezzos, and other music threaten dyspepsia to the soul.

The American women too, are superficial and untamed in spite of all their elegances. I sometimes think when I see the strange movement of their mincing gait that if I but turned my head they would relapse into a wild and ungovernable cat-walk. They are threatened by the primitive things. Beautifully manicured hands and Parisian costumes cannot make me quite assured that they are really civilized – but who was the cynic that said women were the only animal we had not tamed? On his head be my ungallant imaginings!

I intended to describe the Atlantic to you while I was crossing it. The languor of the sea and its thought-effacing influence prevented this: and now that I am on land the heat enervates me.

There is a delight in gazing on unlimited spaces. 'I love all waste and solitary places; where we taste the pleasure of believing what we see, Is boundless as we wish our souls to be: and such was this wide ocean' – I think this is more or less accurate Shelley. And the colour was glorious – the word is not exaggerated or inexact. To see the black-green water furrowed into April green and white – snow in Spring; and an everlasting rainbow shine above the changing waters was a sight that will nourish the soul that may never be able to describe it. And then above the dim red sunset the tranquil yellow evening star. When the great long, slow-moving waters moaned away on either side of the prow one could see beads like strings of pearl stretched from their crests – before they broke – to their bases. This in the evening with Hesperus must have been beheld of Lovell Beddoes when he wrote that lovely lyric, 'How many times do I love you?' At night the phosphorescent stars were really scintillating planets of the ocean or glow-worms of the night. I am now looking *forward* to going *back*! Is this native? I will probably catch the 'Campania' on the 27th and if the dollars decrease not – let it pass my native isle and land me in Liverpool whence I might run down to see you.

In this sequence of letters we may glimpse something of the conversational quality which captivated Edwardian Dublin and later was 'the success of the Season', when Gogarty arrived in London in the 'twenties. For Gogarty had the unusual gift of writing words almost as he would speak them; though the ideas came to his mind with lightning rapidity, he was able to subject them to the discipline of his pen, and keep them before him long enough to perpetuate in ink. Throughout these letters one often comes across the technique of the conversationalist, the feeling for alliteration, the rhetorical balance of words that can make a spoken sentence come easily to the ear, and therefore more likely to charm a listener. Here too it is possible to observe the serious side of Gogarty's nature, the seeker after truth, the artist in pursuit of the methods of his craft, the side that Gogarty, like Moore, seemed to wish to conceal from the world at large, holding to his pose as a cynic and mocker of life.

NINE

ALTOGETHER Gogarty took ten years to qualify as a doctor. After he had got past his anatomy examination in 1905, which had held him back for three years, he set himself seriously at work to qualify. His final year was 1906–7. In the summer of that year he married after a swift courtship, Martha Duane of Rossdhu, Moyard, Co. Galway. The Duanes were landowners who had resided in the west of Ireland since the ninth century at least. An ancestor, James Duane, was the first Mayor of New York after the revolution; another, Matthew Duane, had been a member of Lincoln's Inn and a Trustee of the British Museum, an unusual distinction for an Irish Catholic in the eighteenth century. Gogarty's marriage and new responsibility stimulated him to put his nose to the grindstone for his final year.

Under the Dublin system of medical teaching Gogarty had had to spend six months of his student career *living in* hospital, to obtain certificates in obstetrics, medicine and surgery. There, one attached oneself to a surgeon or physician, and went the rounds of the wards, taking instruction from him at the bedside of the patient. This was the clinical method of teaching invented by Graves, the Dublin physician in the 'forties.

Gogarty was fortunate in being the clinical clerk of Sir Thomas Myles. Myles was another of those larger-than-life personalities, who seemed so numerous in the Dublin of those days. He was six feet three in height with a head like the Kaiser. An insomniac, he read Shakespeare in the hours when others slept. He once paused before a certain operation performed exclusively on males to remark: 'There is a divinity which shapes our ends.' Ingeniously he would relate Shakespearian analogies to the cases under his care, in the course of his lectures. Even the case history of a syphilitic sailor he could embroider with a wealth of picturesque detail, as Gogarty has described in *Tumbling in The Hay*.

He has braved the arctic night and he has heard the thunder of the breaking ice. He has seen the great whale shouldering off the seas as he comes to surface. Ah, but gentlemen, the shore has its dangers as great, if not greater, than the deep and the ways of women can be deadlier than the sea; some dal-

liance, some little sport with Amaryllis in the shade, some
entanglement with Neaera's hair, and the lurking principle
entered in then, that appears on the surface twenty years
later.

We can imagine that a surgeon with such gifts was delighted to
find among his pupils one who discerned an analogy between the
ascent of the soul from the body, and the clouds of steam emitted
in the last stages of kidney disease, as Gogarty had done in his
verses 'To John Kidney Who died of Nephritis':

> What's in a name if the calling
> The essence of fact has not seized:
> The name in this case was appalling
> For it was diseased.

> From the walls of the flesh which immure in
> The spirit: as tubes do their lumen
> Came urine and mixed with the urine
> Were clouds of albumen.

> Thus by the doctors unbidden he
> Passed out through these clouds to his goal:
> Oedema and coma and kidney
> Secreted his soul.

> There came on that dies suprema
> Which comes unto all who draw breath,
> Death, ushered in by Oedema,
> Oedema and death.

Or who had found material for an ode in the curious propensities
which the promptings of the prostate gland can induce among the
middle-aged:

TO HIS FRIENDS WHEN HIS PROSTATE SHALL HAVE
BECOME ENLARGED

> Bear with me friends when ill-defined
> The mortal part shall touch the mind
> And look not askance at me
> And my post-cocious potency.

> When the gland sets my loins on fire
> Urging inordinate desire,

And from the seas 'neath which it lies
A thousand Venuses arise.

When I am contemplating rape
And growing careless of escape
And Lust not art engrosses me –
For who writes old men's poetry?

Then may your minds be set at ease
And learn to pity my disease
Till I with undishonoured head
Join the uncopulating dead.

Occasionally during his lectures when he felt his class were not responding to their theme, Sir Thomas would quote from a labyrinthine ballad of Gogarty's, which he stated once in a letter to Joyce had reached its 236th verse, concerning the adventures of Sindbad the Sailor, a morbid mariner, who had so much mercury pumped into him to relieve the 'bad disorder' that it was dangerous for him to stand near the fire, as the mercury ran up his spine like a barometer, and knocked him out, when it struck the base of his cerebral cortex. His adventures on ship when the compass is upset by the rival magnetic pulls of Sindbad's mercury-packed system and the North Pole, are described in a wealth of fantastic detail. Finally Sindbad is tossed overboard but Jonah-like is swallowed by a whale whose digestive system becomes another victim of the ever-potent mercury.

And where that whale had defecated
A continent is concentrated
From all the food evacuated
Which made no mean land
And from its colour when located
They called it Greenland.

In an airless room, with one window that dripped with moisture, in the vaults of the Richmond Hospital, Gogarty discovered a teacher who was to influence his whole medical career. This was Sir Robert Woods, the ear, nose and throat surgeon. Gogarty attached himself to the great man, and commenced an apprenticeship in the subject he was to specialize in, when he qualified as a doctor. Woods took a liking to Gogarty, and advanced his career later on considerably by sending him patients, though Lady Woods was too nervous to allow him to her dinner-parties because she feared the repercussions of his biting wit. Gogarty never forgot his debt to Woods: 'To him I owe all I know,' he wrote in a letter to Surgeon Doolin, the Editor of the *I.M.J.*, in 1934.

In June 1907 he passed his final examinations with second class honours in two subjects. At last he could exchange the white coat of a medical student for the morning coat, striped trousers and tall hat that were *de rigueur* for a Dublin doctor in those days. He planned to go to Vienna immediately and do a postgraduate course there. This would enable him to specialize in ear, nose and throat surgery on his return to Dublin, and with the help he could expect from friends like Myles, Woods and Sir William Taylor, the prospects of a successful career as a specialist seemed bright enough. Woods had arranged that he should study under Chiari and Hajek, the two leading specialists in Gogarty's line in the world, and Dozent Barany, discoverer of the functions of the non-auditory portion of the ear.

Later Gogarty was to have exceptional success in his profession. He appears to have what only the great surgeon has, the magic touch with his hands. This was pointed out to the biographer by a number of Dublin surgeons, who were themselves noted practitioners in this most individual of crafts. He concealed as well, under a cynical exterior, a deep compassion for the sufferings of his fellow men. The spectacle of suffering humanity brought out in him a kindness that those who knew only the forked-tongued Gogarty of the dining table and salon could never have suspected.

The lofty conception he had of the physician's function is contained in an allocution, printed in his autobiography *Tumbling in the Hay*, which he puts into the mouth of 'Jock' O'Carroll, a Richmond physician. It is set down in the form of a farewell to the students; but it patently contains the kernel of Gogarty's medical creed, and is couched in language which of itself gives it a special place in the annals of the literature of medicine.

Turn back now if you are not prepared and resigned to devote your lives to the contemplation of pain, suffering and squalor. For realize that it is not with athletes that you will be consorting, but with the dying and the diseased. The sunny days will not be yours any longer but days in the crowded dispensaries, the camp of the miner or of the soldier where, unarmed, you must render service in the very foremost positions. It is in the darkened pathological department of some institution that you, some of you, will spend your lives in tireless investigation of that microcosmic world which holds more numerous and more dangerous enemies of man than the deep. Your faces will alter. You will lose your youthful smirks; for, in the end, your ceaseless traffic with suffering will reflect itself in grave lines upon your countenance. Your outlook on life will have none of the deception that is the unconscious support of the layman: to you all life will appear in transit, and you will see with clear and undeceived vision the different stages of its devolution and its undivertible path to the grave. You will see those sightless forces, the pull of gravity, the pull of the grave that never lets up for one moment, draw down the cheeks and the corners of the mouth and bend the back until you behold beauty abashed and life itself caricatured in the spectacle of the living looking down on the sod as if to find a grave.

These are no delightful thoughts, but they will inevitably be yours, and your recompense for them is that your work for a short space may ease pain and baulk, if only for a year or two, the forces of annihilation and decay. You may be able to avert the greatest tragedy in the world – the death of the young mother; you may be able to bring back from the lonely valley of the shadow the babe, and set it again smiling upon its mother's knee.

I have seen as the years of experience progress the wildest medicos, the greatest rapscallions, turn themselves into good, sober and sound physicians. It is by Charity that this miracle is wrought. By Charity. You know too much. You have seen too much. You know what suffering means. You have seen it perhaps at the acutest and most pitiable stage of all when it turns delirious in its attempts at wild delight. You have seen what the wages of sin are.

For this you must be prepared to sacrifice more than your lives. You must sacrifice your delight in Beauty; for, as you gaze on it, your knowledge tempts you to see beneath its bloom the intimations of decay. That is the price that you must pay for this knowledge. That is the sacrifice you must make. Your joy in life must be exchanged for devotion to the service of mankind; sometimes, as in those who are psychotherapists, they lose more than life, they lose their reason. Unselfishly to make this sacrifice is the long-descended tradition and prerogative of our profession ... Good morning.

TEN

GOGARTY did not get off to Vienna immediately, as he had planned. His wife gave birth to a son on July 23rd, 1907. The child was christened Oliver Duane Odysseus Gogarty.

In autumn, Gogarty set out for Vienna with his wife, leaving his small son behind him with a nurse at No. 17 Earlsfort Terrace. Perhaps he did not want to subject his first-born to the aura of the rooms he was leasing in the Austrian capital. They had once belonged to Krafft-Ebing. Before he left, Sir Robert Woods had made an encouraging remark:

> There will be enough in my back-wash, Gogarty, to keep you going for the rest of your life.

The atmosphere of Vienna delighted Gogarty.

> The most civilised City in Europe: the city of music and the waltz; the city where even the girls in the kiosks are embalmed in love; city of the most ineffectual army in the world, not even excepting the Portuguese, and therefore all the more civilised.

The training there was excellent. There were unlimited opportunities for surgical practice.

In Dublin, a junior surgeon might have to wait months before having an opportunity of performing certain types of operation, but in Vienna one could always 'buy' for a few shillings a patient with a particular ailment, suitable to the surgery that an apprentice doctor was currently perfecting. Thus, in a few weeks in Vienna, a surgeon could obtain more experience than in four years in Dublin. Gogarty took full advantage of these opportunities, though he found the conditions under which he worked primitive.

> In Vienna, there were no trained Nurses. Feudalism did not permit its daughters to do menial work, unmarried, so nurses were recruited from retired street walkers. These administer the anaesthetics to a dozen women at a time in the Gynaecological Clinic. The Doctors started when the patients snored. Surgery was savagery in Vienna in 1907. There was

a flag to be flown over the great hospital or Krankenhaus if one day passed without some inmate dying – I never saw it flown.

In March 1908, he returned to Dublin. He had learnt a good deal in a short time in Vienna. Now, if he could obtain a hospital appointment in Dublin, and suitable consulting rooms, the path to a successful career as a specialist lay before him.

Doctors and lawyers occupied a privileged position in Edwardian Dublin. They formed a social elite, and dominated society since the landed gentry had moved out of the city after the Act of Union. In Dublin, titles, which in England were reserved for commerce kings, went to successful surgeons and judges. No new middle class had sprung up to sully the social landscape. Ireland had missed the Industrial Revolution. Even if success in business did secure a title, which was rare, it did not secure admission to society in the city. What H. D. F. Kitto has written about eighteenth-century England can be usefully applied to an estimate of the class structure of Edwardian Dublin.

> One of the reasons why the 18th Century in England was so essentially civilized before the catastrophe of the Industrial Revolution, was that there was no sharp division between the upper middle class and aristocracy, so that the culture of the latter was absorbed in full by the former and kept sane by it.

Since the professional class predominated, Dublin society lacked the rigid codes that were part of bourgeois existence elsewhere. The emphasis was on personality, not wealth. A leading physician or surgeon would be known by appearance in the city streets. Dublin was small enough for important people to be recognized. Eccentricity was cultivated. It was pleasant to be a successful surgeon, and known as a character to rich and poor, as Sir Thomas Myles and 'Johnny' Macardle were.

Though a wit has described Edwardian Dublin as 'the City of Dreadful Knights', because of the number of titles conferred on the professional classes, Dublin medicine nevertheless had reached a remarkably high standard in the previous century, and many of the advances in medical science had been the result of work by Dublin surgeons and physicians. Graves, the founder of clinical teaching, Stokes, Abraham Colles, Andrew Corrigan, have given their names to various conditions, that students throughout the world recognize by these names. Gogarty was always keenly aware of the illustrious history of Dublin medicine; and in an ode written for the bi-centenary of the Trinity Medical School, in 1912, and recited at the Abbey Theatre by Professor Tyrrell, he paid tribute to the doctors and scientists who had brought distinction to their city in the previous century. The 'Hamilton' referred to is Rowan Hamilton, who discovered the formula for quarternions.

> They were indeed a fearless nation
> Whose only sign of hesitation
> At Death was Cheyne-Stokes respiration
> Of Stokes who stood so firm,
> And of that Stokes who taught so well,
> What Graves made so discernible,
> And Hamilton who kenned,
> And made a mirror for the mind
> In which but few have since divined,
> And who called Wordsworth friend.
> His home who into billows hurled,
> The baseless fabric of the world,
> Till, prophet-like, he heard
> The faint, mute, transatlantic cry,
> Of floating cities doomed to die,
> The permeating Word
> Never informed a spirit more clear
> Or kindlier than Fitzgerald's here ...
> What Wilbur Wright achieved
> His mind original foresaw;
> He planned to climb the blue,
> Like Icarus, as free from awe,
> As early-dying too.

Gogarty made his own small contribution to medical science. According to Dr Harry Mellotte, a Harley Street ophthalmic specialist, Gogarty was the first to draw attention to certain aspects of sinus infection. A paper by Gogarty, 'Latent Empyema of the Nasal Accessory Sinuses', that was considered significant at the time, was published in *The British Medical Journal* of 1914, Volume 2, page 1020.

He had brought a bronchoscope back to Dublin from Vienna,

the first one used in the British Isles. This instrument illuminated the throat and lungs, so that the specialist could obtain a clear view of the organs he examined. Gogarty's problem was to find a hospital where he could put it to use. In Dublin, in order to specialize, it is necessary to secure a hospital appointment. Work at a hospital is performed gratis, but it brings a specialist into contact with general practitioners in the city, through whom patients are sent to the hospital. Thus the surgeon makes his professional contacts and builds up his practice, as well as getting experience in his speciality. Within a few weeks of his return, Gogarty had a stroke of luck. Sir Robert Woods resigned from the Richmond Hospital to go to Sir Patrick Dun's. Gogarty applied for the vacancy and was successful. Thus, he began again to retrace the journey he had made daily in his student days, down Red Cow Lane, up North Brunswick Street towards the green copper minarets that crowned the quaint mock-Byzantine towers of the Richmond.

Gogarty found a house in Ely Place, opposite the house where George Moore lived. It had belonged to Sir Thomas Deane, architect of Ruskin's Museum in Oxford, and, though originally built in Queen Anne style, had had various Gothic additions built on, by its owner, that lent a curious effect to the outside of the house, with its numerous balconies and wooden pillars. Its Florentine knocker appealed to Gogarty; this decided him to purchase the premises where he was to reside for the rest of his life in Dublin. George Moore kept the garden in the cul-de-sac, and Gogarty gazed out on the greenery and composed verses while he waited for patients to arrive. This garden, acquired after Moore's departure, he used as a tennis-court and archery ground.

His next step was to purchase an expensive motor-car. First, he bought an Argyll, than a Daimler, and a few years later a 40/50 horse-power, buttercup-coloured Rolls Royce, which became well known in Dublin. 'I'm going to drive myself into a practice,' he told one of his friends. With his fur-collared coat and top hat, he looked impressive as he drove through Dublin, seated bolt-upright in the driving seat of one or other of these splendid vehicles.

Two mishaps befell him in his first year in practice. In March, he had his appendix out in Mount Street Hospital; then four months later, while he was in the car as a passenger, his chauffeur crashed at Bray and killed a child. He cured the nervous shock that followed this incident by going to London for the dinner in honour of Bleriot, who had just flown the Channel, and blowing £100 in six days.

Ear, nose and throat surgery, which was Gogarty's speciality, could, in those days, provide a lucrative income. The work involved mainly tonsillectomies, treating ear infections and adenoids, and washing out antrums: occasionally, a mastoid operation had to be performed. Routine E.N.T. work took up little time and, therefore, the income from it was high in proportion to those operations which occupied long periods. 'I am endeavouring to make people pay through their noses,' Gogarty wrote jokingly to Dermot Freyer, in March 1907. In fact, his practice was growing rapidly. In 1911, Edward Taylor suggested that he should apply for a post in the Meath Hospital. This would be a promotion, as the student fees in the Meath were divided up amongst the medical staff, so that they received payment for their services. On February 23rd, 1911, Gogarty wrote, as follows, to the Registrar of the Meath:

> I have the honour to apply for the position on the Staff of the Meath Hospital left vacant by Mr Conway Dwyer. I have graduated from Trinity College, Dublin, and I am a Fellow of the Royal College of Surgeons. In the Richmond Hospital, I had the appointment of Throat Surgeon.

He was duly elected, and remained on the staff of the Meath for the rest of his medical career in Dublin.

His popularity with the senior members of the profession helped to increase his practice. Sir William Taylor, Sir Thomas Myles and Sir Thornley Stoker occasionally sent him rich patients. Though the greater portion of their work was done for nothing, it was recognized that the surgeon was entitled to make up for this, by charging stiff fees to those who could afford it. Sir Robert Woods once charged a thousand guineas for a mastoid operation. Gogarty's fee for a major operation was a hundred guineas, if he knew that his patient was in a position to pay it. A hundred guineas, pre-war, would be six hundred in today's currency.

The landed gentry at that time in Ireland were extremely wealthy. The fact that Gogarty had begun to move in country-house society, added to his list of wealthy patients. Lady Fingall

122

had taken him up at her dinner-parties. She was a friend of Edward VII. His reputation as a conversationalist spread. Lady Fingall recalls in her memoirs, how Gogarty used to 'keep the air electric with his wit'.

Other titled people with whom he was on terms of friendship at this period included Lady Leslie, the Earl of Granard, Lord Dunsany and the present Marquess Conyngham.

How good a surgeon was Gogarty? In later years, when he had allowed his medical practice to take second place to his literary pursuits, it became the custom among those who were envious of his versatility, to deprecate his talents as a doctor. To arrive at an estimate of his surgical prowess, the biographer went to a reliable source of information, Gogarty's colleagues who had worked with him in hospital.

Surgeons are a special breed of their own. They do not adopt the title 'Doctor', but 'Mr', to distinguish them from other members of the medical profession. They are craftsmen. In some ways they remind one of circus acrobats: they are men with a knack; either you have a knack or you have not, and if you haven't got it, no amount of training or teaching will give it to you. The knack is in the fingers – their deftness and their power. 'Gogarty was extraordinarily dexterous', Surgeon Lane of the Meath remembered: 'He was like lightning with his hands.' And Surgeon Burke, who worked with him as a junior surgeon, recalled: 'Gogarty was a top-notch surgeon – good judgment and good hands.' Surgeon William Doolin remembered Gogarty as 'a brilliant surgeon'.

Stephen McKenna, the writer, who had had emergency treatment by Gogarty for an abscess in his ear, has related that when he went later to a leading ear specialist in Europe, his comment was that he thought there were not two men in the world who could have performed the operation that Gogarty had.

Gogarty seems also to have had a flair for diagnosis. After J. M. Synge, the dramatist, had been ill for a year or so, he was diagnosed as having TB. Gogarty pointed out that Synge was suffering from Hodgkin's Disease (a form of cancer), because the glands in his neck were located posteriorly, where they are very rarely found in TB. The diagnosis proved to be the correct one. Dr Patrick O'Kelly, a radiologist, formerly of the Hammersmith Hospital, has written to the author:

This is a very good indication of Gogarty's quality as a physician, even though he was an E.N.T. specialist. This might seem a small thing in the light of the great advances which have been made in medicine since that time. But in Gogarty's day, when the reliance upon clinical findings was paramount and rarely aided by laboratory assistance, it represented a high degree of competence in diagnosis.

He worked at great speed. Often he removed tonsils with only a local anaesthetic, while the patient was sitting in a chair. In those days, anaesthetics involved a degree of risk, and a surgeon who was skilful enough to operate without putting his patient 'under', diminished the chances of a fatality. As he worked away, with his fingers flying, Gogarty talked continually, telling stories, making jokes, passing remarks, making allusions, sometimes related to his work, sometimes not. In the Meath Hospital, the surgeons operated together in one large theatre. Occasionally, as he operated with exuberance, Gogarty would fire tonsils at his fellow surgeons, across the theatre. Yeats has furnished us with a description of Gogarty at work.

Gogarty, with his usual exuberant gaiety, removed my tonsils. As long as I retained consciousness, he discussed literature, and continued the discussion when I awoke. He would probably have continued it most of the afternoon (he came 6 times) but I had a haemorrhage and was preoccupied with my possible end. I was looking secretly, of course, for a dying speech.

There is no fear that the operation has not been done thoroughly, for as Gogarty looked at me over the end of the bed as I was meditating on the ducks, he said: 'I have been *too* thorough.'

Michael Scott, a well-known Dublin architect, but at that time an actor, remembers coming to during an operation before Gogarty had finished, and hearing the surgeon telling some amusing story to the nurses, as his fingers rapidly made the adjustments necessary to complete the operation. Scott weakly tried to give some indication that he was conscious. He heard Gogarty saying:

Nurse, kindly put your hand over that man's mouth; we are not interested in an actor's subconscious.

Even during the difficult operations, he could seldom resist the chance of a quip. He performed the second laryngectomy ever done in Ireland, when he was thirty-three years of age – an operation which took over five hours to complete. He was watched breathlessly by a crowd of students in the gallery. During the operation, which took place in the Richmond Hospital, a knocking was heard on the floor underneath the operating table. A river flows under the Richmond, which comes from Grangegorman Mental Hospital. Gogarty's comment on the knocking was, as he continued to operate: 'Pinkeens with G.P.I., imagining they are salmon.' A picture of these tiny denizens of the deep, leaping from the stream in delusions of grandeur, drew a roar from the listening audience. At the end of the operation, when he had successfully removed the larynx, Gogarty sent it up with a flip from behind his back, to the gallery, saying: 'There you are, boys, have a look at it.' A typical finish to a brilliant piece of work.

Under stress, he could be cutting in his sarcasm. 'Jesus Christ,' cried a young assistant in dismay, when a lesion burst during an operation. 'Cease calling on your unqualified assistant,' Gogarty hissed, as he searched for the instrument that the assistant should have handed him. He found it difficult to resist the temptation to make a witty remark at the expense of a colleague, even if it happened to be someone he admired particularly, like a famous surgeon who was the defeated defendant in a divorce action. 'He is the only person who made his fortune with the knife, and lost it with his fork,' was Gogarty's summing-up, which, needless to say, made the rounds of the Dublin hospitals and was probably appreciated by the victim as much as by anyone else. On another occasion, referring to a specialist, not specially noted for self-effacement, who had read a paper on 'Advertising in Medicine', Gogarty remarked afterwards to Oliver Chance 'It was like listening to a loudspeaker blaring out "Mum's the word".'

An instance of his quickness of mind occurred on an occasion when he was waiting for a Surgeon Diamond of the Meath, to come down in the lift. As the lift appeared, it revealed a pair of woman's legs. 'Legs,' murmured Gogarty, 'but not Diamond.' The allusion is of course to 'Legs' Diamond the Chicago gangster.

'He educated the Boardroom at the Meath', recalls Mr Lane, who became attached to the Staff some years later. 'He often conducted long contests in Shakespearian quotations with Lane-Joynt. Dr Boxwell and Sir John Moore were others who were able to keep up with him in literary allusions.'

Mr Lane remembers Sir Lambert Ormsby, who was a great admirer of Gogarty's, stopping on the stairs one day and actually overhearing Gogarty telling a story against Ormsby himself. Ormsby's only comment was, with a smile: 'Funny fellow Gogarty, isn't he?'

'He would burst into the Boardroom,' remembers Surgeon James Quinn, 'and regale us with the latest scandal of the city, and keep us amused for a half an hour or so. His usual opening was "Listen, boys, did you hear this one?" He had a habit of throwing his head back and gazing round the room with those remarkable eyes of his whose appeal it was impossible to resist. No one minded in the least what Gogarty said about them; it was always so brilliant.'

One aspect of his personality that the medical profession brought out in Gogarty, was the kindness and generosity which were inherent in his character, a character often misunderstood by those who saw him only as a biting satirist. He never charged poor people, even when they came to his consulting rooms. Actors, priests and nuns and clergy of all denominations were others for whom he reduced his professional charges when they came to him. One little boy remembers having his tonsils removed to improve his singing voice, for he was in the choir of St Patrick's Cathedral. The operation was painful, and he was crying as he left the surgery. He felt something being pressed into his hand. Outside, he discovered to his delight that Gogarty had given him five shillings, though there had been no fee for the operation. After forty years, the former choirboy remembered the keen pleasure he felt at receiving what was, for him, a princely sum. The irony of the tale is that when he reached home, his mother wouldn't believe that he had got the five shillings from Gogarty. 'That fellow never gave you that,' she said. All she had seen was her child in pain, and an apparently callous surgeon. As a matter of fact, Gogarty had a low pain threshold himself, and found it difficult to conceal his surprise when patients under treatment from him complained that he hurt them.

On another occasion, after he had operated on a rich patient, a junior medical student who had assisted found something pressed into his hand by Gogarty. He thought it might be a ten-shilling note – a generous present in those times for students, who were not usually paid for assisting at operations. He found he had been given a five-pound note, which he immediately brought to the Students' Room in St Vincent's Hospital, brandishing it over his head so that all might hear the good news, and join him in those celebrations for which medical students are noted.

Once, Gabriel Fallon, at that time an Abbey actor, whom Gogarty had refused to charge, asked him how was he going to make an evening's profit out of the numerous poor people who were crowded in his surgery. Gogarty replied, with a toss of his head: 'I have a Duchess coming from London, and I'll settle her snout for a century.'

To a political opponent, Robert Briscoe, he showed great kindness by operating in an emergency and absolutely refusing to accept any fee from a fellow member of the Oireactas.

Violet Clifton, wife of Talbot Clifton, a friend of Gogarty, who was living in Ireland before the Great War, and who later became in her own right a distinguished writer, remembers a particular instance of Gogarty's generosity as a doctor when a burst appendix nearly cost her boy his life.

Gogarty had great wealth of quick generous kindness and a wealth of courage. He proved both virtues to me by two signal deeds of friendship. My elder son, on an Xmas day in Connemara, was plunged in sudden unaccountable agony. Gogarty, leaving his children and his festal friends, drove the child and myself through snow and over ice many miles into Galway. The boy was not his patient. In the snow-storm of Galway, I jumped out of the car stationed before the only nursing home. I stretched out my arms to stop the doctor in charge, to beg him to instantly admit and to attend my son. A male nurse had already carried the child half way up the stairs. When the doctor in the street became aware of Gogarty, he refused us admittance to the Home – and that on account of political unreason. We went on to the poor hospital; the good nuns allowed me to share the cold room with my son, until he left ... (Gogarty seeing a statue of the Sacred Heart murmured to me that he disliked 'anatomical devotions').

127

Oliver had said to me that the most grievous loss is the death of a child to its parents. That the givers of life should behold the life jessant from them cut off is an insult to their mutual expectation; an insult to the run of nature.

He was also remembered by his colleagues for his generous qualities. 'One of the most generous of men,' recalls Surgeon Doolin. 'He never forgot a kind act, but always repaid it. Yet, he hated pretence and pomposity, and he could be merciless at Academy meetings, at the expense of any colleague whom he considered guilty of sharp practice or bombast.'

Curiously enough, Gogarty was something of a hypochondriac. Once, he rushed to Stokes, the physician in the Meath, asking him to investigate what from a glandular swelling he thought might be an attack of typhoid. Stokes diagnosed the illness as merely a boil under the armpit which he lanced and thus cured. This did not prevent Gogarty from presenting him a month later with an expensive antique chair.

There was method in his kindness. When Gillman Moorhead, a brilliant Dublin physician, lost his sight, Gogarty organized a rota of doctors to accompany him on Saturday walks, so that Moorhead could get out at week-ends to the hills. A sonnet which Gogarty wrote privately for Moorhead reveals the depths of his affection for his stricken friend.

> It takes us all our time with all our eyes
> To learn to know, since knowledge comes from sight,
> And, long before we give back light for light,
> Evening is on us and the daylight flies.
> But you were swifter and your faculties
> Gathered more quickly, so the mind is bright
> That long before the evening fell on night.
> And it shall comfort you to realise
> That when we all are into darkness sent
> The dark, of which you had more than your share,
> If there be succour in Time's banishment,
> Pre-eminent again, you'll help us where
> The sudden dark, the vague beleaguerment
> Calls for such fortitude as you can spare.

Sometimes, the sufferings of his patients revealed to Gogarty a splendour of personality beneath the outer mask. One day, when he told a patient that he had no hope and would soon be dead, the man replied: 'I have seen all the pictures.'

As soon as his surgery was over, Gogarty rushed out to Philip Sayers's printing office in Suffolk Street, and scribbled down this little poem, 'All the Pictures', written, as many other of his poems were, 'off the cuff'. This is the explanation of one or two indifferent lines.

ALL THE PICTURES

I told him he would soon be dead.
'I have seen all the pictures,' said
My patient. 'And I do not care.'
What could a doctor do but stare
In admiration half amused
Because the fearless fellow used
'The pictures' as a metaphor,
And was the first to use it for
Life which he could no longer feel
But only see it as a reel?

Was he not right to be resigned
To the sad wisdom of his mind?
Who wants to live when Life's a sight
Shut from the inner senses quite;
When listless heart and cynic mind
Are closed within a callous rind;
When April with its secret green
Is felt no more but only seen,
And Summer with its dusky meadows
Is no more than a play of shadows;
And Autumn's garish oriflamme
Fades like a flickering skiagram,
And all one's friends are gone, or seem
Shadows of dream beyond a dream?
And woman's love not any mo,
Oh, surely then 'tis time to go
And join the shades that make the Show!

His special regard for priests and nuns may surprise readers, who see him only in the light of A.E.'s description. 'A gay mocker, who spared neither the Maker of the Universe nor His creatures.'

But Gogarty never cut himself off from clerical company, an integrated part of Irish society. An intimate friend was the Most Reverend Dr Fogarty, Bishop of Killaloe, one of whose great delights in life was to spend an evening in Gogarty's company, where he laughed without ceasing from beginning to end. Another close friend was Archbishop Gilmartin of Tuam. Mother Eucharia, of Loreto Convent, St Stephen's Green, invited him regularly to tea. But there were other nuns who took a different view. Once a nun said to Brenda, his young daughter: 'There are three men who will destroy Dublin; Yeats, A.E. and ——' She was about to mention the third when she realized it was the child's father. Gogarty particularly admired the Christian Brother Order, who provide free secondary education in Ireland. This Order ran an industrial school near Renvyle, and Gogarty often helped them when they were in need. At his funeral, boys from this industrial school sang the Requiem Mass.

He was a church-goer, though sometimes a rather unorthodox one. Once a woman at church was impressed to see his lips moving as if in prayer, as he read from a Missal. She looked over his shoulder to find he was reading Horace's Odes.

One of Gogarty's closest friends in the second decade of the century was Dr Patrick Browne of Maynooth College. 'Paddy' Browne had a European reputation as a mathematician, was fluent in German, French and Irish, as well as being a noted classical scholar, and a fine horseman. He is 'Fr Paddy' in Gogarty's *As I Was Going Down Sackville Street*, the witty priest with 'one of the greatest brains and with the best memory of anyone in Ireland'. He was a striking-looking man, six feet three inches in height, with a leonine head and an aquiline profile. Most evenings when he was in Dublin, he would saunter into Gogarty's surgery at five o'clock and exchange the latest scandal of the day with him. Browne had a strong Rabelaisian streak, more akin indeed to a Renaissance cleric than a twentieth-century Maynooth professor, and on one occasion is said to have shocked Sartre at John Huston's home in Galway, sending him up to bed in dismay at the outflow of Rabelaisiana from this unusual priest. He and Gogarty were well met, and, in the evenings, over a cup of tea in the surgery, they would discuss with sardonic pleasure the failings of their fellow countrymen in every aspect of life. They parted, however, over political matters in 1922 and seldom met or talked to each other afterwards. It was from Dr Browne's blotting-paper memory that I succeeded in salvaging a number of Gogarty's Rabelaisian poems, and those of the group with whom he mixed at that time. 'Fr Paddy', like Gogarty, could remember a poem that he admired, on only one hearing.

Despite the demands on his profession, Gogarty remained a prominent figure in the literary life of Dublin, which, if anything, had gained in brilliance in the last years before the First World War. A.E. and Yeats held their 'evenings' on Mondays and Fridays. Tuesdays, Stephen McKenna, the translator of Plotinus, held open house, provided those who came conversed either in Irish or Greek. Sara Purser was another noted hostess. Gogarty had his 'evenings' on Friday, at which his wife acted as an energetic and thoughtful hostess. Ernest Boyd has recalled the atmosphere of Gogarty's 'Fridays'.

Yeats was there in that old Queen Anne house with windows looking on to the garden the leased demesne of George Moore and celebrated by him. A.E. is there too, and these two life-long friends with the stimulating seriousness and wit of their host to give edge to their conversation, talk of Gods, of heroes, of visions, and beliefs, and running through it all is the thread of common culture, hopes and dreams.

Dublin's reputation as the centre of a Renaissance had begun to spread. At the various Dublin literary gatherings, famous figures in the arts from England, France and Italy, could often be met with. D'Annunzio, Edmund Gosse, Augustus John, Mancini, Sargent, Bernard Shaw, were among those who came to Dublin to visit Lady Gregory, Yeats, or A.E. in this remarkable period. Lord Conyngham remembers how excited he was when Gogarty began to invite him regularly to his 'evenings' about 1910.

They were, to say the least of it, an education for a young man, as I was then, 22 years old ... His parties at his house were noted for the inclusion of the intelligentsia of Ireland, and for that matter, of Europe. I mention some names who later became famous. J. B. Yeats, Augustus John, Sir William Orpen, Sir Horace Plunkett, Daisy, Lady Fingall, Lord Dunsany, and many more.

Gogarty had met Dunsany at a Hunt Ball at Dunsany Castle. Observing a fair young man with regular, well-cut military features, sitting by the fire, Gogarty went over to talk to him during the dance. He soon discovered that they had in common a love of literature. From that moment, a close friendship was born. Dunsany was already a prolific novelist, poet and playwright, though he lived the life of a country gentleman, and was one of the best shots and fishermen in Ireland. He and Gogarty formed a friendship that was to last until Gogarty's death in 1957. Both were men of action, who lived their lives in the world, yet felt the need for communication with that other world where beauty hovers on the edge of consciousness. Their attitude to art had much in common. Dunsany's work had an enormous vogue in its own day, and at one time he had plays running in Prague, London and Moscow, simultaneously. A true aristocrat, from one of the oldest families in Ireland – his lineage went back to the twelfth century – his natural reserve was no proof against Gogarty's bubbling gaiety, and he enjoyed nothing better than a visit from the surgeon-poet who would come down to Dunsany Castle during the week and spend the evenings in Dunsany's private room, where they discussed literature, poetry and drama.

When Dunsany wrote in November 1911, asking Gogarty for the text of 'On the Death of Diogenes, the Doctor's Dog', Gogarty's reply shows that his attitude to his old professor had mellowed:

> I will send tomorrow a typed copy of that Threnody – 'The Death of Diogenes, The Doctor's Dog'. But remember when reading it that I like and respect Mahaffy very much. I have changed many an opinion since I wrote that doggerel. And with others my objection to his tuft-hunting. I see in it something that, if it does not exactly 'make for righteousness', is diametrically opposed to democracy. Then too how splendid it must be to talk only to Emperors and Kings; and to think only of 'lords that were so great of hand, and ladies that were queens of fair green land'. What a Tamburlaine of the intellect he is! He rides in Triumph thro Persepolis by dint of company! He reigns without anxiety and legislates without reproach. Therefore, in his mind he is royal and I am loyal to him.

Dunsany had discovered a remarkable ploughboy poet, Francis

Ledwidge, working on his estate whose books still run into new editions. Ledwidge was killed in 1917 in France. His delicate pastoral imagination was occasionally disturbed by melancholic fantasies which he confided to his patron. Gogarty couldn't resist satirizing these phantoms of the ploughboy protégé's brain, in verses which he sent to Dunsany.

P.O. & Telegraph,   Station, Drumree,
Dunsany   Meath Ry

DUNSANY CASTLE,
Co. Meath.
'My Lord,' said the Singer of Slane,
'I fear I'm becoming inane,
 For ladies vampiric
 Attend on each lyric
And banish the sleep from my brain.'

'Rejoice O you wakeful of brain,
So few to a frenzy attain!
 Now sentiments, Ledwidge,
 Will come to your head which
Could hardly have come to you sane.'

'But what of the maidens severe
Who out of the plaster appear?
 And an eye I discern,
 Wherever I turn,
That drives me to madness with fear?'

'Now really your fancy obtuse is –
The manifold maidens are Muses,
 And the Eye don't you follow
 Belongs to Apollo
Who searches the soul and accuses,
Whom lethargy always accuses.'

Gogarty continued to contribute to *The United Irishman* and to write poetry, most of which he sent off to his friend, Dermot Freyer, as soon as he had written it. Later, this poetry was to figure in Gogarty's first published work, *Hyperthuleana* (Beyond the Beyonds), a collection of verse of which he only printed five copies. These copies were given to George Moore, Augustus John, Dermot Freyer and Seamus O'Sullivan, and he kept one for himself. Freyer was the son of Sir Peter Freyer, the inventor of the prostate gland operation, which kept him in luxury for the rest of his life. Gogarty was extremely fond of Freyer junior and was always asking him to come to Dublin for a few hours to have the pleasure of his company.

> Oh, leave the prostate in its press,
> The Pater in his study,
> And seek this Isle of green access,
> Where everything is ruddy.

In 1908, when Tyrone Street was knocked down by the police, the event moved Gogarty to compose a sonnet which he forwarded to Freyer on April 22nd. This sonnet later appeared in *Hyperthuleana*.

> *When the Clearance was intended to the Kips*
> Sergeant with manners like an Inspector's
> Who chance on these defenceless walls may seize,
> If nights upon us did you ever please,
> Spare us, and we will stand you free encores.
> Against lust, rampant most, our business scores.
> We bring the hardest roués to their knees.
> And those temptations that by no means cease
> Are cured by yielding kindly to the whores!
> Lift not your baton 'gainst our bawdy bower!
> Has Hercules not laboured once till day?
> And Jove come – capital! – 'a golden shower',
> (Damn the expense!) to spend on Danae?
> If gods found comfort in a paramour,
> We, too, can take the 'perilous stuff' away.

Another poem which Gogarty forwarded to Freyer on November 16th, 1910, and which also appeared in *Hyperthuleana*, combines theological speculation with Rabelaisian fancy; but despite the change of key in the last two verses, the poem is a serious examination of the nature of free will, revealing again Gogarty's preoccupation with theological and metaphysical problems.

At the Abbaye la Trappe, on hearing the cry
        Memento homo quia pulvis es
The strong sound of the deep bell burns
The darkness and my soul resumes
Its meditation now, and turns
To think exclusively of tombs:
Ah no! – Those Greek funereal urns
Were not intended – I've been told –
Merely to meditate on mould.

I meditated: Man is Dust,
And into dust he shall return.
Until I wondered why God thrust
His breath into the dust to burn.
He gave it life, who gave it lust?
And who's to blame? If dust is Man,
The trouble in God's breath began.

God damns His breath, which is man's soul,
For misbehaviour of the clay:
His breath must be beyond control
To leave man Freewill anyway.
And then His breath must be most foul.
That thereby it should damn a soul.

Freewill to do or leave undone,
Means, first, repudiating laws
Lest they have influence thereon.
And then, effect without a cause:
For that Freewill should have effect,
All casual things it must neglect.

And when I think of all the work
And time they spent in teaching me,
A little doubt begins to lurk,
Of even the power of thinking free,
For what must I all danger shirk?
The value of a Saint's vocation
Varies directly as temptation?

A slight distraction unawares
Beset me in a twofold way:
I saw the legs of one who chars
And cleans the chapel out each day,

As she was washing down the stairs.
And I was bending down to pray.
I said 'If hers are not so trim,
Her daughter's might be tight and slim.'
And then I prayed a little space:
'O Thou, Lord God, what is this thing
Besets me in Thine Holy Place?
Why must Thy washerwoman fling
Her petticoats before my face
And set me wild with wantoning?
O, cool me with Thine Holy Water,
That I may think not on her daughter.'

'I am reading only Rabelais now,' he wrote to Freyer about this time. He never lost his enthusiasm for the 'Fornicating Friar', or his desire to venture on fancy's wing into the fantastic realm revealed by Rabelais, where the aphrodisiac is dissolved in the delight the image kindles in the reader's mind.

How can we reach though sail be bent
Beyond the horizon's verge
Those isles of your astonishment, Panurge?

At this time too, he kept up his friendship with Yeats. In 1910, Yeats actually came to live for a while at Fairfield. We find, the same year, that Gogarty was active in using his influence with Tyrrell, trying to get Yeats appointed Professor of English in Trinity, after Dowden had retired. He was unsuccessful, mainly because the poet had no academic degrees, and a Doctor Wilbraham Trench was appointed, whom Yeats later described as 'a man of known sobriety of manners and mind'.

Another friend was William Orpen, later to become famous as Sir William Orpen, the portrait painter, who could command up to £60,000 a year in portrait fees, in post-war London. Orpen painted Gogarty in 1911. Later, Augustus John was to paint him twice. The Orpen portrait is more subdued than any of the others. It shows Gogarty preoccupied, perhaps by the demands of his profession. The elfin vitality that is in the John portraits, painted in 1917, is not apparent here. But there is a hint of laughter on the edge of his lips, and the inquiring look of an artist in the fine eyes and high brow.

When Gogarty had an hour or so free, he would rush over to

Orpen's studio and make for the nearest mountain in a fast car. Orpen loved these jaunts into the Dublin hills, but he was always apprehensive of Gogarty's habit of talking as he drove, commenting on every inch of country-side they passed, and turning to Orpen with his hands off the wheel, to emphasize a point, or quote a passage of poetry.

How pleasant it was of a summer morning, 'when we were free! and all was hospitality' to drive out in the doctor's big car to 'Lamb Doyle's', that wonderful inn on the Hill of Step-a-Side which lies near the base of the Three Rock Mountain, so named from the three enormous rocks on its summit, which one can see clearly from Howth twelve miles away! The view from 'Lamb Doyle's' pub on a summer morning, as you sit in the shade on a bench outside the house and look back over the bay, with Dublin on the left, and Howth and Ireland's Eye, and Lambray behind! On the right Kingstown, Dalkey and Bray Head, all of them in the blaze of the midday sun! This view, with the sweet fresh smell of the country in your nostrils, a cigarette in your mouth, and your glass beside you, truly you could feel life in all its glory, yourself having only left the crowded hot city some twenty minutes before; in fact you could leave Dublin at noon and get all this joy and be back in the city, have lunch, and be ready for work at two o'clock. In no other town in the world that I have seen, could you have a pleasure like this in the middle of a day's toil.

Gogarty had a passion for fast cars at this period. 'It is not generally known', writes the present Marquess Conyngham, 'that Gogarty was a very fine driver and had a sound knowledge of internal combustion engines. We drove thousands of miles together, all over Ireland during the years 1911 to 1914.'

He owned two cars, a 10 horse-power Ford, and a 40/50 horse-power Rolls, which he bought in 1912. Lord Conyngham writes that Gogarty liked to drive in weather which other drivers considered suicidal. One day in torrential rain, Gogarty lured him into his Rolls and then drove to the Phoenix Park where he approached the Gough Monument at eighty miles an hour. At the last moment, he went into a deliberate skid, which brought the car completely round, about face, in front of the monument. This sort of acrobatics terrified his passengers; but it is typical of Gogarty's attitude to danger that he indulged himself in this way, as others might satisfy themselves with a special brand of drink or food.

After surgery, between five and seven, Gogarty usually slipped down to The Bailey Restaurant in Anne Street, which was about five minutes' walk from his rooms. Upstairs, he and a group of friends had been allocated a special room by Mr Hogan, the proprietor. Here, the best wit, epigrams and political talk in Dublin were to be heard. James Stephens recalls his first visit to The Bailey:

> I had my first adventure in the Bailey in the air, oxygen and gin, which we call wit, and which I watched as a cat watches a mouse, hoping to catch it; and for the first time I heard poetry spoken of, with the assured carelessness with which a carpenter talks of his tools and of the chairs and tables and oddments he will make with them.

Stephens soon became one of the 'regulars'. He sat in a corner, his legs curled round a stool like a leprechaun, his large expressive eyes lighting up as he sang a ballad or told a story, in a low musical voice, that was later to exercise its charm on B.B.C. listeners during the Second World War. So poor a few years before that he had fought with a swan for a crust of bread, he was now an established writer as a result of the success of his book, *The Crock of Gold*. Arthur Griffith presided at The Bailey. He seldom talked but listened with a twinkle in his blue eyes. On rare occasions, he sang his own composition, 'The Ballad of the Thirteenth Lock'. Most of the members of the circle were Sinn Fein supporters, but this was not exclusively so. Tom Kettle had been a member of the Irish Party before a speech in favour of the suffragette movement had resulted in his dismissal. Kettle was, according to Robert Lynd, 'the most brilliant mind of his generation, the generation after Yeats and Synge'. And Balfour had declared that Kettle's maiden speech at Westminster was the best maiden speech he had heard in the House. Kettle had been at Clongowes with Gogarty, who always admired him immensely.

> Tom Kettle [he wrote] had laughter in his soul. He spoke to you as from some Elysium wherein everyone was merry and full of wisdom.

Kettle had a fine presence and a pair of dark eyes, with a glow in them that could light a room; he was the epigrammatist of The Bailey. 'Home Rule,' he once said, 'is the art of minding your own business well. Unionism is the art of minding someone else's business badly.' On another occasion: 'The tram-car is the social confessional of Dublin. Sixpence prudently spent on fares, will provide you with a liberal education.' He dismissed the Ulster problem with: 'Orange-ism consists mainly of a settled hallucination, and an annual brainstorm.'

Then, there were Joe Boyd Barrett and James Valentine Nolan-Whelan, doctor and barrister respectively. Boyd-Barrett had a phenomenal memory for classical quotations, in which he used to rival Gogarty on occasions. Nolan-Whelan, who had been a double Blue at Oxford, squandered three fortunes on the race-course, but always retained a sense of gesture. Once he entertained the Viceroy, Lord Dudley, to a dinner. 'Make sure the boys are well fed,' he enjoined the butler at each course. When the Viceroy inquired, politely, who were 'the boys', he learnt that his host was referring to the bailiffs who were at that moment removing the furniture from some of the other rooms.

George Redding seldom spoke, but kept his genius for his poems, which, according to Gogarty, were the best satiric verse written in Dublin. He was head of the coopering department in Guinness. A Protestant Sinn Feiner, he was devoted to Griffith. Gogarty thought Redding's verse Swiftian in quality. It is difficult in retrospect, to select stanzas from the large repertoire of Redding's compositions which reproduce the effect of lines written to satirize current events. But his satire directed at a notorious woman-chaser, reputedly impotent, whose marriage had produced a man-child, has a verbal balance that would not, I think, have displeased the sardonic Dean.

> Hail seedling from the lawful sheets,
> Your father who went wild,
> A prowler in our lighted streets
> Acclaims his first man-child.
> And laughs at those who would deride
> His preference for the distaff side.
>
> Were you the aftermath that grew
> From elephantine frolic,

Or merely incidental to,
Adventures alcoholic?
Or did you spring from spiteful zest
To crown an evening's fruitless quest?

Your sire provided fore and aft
The gifts that make a fit man.
Guile without end, a touch of Kraft
A hint perhaps of Whitman.
The Hebrew too in your extraction,
Was but a very vulgar fraction.

Yet spare us when you grow to be
Plump, hairy and erotic,
His artificial ecstasy
Uneasy, vain, chaotic.
And if you would attain salvation
Avoid his style in conversation.

It is interesting to note that it may have been Redding who wrote the verses which were the subject of a successful action for defamation when they appeared in *As I was Going Down Sackville Street*, Gogarty's first book of prose.

According to Gogarty, Jimmy Montgomery was 'the greatest Dubliner of them all'. Montgomery's wit was prolific and he did not mind others appropriating it to their own use, as indeed, Gogarty often did. 'I am between the devil and the Holy See,' he remarked when he was appointed film censor, and added that his task was to prevent 'the Californication of Ireland'. There was hardly a day when he hadn't a new epigram or verse to show at The Bailey. Even when dying, he could murmur to an acquaintance who asked him how he was doing: 'Hovering between wife and death.'

Seamus O'Sullivan, wit and poet, was a close friend of Gogarty's. They had lived together in the Martello Tower, and spent days swimming and writing verses in the sun. His verse has the fragile quality of Verlaine, seen against an Irish landscape. He was not a 'Celtic poet', though, curiously enough, Yeats accused him of being an imitator of his. When asked what he thought of O'Sullivan's poetry, Yeats replied: 'Why should a wild dog praise his fleas.' It was just one of those unaccountable Dublin dislikes. Professor Heinz Hopfl, in 1938, devoted a special issue of *Neuphilo-*

logische Monatsschrift to O'Sullivan's work, and placed him in the highest rank of English lyric poets. O'Sullivan's reply to Yeats was sad but pointed.

I too, with Ireland, loved you long ago
Because you sang, as none but you could sing,
The cause we held the dearest; now I know
How vain your love was, and how mean a thing.

And not to you whose heart went anywhere
Her sorrow's holy heritage belongs:
You could have made of any other air
The little careful mouthfuls of your songs.

It was in this atmosphere created by the thrust and parry of lively intellects that Gogarty relaxed after his day's work.

General Piaras Beaslai, later Director of Publicity in the I.R.A. and then a journalist, has left a description of the sort of conversation one might encounter in The Bailey of an evening.

I found Dr. Oliver St. John Gogarty at a table, smoking a cheroot. Opposite him, Dr. Joseph Boyd Barrett had his head bent over a book. They had drinks before them.

'I was showing Joe a passage from Catullus,' said Gogarty. 'You may know it,' and he rolled out the lines with relish.

'I don't,' I said, picking up the book and looking at the passage. 'My copy of Catullus hasn't got these lines.'

'A bowdlerised version,' said Gogarty pityingly. He ordered a drink for me and resumed: 'All the Latin poets have been maltreated by bowdlerising editors. It is bad enough when they show the omissions by stars, but to print a bowdlerised passage as if nothing had been omitted is damnable.'

'I was showing Oliver something,' said Joe. 'You read of Drinkwater's death the other day and what the critics said of his poetry?'

'This is good!' said Oliver.

'Do you know,' said Joe, 'I found a criticism of Drinkwater in Horace.'

I looked surprised and waited. 'Here it is,' said Joe triumphantly. He drew a small book from his pocket and read out: 'Nulla placere diu nec vivere carmina possunt, Quae scribuntur aquae potoribus!'

('No poems can give pleasure or live long, which are written by drinkers of water.')

Gogarty talked on, quoting some clever parodies of famous poets which he had composed in his student days, discussing the style of Arnold and its origin, dismissing Browning as a tuneless jingler who must have had some negroid strain in him, quoting Goethe's 'Ueber allen Gipfeln', wandering off into an anecdote about a German girl he had met in London, expressing some unusual views about Heine, and telling a number of anecdotes, decorous and indecorous, until Louis came with the news that the time was up.

He still talked in the car as he drove us home, chiefly about Arthur Griffith.

At The Bailey, the passion that Dubliners have for the clinical observation and exploration of character was given full rein. Local personalities were incorporated into anecdotes, illustrative of their personal idiosyncrasies or eccentricities. It did not matter if the tales concerned friends of the group discussing them. The artist's licence was allowed to the teller of the tale. 'They would sacrifice their mother for a witty phrase,' was how a contemporary described them. Out of 'The Bailey' poured limericks, verses, epigrams, witty sayings, that did the rounds of Dublin before the evening was out. It had a Johnsonian reputation for wisdom and wit, combined with the inevitable Dublin predilection for derisive comment.

With Mahaffy's training behind him, and his early triumphs at Moore's soirées, Gogarty was able to shine in this lively company. Once, he capped a saying of Stephens, who, lamenting the departure of 'the grog-blossomy nose' from Dublin, punned: 'A nose-red city half as old as time.' Gogarty's riposte was: 'Où sont les nez d'antan?'

When a friend, after a serious operation, entered with a patch over one eye, Gogarty said instantly: 'Drink to me with thine only eye.'

Once when Gogarty was walking in the hills with Seamus O'Sullivan, they dropped into 'Lamb Doyle's' public house for a drink. Present, also in pursuit of refreshment, was 'Davy' Byrne, who owned a famous drinking establishment across the road from The Bailey.

'Why Dr Gogarty, my turn now to stand,' Byrne said, 'I often served you from the other side of the counter.'

'Yes. They also *stand* who only serve and wait,' was Gogarty's instant reply.

He could be biting in his wit, if he thought it necessary. When Archbishop Bernard resigned the archbishopric of Dublin to become Provost of Trinity, Gogarty, who had reason to dislike Bernard, remarked: 'He has sold the Thirty-Nine Articles for the thirty pieces of silver.'

About a deceased judge with indeterminate sexual characteristics, Gogarty said: 'He died of an undelivered judgment.'

A remark of this kind might seem outrageous to an outsider. But Gogarty seemed to feel a compulsion on such occasions. A witticism was entitled to an airing. Lord Glenavy has said to me, 'He would choke if he couldn't "get it out".' When Orpen died, despite the fact that he was speaking to one of Orpen's best friends a few days after the funeral, he could not resist saying, 'Our painter! He never got under the surface till he got under the sod!'

On another occasion, interrupted in the middle of an anecdote by one whose race are noted for their flair for finance, who said: 'You can't believe eighty per cent of what Gogarty says,' Gogarty replied in a flash: 'The trouble about you is that you never forget your percentage.'

He disliked snobbery, and remarked of a social climber who was becoming notorious for the number of times he had fallen off his horse: 'Acquired concussion won't open the doors of country houses. The better classes are born concussed.'

Piaras Beaslai has said: 'Though Gogarty said many brilliant things, he rarely gave an impression of spontaneous witticism, and neither did James Montgomery. Of that circle, Seamus O'Sullivan's wit was the most spontaneous arising in answer to something said by somebody else in conversation.'

This is not quite fair. In the strict sense of the word, there is no such thing as prepared wit. A witticism that has had its birth elsewhere may be introduced into conversation. But the spontaneous mental combustion that has given birth to the original witticism is what determines its nature. The mind, through the imagination, discerns a comparison between two hitherto unrelated objects. The more far-ranging the imaginative leap that produces the analogy, the more does the witticism gain its effect in the ears of the listeners. Thus wit has an inherent quality of its own which gives it kinship with the poet's art. It is this lightning intuitive process which makes a witticism as elusive of analysis as a line of poetry is. In wit of the first order the mind is delighted by the ease of apprehension because of the perfect congruity of the images presented to it.* That Gogarty and Montgomery repeated their witticisms on various occasions is of no importance provided these remarks originated in the spontaneous intuitive process that alone achieves true wit.

Of course Gogarty's personality helped to make even his less brilliant witticisms successful. Seamus Burke, a friend of The Bailey days, remembers how Gogarty could raise the spirits of a whole group instantly he entered a room. The delight in his eyes kindled joy in his listeners. 'Wit flowed from him like fresh water,' was a phrase of Violet Clifton's. 'It flashed out of him like water from a fountain,' is how Philip Sayers, a Jewish friend, recollected it. Susan Mitchell also used a liquid simile to conjure up the effect of a Gogartian display. 'He nipped the wires of the champagne of his wit, and sprayed a pungent froth around him.'

Another Irish writer, Lynn Doyle, has recalled that Gogarty was not a funny man in the ordinary sense.

> He was funny because of his outlook on life. He was amused with life and it coloured his conversations. He rarely left me that I wasn't laughing. He enjoyed living and enjoyed passing on his joy to you. He caught you by the arm and bursting with life, passed it on. A damn good man to meet. He held up his torch for a moment or two, and then went his way.

Violet Clifton, too, thought Gogarty even more of a satirist.

> Gogarty, I think, envisaged men and women as moving with ridiculous gait and ridiculous grimace, through godless life towards godless death. He was the abstract, the epitome of age-long Jesters, shaking their bells at Kings, mocking at both the majestical and at the mean.

* Sidney Smith remarked that 'a man might sit down as systematically and successfully to the study of wit as he might to the study of mathematics,' and that 'by giving up only six hours a day to being witty he should come on prodigiously by summer.' This is a negation of the ingredients that should constitute wit of the first order. The majority – but not all – of Smith's most celebrated sayings are less than spontaneous and bear the imprint of his philosophy of humour.

144

I remember how, when one night Gogarty and his wife arrived to dine with us in our house in Connemara, Mrs Gogarty whispered to me: 'I am afraid that Oliver will not be in top form to-night, he was annoyed just as we left home.' The words conjured up a fantasy: a paid musician, his violin strings all muddled irreparably, seemed to stand before me. However, I restrung the lute by telling Gogarty that I had just pressed some stick-jaw sweet upon dear Judge Ross so that he, Gogarty, could have the first start.

Sir William Rothenstein saw him as:

An intellectual aristocrat like Yeats, an Irishman, glorying in the Aristophanic spirit of which he has such a noble portion. He has the high Irish pride of wit, a splendid zest for life. He has a genial tolerance of barmen, drunkards and whores, unrelated to the conventional left-wing sympathy for the bottom dog.

Gogarty had a special gift of piling imagination on imagination, and it was the very fire-cracker quality of his wit, each mot igniting the next one, that lent his witticisms this individual quality and that lessens their effect when quoted in isolated examples.

Certain passages in his *As I Was Going Down Sackville Street* suggest this fire-cracker technique, and when Mr Leslie Luke told me that part of *As I Was Going Down Sackville Street* was taken down by him at Gogarty's dictation, it occurred to me that in passages from this work, one might find something perhaps of the quality of the wit that entertained The Bailey, the salons, the board rooms, and the Anglo-Irish house parties of those days. But the printed page dissolves so much of the spoken word's effect that it is necessary to imagine the words pouring out with machine-gun-like speed from Gogarty's lips, spontaneously and without preparation, to conceive the effect of a Gogartian monologue in full swing.

The truth is that every Englishman's house is his hospital, particularly the bathroom. Patent medicine is the English patent. Liverpool to London, judging by advertisements for food, sauces, soups, purgatives and hygienic porcelain, is an intestinal tract. Millions have been made out of patents for purgatives, not to include patent medicines which are intended to deal with the various results of eating too much. And most of these patent medicines, very nearly all of them, are taken in the bathroom. The most amazing results are advertised. You can lose pounds of flesh by taking a patent form of Glauber's Salts, or put on pounds (only if you are a lady) by the same taking. Agonizing aches in people unseen and unheard of by the patentees, disappear, regardless of idiosyncrasy or a positive Wassermann. And the English believe all this. He believes that a purgative can fatten or make him thin; he believes that either there is only one kind of ache or that one medicine can cure various kinds. His empty churches would be filled twice over by the faith he wastes on the permutations and importance of his lower bowel. And yet in spite of his faith in one medicine for many unseen and unknown diseases, he cannot accept miracles; he burks at the infallibility of the Pope, but unquestionably accepts the infallibility of the pill. 'Just as much as will fit on a threepenny piece', instead of as many angels as will stand on the point of a needle. So faith has fallen England to the level of the lavatory. And yet it cannot be said that it gives rise to less appreciation of love of righteousness for it makes Mens conscia recti. But it saddens me to think of the pent-up faith misdirected, that liberated could rise to Heaven in minsters with flying buttress, curious pinnacle, and soaring belfry. Perhaps, fearing lest he be made to hop on the Day of Judgement, the Englishman is keeping something in reserve.

Gogarty's family was growing up. Dermot was born in 1908 and his daughter Brenda in 1912. He took a keen interest in the children. The boys were taught to swim at an early age. First of all they learnt how to breathe, with their heads in a basin of water. Then, carried by their father, one on each shoulder, fairhaired and dark-haired in contrast, they went down to Garranbaun Strand, to learn how to equip themselves against the mysteries of the wily tide. Any signs of athletic skill in his children, Gogarty observed with special pleasure. Later, one of the disappointments of his life was that Dermot failed to get his rowing Blue at Cambridge, by a hair's breadth, although the same year he won a gold medal at Henley, rowing at No. 2 in the London

R.C. boat. These years seemed happy ones for Gogarty; indeed in retrospect they seemed the happiest of his life. He had many friends. He was a success in his profession. He had his wife and children. Often with his family he would spend afternoons picnicking at the sea, or in the hills around Dublin. One evening at Ticknock as he lay watching the sun glint off the granite with the blue bay of Dublin below, his little daughter Brenda came running back with a look of annoyance on her face. She had been playing in the long grass and her shoes had become stained yellow in colour. Her father explained that this was the pollen from the buttercups and later used the incident as the basis for one of his best-known poems.

> Golden stockings you had on
> In the meadow where you ran;
> And your little knees together
> Bobbed like pippins in the weather,
> When the breezes rush and fight
> For those dimples of delight,
> And they dance from the pursuit,
> And the leaf looks like the fruit.
>
> I have many a sight in mind
> That would last if I were blind;
> Many verses I could write
> That would bring me many a sight.
> Now I only see but one,
> See you running in the sun,
> And the gold-dust coming up
> From the trampled butter-cup.

Fairfield was sold in 1912. For a while, Gogarty had been on the look-out for a house in which to entertain his friends, and one day in 1917, he saw an advertisement for a mansion in one of the most isolated parts of the West. Gogarty realized that the growth of car travel would make the place accessible in half a day. He bought the premises at a bargain price. It was named Renvyle, and was situated on the edge of the Atlantic in Connemara. The haze around it was diaphanous: the mountains had the soft colours of pearl. Augustus John maintained that Renvyle was the most beautiful landscape in the world. The climate was moderated by the Gulf Stream. Daffodils and snowdrops broke out a month earlier than the market. This was Gogarty's haven from the frenzy of city life for years to come. He would drive down at seventy or eighty miles an hour at the week-ends to:

the fairy land of Connemara at the extreme end of Europe, where the incongruous flowed together at last

and return refreshed to his medical work on Monday mornings. Renvyle had been owned by the Blakes, a Norman-Irish family of fabulous and eccentric legend, straight out of the pages of Charles Lever. Before the Blakes the O'Flahertys had lived there who had intermarried with the Duanes, hence the double attraction for Gogarty. The house was built in an H-shape, with the cross-piece near one end. It was solid: some of the walls were six feet thick. It looked out on to a small beach, and the next parish was America. There was a small fresh-water lake, Rusheen Dubh, twenty yards from the house. Behind Renvyle was Tully Lake, with an island of eleven acres in the centre. The island had a house on it, with a heronry, and otters barked around it in the early mornings. Beyond the lake were the Connemara mountains, which Mahaffy announced, when he arrived down, were 'plum coloured'. At night-time, these mountains, as the sun faded, turned from purple to blue-black. Here came Augustus John, Lord Tredegar, Lady Leslie, Lady Lavery, Viscount Castlerosse, Mrs Valentine Fleming, Lord Beaverbrook, Lady Leconfield the painter, and other distinguished guests. One of the first visitors there was Yeats, who came to stay at Renvyle with his wife, after his honeymoon in 1917. Later in the 'thirties his 'Hawk plays', with masks by Edmund Dulac, were performed there.

At Renvyle Augustus John painted numerous landscapes. Normally he concentrated on portraits, but he found the panorama at Renvyle irresistible. Here too he encountered authentic Irish magic. One day he felt an invisible figure creep up behind him in an empty car as he drove along.

John and Gogarty had become friends in 1912. Gogarty never forgot his first image of the painter when he arrived in Dublin with large earrings in his ears, golden hair tumbling down his back, and a green velvet shirt open at the neck. John found the intellectual pace of Dublin faster than he was accustomed to, but was 'never better entertained'. He accepted Gogarty's injunction to 'float his intellect' as a rule for enjoying Dublin life. But he had floated so much on John Jameson that by the time he arrived at Coole to stay with Lady Gregory, he was in no condition to paint Bernard Shaw. Robert Gregory, Lady Gregory's son, gave him a cure by putting him on a Galway hunter and sending him out into the country-side. When he returned next morning he began painting with exultation. Gogarty taught him to drive in the same way simply by putting him in a car, and sending him off. He took the corners at sixty and didn't stop till he ran out of petrol at Lough Fee.

At the Railway Hotel in Galway, near Renvyle, John became the first person to stop Gogarty when he was launched in full flight of conversational monologue. Tiring of Gogarty's brilliance, for he was himself a Celt and desired perhaps a share in the lime-light, John threw a bowl of nuts full in Gogarty's face. The effect was instantaneous. Gogarty stopped in the middle of a sentence.

'He had become pathological after three hours non-stop,' John explained, excusing his drastic remedy and recalling how un-suited Gogarty's temperament was to the pose of injured dignity which he adopted as a defence to the painter's stratagem, taking his wife by the arm and walking slowly from the room.

Renvyle became an escape hatch for Gogarty, to which he returned whenever he was beset by the worries of professional life in Dublin. Even at night in sleep, when his body took up wings, it chose for its resting-place:

> Far off on the margin of the west
> A sea-gray house, whereby the blackbird sings.
> The waves come up like Berserks from the sea,
> The crystal mountains yield a little sound,
> Through level light, the bird of valour calls,
> Adventurous as a Viking must that be,
> Which will not rest, when sleep on Nature falls,
> But hastens to the confines of the Land.

ELEVEN

BEHIND the splendour of the Georgian drawing-rooms, the dazzle of the Viceregal court at the Castle, the excitement of the Literary Revival, Dublin had its private shame, the most fearful slums in Europe. A priest appearing before a Government inquiry in 1913 stated in evidence that he knew of a tenement house in which 107 people were living. According to the *Medical Press*, 1913, the death-rate in Dublin was the highest in Europe, exceeding that of Moscow, and even Calcutta where plague and cholera were rife. The conservative *Irish Times* in a leader in February 1914 compared the conditions in the Dublin slums to Dante's Inferno. The slum area was mostly composed of old Georgian houses left vacant on the north side of the city when Society shifted across the river. In rooms of gilded splendour, with ornate ceilings and elegant fireplaces, the poor languished from hunger, disease and cold. At twilight the gaunt spectral mansions in silhouette regained some of their old grandeur, as darkness covered the filth on the classical doorways and unpainted windows, summoning the living back to the hopeless hell inside.

These slums have vanished today. That they could have existed in the twentieth century was an indictment of the system which had allowed them to accumulate, and which did nothing to alleviate the condition of the people who lived there.

Gogarty's medical duties brought him into direct contact with the conditions in the slums. As a student and intern, he had come across houses with one lavatory for seventy people. He knew the frightful incidences of tuberculosis and venereal disease among the tenement dwellers. The fate of little children growing up in these living hells tortured the side of his nature that was compassionate and kind. In 1913, he delivered an address 'On the Inspection of Dublin school children' at the Academy of Medicine that excoriated some of the evils of slum life. A report of the address that appeared in the *Irish Times* the next day, evoked a congratulatory letter from Maud Gonne, the adored of Yeats's early love poems, who was at that time engaged in social work in the city. She thanked Gogarty for being the first to have the courage to speak out 'publicly and frankly' on the state of child life in Dublin.

In the poorest districts only about half the children bring even a piece of bread with them and when at 3.30 they return, the family dinner is over. The breadwinners of the family have very naturally eaten any meat that may be there and little is left for children but bread and tea.

Hundreds of children are literally starving in the schools and we cannot get the Irish M.P.s to pay the slightest attention or to get the free meal for children, which provides feeding for children in England, Scotland and Wales, extended to Ireland.

To try and arouse some sense of the reality of slum life among his fellow townsmen, Gogarty decided to write a play about tenement life.

Blight opened at the Abbey Theatre on December 11th, 1917. The production caused a sensation. There had been rumours during the week that the play might be suppressed because of its hard-hitting dialogue.

'Such an audience,' stated the *Irish Independent* next day, 'has not been at the Abbey since the night Shaw's *Blanco Posnet* was first produced.' *Blanco Posnet* had been banned by the Lord Chamberlain in England and received its first production in Ireland.

The *Independent* critic went on to say, '*Blight* is the tragedy of Dublin – the horrible, terrible, creeping crawling spectre that haunts the slumdom of the capital of Ireland. It is not horror for horror's sake. That charge may not be levelled against the authors with any hope that it can be maintained, for if I understand aright the meaning of the painters of this lurid picture it is this : Slumdom is the nest of vice; charity as a palliative is no cure. The charity in fact that endows hospitals and helps those institutions to extend their premises and cater for increased cases is misdirected charity. Away with the seat of the disease !'

The *Irish Times* thought the play 'revealed the horrors of slumdom in the naked light of truth'.

Gogarty's name did not appear on the programme; the pseudonym was Alpha and Omega. Omega was Joseph O'Connor, later a judge, who had helped Gogarty revise some of the dialogue, and who just before his death two years ago, told the biographer, '*Blight* was written to scarify the tenements.'

The play deals with the life of a Dublin labourer Stanislaus Tully who is awaiting a court award as a result of injuries he incurred when a bag of cement fell on his back. He is living on credit in expectation of the damages he will receive, and carefully nursing his injuries in the meantime so as to extort the maximum of compensation when the time comes. Like others of his kind he has a quick intelligence, bred from a lifetime of fighting for existence, and his judgment of events around him is shrewd. He unleashes a flow of heavy sarcasm on the efforts of the 'charity visitor' who has reproached Tully's landlady, Mrs Foley, because she has hidden drink in her one-roomed premises.

Why do we drink? Because we want to sleep, because it's cheaper than chloroform! Who could stand this living hell without drink? Suppose ye had three childer in the bed with ye like Mary there and was expecting a baby, how are ye to get up and cook food? Isn't the milk of the city liquid filth, and if it wasn't wouldn't it get filthy standing in a room with all the slops – while a pint of porter is eating and drinking. Was it drink gave Jimmy his diseased hip? The worst thing drink does is that it brings us visits from the likes of you. For it's not to do good ye came here; ye kem here to get yer self-complacency stroked down wud the smoothing-iron of our vices. It's all drink, drink, and nothing else. Yer putting the cart before the horse, me lady. Poverty first, then dirt and disease, and discontent and vice follow you and your preaching. Was it drink sent Georgie to the war for the sake of the Separation Allowance? Did it ever strike you that nothing good was ever done by preaching in this town? What built Findlater's Church? Was it preaching or drink? Drink. And the new hostel in Hatch Street? Drink. What put a roof on Christ Church Cathedral? Drink. What renovated St. Patrick's and cleared Bull Alley? Drink. What gave us Stephen's Green – Drink – and the ducks swimming in it! Drink doesn't keep us poor; but poverty makes us drink.*

The acquisition of sudden wealth however dilutes Tully's social wrath. When he wins his case, and receives his award, he becomes a slum landlord himself. In the last act he is shown as a

* The Guinness family had provided funds for the restoration of Christ Church cathedral and had given St Stephen's Green to the city.

member of the Corporation and a delegate to a Hospital Board on which he engages in dishonest deals to sell tenement property to the Board, without disclosing that he is the landlord.

It was within the framework of this plot that Gogarty attacked the complacency of the middle classes who refused to face up to the reality of the sickness and poverty in their midst. An incident in the first act underlines the hypocrisy that surrounded the treatment of venereal disease in Dublin at that time. Lily Foley, the landlady's daughter, a prostitute, is reproved for her way of life by the District Visitor, 'The wages of sin is death.' Lily's reply is: 'The wages of sin is a month in the Lock.' When inevitably she collects her 'wages', Gogarty uses the occasion to initiate a discussion between those two survivals from the ballads of his student days 'Medical Dick' and 'Medical Davy' and inserts a neat propaganda piece in favour of prophylactic treatment for the disease:

MED. DICK. Lily was a nice little girl ... it's a damn shame!

MED. DAVY. So it is; but what the devil is one to do?

MED. DICK. What the devil did they do about small-pox! Isn't every child in the country taken before it's able to talk and injected with cow-pox? Wouldn't it be just as simple and neither dirty nor dangerous to test a drop of everybody's blood, and then we'd know how to get rid of it, once we knew where it was? How can it be avoided until its whereabouts is known?

MED. DAVY. But can that be done?

MED. DICK. Of course it can! D'ye mean to say ye've never heard of Wassermann's test?

MED. DAVY. Of course I have. That's what they did to me when I only had sciatica. But why isn't it done?

MED. DICK. Because of our imported hypocrisy, and because we haven't the courage to face facts; because we won't realise that prevention is better than cure, because charity must prey on suffering; because we mix morals even in our medicine.

In the third act one of the main points of the play is introduced on the lips of Mr Tumulty, a practical minded member of the Hospital Board, who makes a proposal for the demolition of tenement dwellings, but the Hospital Board are intent on building a new mortuary chapel and the proposal is ignored. This mortuary is a symbol of the ineffectuality of the governing classes. They will build a place to house the dead, but won't take steps to see that the death-rate is diminished. In fact, *three* mortuary chapels require to be built as even in death Catholic and Protestant cannot lie together, and the Nonconformist member of the Board demands 'muffled glass' for his chapel so that Quaker corpses won't be compromised by stained glass windows. Tumulty departs in disgust. 'I leave you,' he says, 'to erect your tripartite edifice over the children of the city of blight.' He has a final fling at the Government for their refusal to alleviate the conditions that have produced the slums.

> Until this Moloch of a Government realises that they must spend more money on education than on police, this city will continue to be the breeding ground of disease, vice, hypocrisy and discontent.

Earlier he states, referring to Mrs Foley's husband, who had returned from the front and found his little boy dying of TB.:

> He went out to fight for you, and the continuance of the system that betrayed him, did his son to death, and sent his daughter to hell.

Such criticism of the Government and the war effort was hot stuff in 1917, with the allied forces in retreat, and the resurgence of revolutionary activity in Ireland. In fact, the play was strong meat even for Lady Gregory, and perhaps reacting to external pressure (for the Abbey was in a precarious position) she took *Blight* off after only ten days' run. But it had played to packed houses, and taken in £160, a record for the Abbey. A week later Sir John Russell, speaking at a public meeting of a charitable organization, said that when he had gone to see *Blight* he had seen the truth about the Dublin poor as it had never been told in Dublin.

Blight's importance in dramatic literature is that it marked the first appearance on the Abbey stage of the 'slum play', which was to have such a vogue six years later, when O'Casey produced his three masterpieces. It was the first play to reveal the poetic undertones in Dublin proletarian dialogue. Synge had discovered that the Western peasants spoke language as 'fully flavoured as a nut or an apple'. Gogarty knew of the striking language current among the Dublin poor and was the first to see its possibilities for the stage.

The Charwoman's summing up of the weaknesses of the hospital system:

> What's the good of feeding the little creatures for a few days, and then throwing them back where they caught the diseases? It's like spittin on a herrin' when the sea's dried up,

and Tully's roar to the mob:

> We will shake capitalism off our backs as a terrier shakes canal water out of its hide,

are examples of the type of vocabulary that O'Casey later made use of to give his dialogue its distinctive quality.

The weakness of *Blight* lies in its construction. Primarily concerned with getting his propaganda across, Gogarty allowed his characters to become victims of the exigencies of the plot. Stanislaus Tully, a well-observed and vital character in the first two acts, virtually fades out in the last act. His place is taken by Mr Tumulty whom we have not met before, and who strictly speaking is merely an indignant voice, and not a character at all. Despite these serious weaknesses of plot, *Blight* shows that Gogarty possessed a flair for dramatic dialogue and comedy. He also had a gift for character creation, as his treatment of Tully shows before it tails off in the last act. Tully's character too has a special significance in that it is a forerunner of the personality that was to form the basis of O'Casey's three famous characters: Joxer Daly, Fluther Good and Captain Boyle. He has the same curious mixture of sardonic sarcasm, combined with a natural courtesy and dignity that endears O'Casey's principal characters to us. Tully affects imaginary pains in his back as Captain Boyle does in *Juno and the Paycock*, and for the same reason a disinclination to do any hard work. In both *Juno and the Paycock* and *Blight* the plot turns on the reaction of a tenement family to the prospect of a large sum of money coming to them. The opening scenes of *Blight* and O'Casey's *Shadow of a Gunman* are similar; in both plays the curtain goes up on a silent stage: there is a bed in the middle of a tenement room and a man asleep on it. O'Casey must have been struck by the marvellous possibilities for comedy inherent in this device when he saw it in *Blight*. In fact, before he wrote his first tenement play, O'Casey according to Horace Reynolds who asked him about the matter, had only seen two plays, *Blight* and *Androcles and the Lion*. O'Casey's flashing dialogue later captivated critics like Agate and Nathan. Agate thought O'Casey was the greatest master of tragi-comedy since Shakespeare. But it was Gogarty who first saw the possibilities for stage purposes of what Joyce has called the 'sacred eloquence of Dublin'.

Gogarty received £2 10s. from Lady Gregory as his share in the profits. He immediately sent the cheque to the Herald Boot Fund (which published its list of subscribers) to revenge himself on the Old Lady by revealing, in public, her noted parsimony towards playwrights.

TWELVE

N 1914, Gogarty wrote to his friend, Lord Dunsany:

I think that if not only you patronised the meeting of Volunteers of which you spoke, but were to raise a force yourself, you would be doing an effective thing for each member of it, and the Country.

I would have joined the Volunteers long ago – Sir Thomas Myles asked me to send in my name for the Limerick Company – but I did not wish to join when others were joining for party-political motives. If there were to be enrolled a company of Volunteers whose members were banded together with neither bigotry nor politics to influence them, I would welcome it: for I think the time was come when we must do the rigid thing if we are to save ourselves from being herded by the vagaries of corrupt placemen.

North and South must in the end, see through the clay-footed Generals that are keeping them separate; and the constraint of a common interest will unite them. If you think of raising 100 men in a Corps that will hold itself aloof from being the pawn of any political party, I will throw in my lot with it. I am sure it would give a lead where a leader is sorely needed by the many Volunteer Corps that are being forced to be the prey of Carson, Redmond or Devlin, and other demagogues.

Yours sincerely,
OLIVER GOGARTY

You could drill them as well as Col. Moore or Capt. White, and better than Carson! The dissension caused by different views of union, and the disunion caused thereby, makes it urgent that someone with some authority should fix the purpose and direct the will of as many as he can influence at the present time.

N.B. How hard it is to keep words from contradicting themselves or becoming irresponsible for their own meanings when we write of politics!

There was a plethora of 'Volunteers' in Ireland that year. In the North, there were Carson's Ulster Volunteers, fully armed since the illegal landing of rifles at Larne in April, pledged to defend Ulster against Home Rule. In the South, there were the Irish Volunteers, formed by Professor Eoin McNeill of the National University, as a rival body to Carson's 'vigilantes'. A third body of Volunteers had grown out of the strike which had paralysed Dublin in the summer and autumn of 1913. This was the Citizen Army, drilled and commanded by Captain Jack White, son of the defender of Ladysmith, Sir George White, v.c. The strike had been organized by a Messiah-like figure, James Larkin, who had welded the workers, many of them half starved and disease-ridden, into a solid mass of resistance. To use a phrase of Tom Kettle's about O'Connell, Larkin 'shouted slaves into the status of manhood'. His language was a mixture of the Bible, Milton and Shakespeare:

I have come to preach the divine Gospel of discontent. They shall crucify Christ no longer in the streets of Dublin,

he roared to the assembled thousands. His great face, long and leonine like a rugged St Francis, glistening in the night air, aflame with eloquence, became an image in the minds of his listeners that sustained them as the symbols of their religion might have, through the hunger and agony of the strike. Over 24,000 were unemployed at that time.

The aims of the Ulster Volunteers at least had the virtue of clarity. They intended to use armed force if Parliament attempted to enforce the Home Rule Bill which had been introduced in 1912, by Asquith, and which would have transferred to a Dublin Parliament executive control of the whole country. An interesting book, *The Grammar of Anarchy*, compiled by J. J. Horgan, sets out different statements by the Ulster leaders, Carson, F. E. Smith, Bonar Law, Lord David Cecil and others, which leaves no doubt that the intention to use physical force was clearly envisaged by these men. General Crozier, who was in command of a section of this irregular force, has stated in his book, *Ireland For Ever*, that he would have given the order to fire on army and police on one occasion had not some fortuitous incident intervened.

These treasonable activities were actively assisted by sources inside the regular army. The Director of Military Operations, Sir Henry Wilson, a Southern Irishman, was not above imparting confidential information to the leaders of the Ulster movement. One result of his willingness to share secrets was the so-called Curragh Mutiny, when certain officers were quite improperly asked what course they would take if armed force were to be used against Ulster. Wilson's sinister figure, flitting from Cabinet Minister to Leader of the Opposition, from his own Intelligence Service to the confidences of the Ulster rebels, foreshadows disrupting tendencies which were to have a powerful influence in the destinies of nations in post-war Europe. The Ulster Volunteers were, in fact, modern Europe's first Fascist force. They were prepared to oppose majority decisions by violence. During their existence, parliamentary authority was constantly impinged on by military interference.

In the South, the introduction of the Home Rule Bill had at first been hailed with enthusiasm. Padraic Pearse, later to lead the rebellion in 1916, welcomed the Bill in a public speech made in conjunction with John Redmond and Joe Devlin, in March 1913. Arthur Griffith also favoured the Bill at first but, by April 1914, it had become clear that the Liberal Party were not strong enough to resist the interference of right-wing reactionaries, whose opposition to the Bill had by then assumed hysterical proportions. The *Irish Churchman* talked about welcoming 'a powerful Continental deliverer' should the Bill receive Parliamentary assent. An amending Bill to deal with the Ulster question was introduced. This, and the refusal of the army to enforce the law in Ulster, were probably the root causes of the defection of the extreme Nationalist element in the South from the Home Rule movement. A phrase:

> The Liberals of England, the lackeys of the moneybags, are capable only of cringing before the Carsons,

might have been written by Griffith. In fact, it was a phrase of Lenin's.

The Irish Volunteers had been formed in November 1913. Their purpose was to secure the passage of the Home Rule Bill, without interference from the North.

Their motto was: 'Defence, not defiance.'

The outbreak of the war split the Volunteers in half. Redmond, without consultation, committed the Volunteers to the Allied cause. It was the fatal mistake of his career. Had he held his hand

and bargained the potential manpower of Ireland, in return for the instant operation of the Home Rule Act, he must have gained his point. By Christmas 1915, when the Allied war effort was at a low ebb, England could not have refused Home Rule in exchange for the enlistment of able-bodied Irish Volunteers. Those members of the Volunteers who did not subscribe to Redmond's policy, continued to drill. After the war, their time would come. Their purpose was still 'defence, not defiance'. However, a minority among them had met in secret in the first week of the war and decided that there would be an armed insurrection before the war ended.

Despite the 'split', over 400,000 Irishmen joined the British army. Fifty thousand were killed during the war. The majority of these were from Southern Ireland. The war had barely begun when Redmond received a practical demonstration of the dislike of the Tory clique for Southern Irish Nationalists. Kitchener refused to let an Irish brigade be formed. It became virtually impossible for a Catholic to receive a commission in an Irish regiment. Redmond's own son was refused a commission in the Munster Fusiliers. Lloyd George declared later: 'The flag of Ireland was torn from the hands of men who had volunteered to die for the cause which the British Empire was championing.'

Lady Fingall and Lady Mayo had been embroidering a flag for the Irish Brigade, when they heard of Kitchener's refusal to allow its formation.

We can see from Gogarty's letter quoted at the beginning of this chapter, that, by 1914, he had lost faith in Redmond's methods. His attitude to the war would have been that of Griffith.

Give us Home Rule and we will fight with you. While you withhold it, we withhold our manpower.

Despite his attitude to the war, we find Gogarty writing to Dunsany again in November 1914, enclosing a little phial which contained a prophylactic against infection from wounds.

Dunsany had volunteered on the outbreak of the war. In a poem which accompanied this life-saving gift, Gogarty refers to his own policy of 'stand and wait'.

Before you go to the war, I want you to have a little phial to prevent any grave complication from an infected wound

The Gogarty family, with Oliver in the centre,
between his parents.

Oliver's mother, c. 1880

Gogarty, aged 21, as a student of Trinity College, Dublin

Gogarty cycle-racing at Trinity College, Dublin

These 'worthies' were invited by Gogarty and the Irish Free State to the Tailteann Games of 1924. They are gathered in Gogarty's garden. *Back Row (left to right)*: G.K. Chesterton, James Stephens, Lennox Robinson. *Front Row (left to right)*: W.B. Yeats, Compton Mackenzie, Augustus John, Sir Edwin Lutyens

Below: Oliver on board the cruise ship SS *Aguila* 1928

Gogarty presents two swans to the Liffey at the Trinity College Boat Club in Islandbridge, 1924.

Left to right: President William Cosgrave, Gogarty, Martha Gogarty, W.B. Yeats, Col. J. O'Reilly (aide-de-camp to President Cosgrave)

Below: Yeats and Gogarty arriving for the presentation of the swans

Gogarty arriving at the Dublin Horse Show with Augustus John (left), Martha Gogarty and Oliver Duane Gogarty

Below: Gogarty at the Horse Show with General Eoin O'Duffy (left) and General Sean MacEoin (centre)

Portrait of Gogarty's son, Oliver Duane Gogarty,
painted by Sir William Orpen

Portrait of Gogarty's daughter, Brenda, the subject of
Gogarty's poem 'Golden Stockings', painted by his
friend, Augustus John.

setting in. It is a 'terrible gift' such as Nietzsche would delight to impose on the people. But even a slight wound can be dangerous if not treated at once owing to the grief of campaigning.

Ledwidge, your harper whom you bring with you, met a friend of mine and said that he had hoped to preserve some individuality: but 3 weeks of discipline took it all away. When the war is over, new and more vigorous dreams will urge themselves on the world. After all, if there were perpetual peace, manhood would have recourse to war in order to hold its honour high. Its touchstone is valour.

> If fighting were the worst of War
> For you I'd have no fear,
> For there is Honour in a scar
> And Glory on the bier;
> And since Disease has killed far more
> Than all the Dreams that lead to War,
>
> I send this transport out to you,
> A millioned mighty arm,
> Against a foe that skulks from view;
> And know that, saved from harm,
> You will, with this within your veins,
> Win inconceivable campaigns!
>
> Tell me what Hero ever brought
> To war a battlefield.
> You know how Alexander fought,
> You know what made him yield.
> By you that foe may be withstood
> For you have Victory in your blood!
>
> To you who made lines live once more
> The Fates be not unkind!
> For few have ever gone to War
> Who leave so much behind;
> And if his death you may not share
> Be you like him unscathed in war.
>
> For me when Glory walks abroad
> Where I may not endure,

It is a rigid thing, My Lord,
To will to live obscure;
When every man strikes for the State
To bear the brunt of 'stand and wait'.

But if by any means of mine
Your life may be preserved
To this my lot I will resign –
I shall have also served,
And kept – I have not far presumed
A mind like yours from being fumed.

If you do this I'll ask you down
To rest till Sunday morn,
With leave to hang your hat upon
My great rhinoceros horn
Who have for style and line and gloss
'A nose like a rhinoceros'.

In Easter Week 1916, the insurrection broke out in Dublin.
Gogarty was on his way from the West on Easter Monday when
he was stopped at Mullingar by armed police. He learnt that the
Volunteers had seized Dublin. He pushed on towards the city in
a hired car: he had patients to see on Tuesday. When he arrived,
he found that the General Post Office had been taken over by the
Volunteers and the Citizen Army. Throughout the city, the rebel
forces had taken charge of key positions; in fact, the insurrection
was intended as a general rising throughout the country, but the
interception of a German arms ship, off Kerry, had made this
impossible.

Sinn Fein was not in favour of the rising. Arthur Griffith was
definitely against it, but Irishmen have ancestral memories of rebellion and Gogarty found himself thinking, as he drove into the city

of the brave men in every century, who had risen in dark and
evil days to right their native land, and had been met with
the pitch cap, the rack, and the gibbet, Lord Edward Fitz-
Gerald, Robert Emmet, Wolfe Tone, all done to death and a
divided Ireland left.

When he arrived in Dublin, Gogarty learnt who the leaders of
the rising were. The intellectuals were represented by Padraic
Pearse, Thomas McDonagh and Joseph Plunkett, one a school-

teacher, the other a university lecturer, all three, poets. Tom Clarke, a veteran of the rising of '67, stood for the old Fenian tradition. James Connolly led the revolutionary Socialist element. His group had been probably more determined than any of the others to resort to physical force. The 1913 strike had left an ulcer on the working-class mind, that made militant action of some kind inevitable.

George Moore, who was in Dublin at the time, met Gogarty the next day, standing unconcernedly watching the troops go past, at the door of his rooms next to the Shelbourne Hotel. Typically, he told Moore that the insurrection could do nothing but good for the British army, as it would redeem their credit in Europe, bringing them their sole current victory.

At the end of the week, the rebels surrendered. Then the blood-letting began in earnest. Under General Maxwell's orders, sixteen of the leaders were shot before Asquith could come over and stop the massacres. In fact, fifty had been condemned to death, but the remaining sentences were commuted.

As a whole, Ireland was opposed to the rebellion. The war had enriched the farmers and merchants. Large numbers of families were in receipt of remittance money from the front. The insurgents were looked on, at best, as misguided idealists, at worst, as German agents. The executions, however, focused attention on the character of the men who had taken part. They died with dignity. The three soldier-poets, men of priest-like purity of purpose, with strong elements of mysticism in their make-up, in particular caught the public imagination. In a country like Ireland, saturated with the Christian story, it was not difficult to recognize the analogy which Pearse had drawn when he spoke of Emmet.

> This man was faithful even to ignominy of the gallows, dying that his people might live, even as Christ died.

The blood sacrifice which each had made could have been understood in fourteenth-century England or France; but in the twentieth century only in Ireland could it have had an effect. The executions in 1916 opened secret reservoirs in the national mind. They were eventually to lend the people a purpose as fervent as that which inspired the Crusades or the pilgrimages of Peter the Hermit.

163

Its effect upon the writers and the poets was typical of the general mood. Within a few weeks, Yeats had written that: 'a terrible beauty is born.'

Other poems he wrote about the rising in this period were 'The Rose Tree' and 'Sixteen Dead Men' with its verse:

> Oh but we talked at large before
> The sixteen men were shot,
> But who can talk of give and take,
> What should be and what not
> While those dead men are loitering there
> To stir the boiling pot?

James Stephens, moved by the turn of events, wrote some fine lines beginning:

> Be green upon their graves, oh, happy Spring.

Later, he contributed, along with Seamus O'Sullivan, Padraic Colum, A.E., Francis Ledwidge and Oliver Gogarty, to a book of verse published to raise money for the dependants of the prisoners of Easter Week. Gogarty's sonnet defends the insurgents and is a stern denunciation of British misrule in Ireland.

THE REBELS

> Not that they knew well, when they drew the blade
> That breaks for victory if gain were planned
> You never gave without a trembling hand.
> But, when they heard of Sacred Truth waylaid,
> And freedom in the name of freedom banned,
> And friendship in this foulness, this England,
> This was the cause of that good fight they made.
> They heard your mobster's mouthing at the hordes
> Who care not so the fight increase their store,
> Hawking your honour on the sandwich boards,
> But theirs is safe, and to these things unlinked
> They stood apart and Death withholds them more,
> Separate for ever and aloof – distinct.

Despite a wave of sympathy for the executed leaders, the country did not immediately swing over to Sinn Fein; but in April 1918, an event occurred which was to change the whole course of Irish politics. Sir Henry Wilson, after persistent nagging, succeeded in getting Lloyd George to proceed with a plan for the conscription of Irishmen. No move could have been better calculated to upset sympathy for the Allied cause in Ireland, and to play into the hands of the physical force movement. It had the unprecedented effect of driving Sinn Fein, the Irish Volunteers and Redmond's Party together on one platform, and led to the formation of a National Cabinet composed of members of these groups. The bishops of Ireland stated in a pastoral that it was lawful to resist conscription by armed force. The temper of the country was up. Even as late as November 1918, three weeks after the Armistice, Gogarty could write to Lady Leslie: 'The Country is on the brink of rebellion.'

The General Election took place in December. One of its results was the obliteration of the Irish Party. Sinn Fein won an overwhelming victory. They had seventy per cent of the electorate in their favour. They had gone to the polls with Griffith's mandate of abstention from Westminster as their policy, and the setting up of a Home Parliament on the Hungarian model. It remained now for them to put their plan into force.

Tom Kettle, on one occasion, denied the assertion that Dublin Castle did not understand Ireland:

Did it not know what the Irish people want, it could not so infallibly have maintained its tradition of giving them the opposite.

In January 1919, the Castle found themselves faced with a *fait accompli*. The people had declared for a Parliament which was to sit in Dublin and not at Westminster. But the Castle authorities, with two centuries of authoritarianism behind them, and largely composed of Orangemen imported from Ulster, were not likely to be impressed by manifestations of democracy. The Dail assembled in the Mansion House, Dublin, in January 1919. Within a few days, the familiar pattern of arrests and repression had begun. In September, the Dail itself was suppressed. Between January and June of that year, 18,215 arrests and raids were made. In June, the Bishops meeting at Maynooth described the British regime as: 'the rule of the sword, utterly unsuited to a civilised Nation, and extremely provocative of disorder and chronic rebellion.'

It should be noted that Griffith's policy was not one of physical force. He merely set up institutions, as he believed he had a mandate to do from the people. When the Dail was suppressed and its leaders arrested, a campaign of armed resistance was initiated by the Volunteers, which was to involve the country in two years of bloodshed and terror.

In August 1919 Gogarty's second play was produced at the Abbey. It was called *A Serious Thing* and was written under the pseudonym of 'Gideon Ouseley'. As it was a satire on current British rule in Ireland, it is worth considering at this stage. *The Freeman's Journal* (Wednesday, August 20th, 1919) said the play 'kept the house in shrieks of laughter', while the *Irish Times*, though not exactly approving of the play, because of its political implications, referred to 'its clever sarcasm'.

A Serious Thing deals ostensibly with the Roman occupation of the Holy Land in the Augustan Age. But the soldiers are dressed in khaki uniform, because the author explains in a programme note:

> he has followed the practice of writers and poets, who coloured eternal themes with their own day (as he did, who called Hector 'that sweet Knight', and as they who depicted men with hounds and matchlocks on the way to Calvary) and has therefore represented the Players in uniform that seemed to him most appropriate.

The play opens with the tomb of Lazarus being guarded by two Roman soldiers. It is soon made obvious that Lazarus symbolizes the dead Ireland about to rise to life again, and that the First Soldier talks with the voice of the British Establishment in Ireland. (The Second 'Roman' is a Jewish conscript.)

> FIRST ROMAN. It's not only guarding a tomb we are, but guarding the interests of the Roman Empire. D'ye think Imperial Rome is afraid of a corpse? Our great Empire fears nothing, living or dead.
> SECOND ROMAN. Well, why are we here?
> FIRST ROMAN. To preserve peace and stamp out sedition.
> SECOND ROMAN. But it is because we are here that the people are seditious.
> FIRST ROMAN (*firmly and rather oratorically*). And because they are seditious we are here.

SECOND ROMAN (*with an irritating smile*). So the effect is an excuse for the cause?

FIRST ROMAN. There's no excuse for anyone objecting to law and order. Surely you don't sympathise with illegal assemblies, seditious speeches, with blackguardism like that recent cattle-driving in Gadara and all that orgy of crime?

(*Pointing over his shoulder*)

SECOND ROMAN. Ah, but eef a man walks straight he is arrested for illegal drilling, and if he walks crooked, for being drunk, and if he remains still he is asked to move on. Be just before you sit in judgment.

FIRST ROMAN. Don't talk nonsense. Do you think justice could have any effect on a lot of rebels? Answer me that. What are you thinking of? Answer me that.

SECOND ROMAN. I'm thinking it's an extraordinary thing that every country we occupy seems to be inhabited exclusively by rebels.

An outburst by the First Roman is a satire on the speeches of contemporary Tory politicians about Ireland.

At the present time Galilee's condition is such that any political experiment must involve the greatest danger. If it should satisfy disaffection the Empire would be betrayed; if it should fail to satisfy disaffection, no good and much harm would be done. There remains then, the course which duty and interest alike dictate – firm and honest government under the existing Constitution. With that responsibility of the Roman Government neither Persia nor Africa has any right or, as we believe, any desire to interfere.

A crowd gathers around the Tomb, and a Voice is heard: 'Lazarus arise.'

The arrival of the corpse in full fig is greeted with aplomb by the First Soldier.

All right, Lazarus, I can identify you. You'll be court-martialled for being in a military area without a permit.

But the Second Soldier has seen the light:

SECOND ROMAN (*amazed*). And he was dead and buried three

days ... I think I'll go away (*rising*). I'll go away out
of this ...

FIRST ROMAN. And join the movement, will you? Ah, man,
have sense, take up yer musket and try and have some
self-respect. It's only a dead Jew.

SECOND ROMAN (*takes up musket and looks at it*). I'll ask the
officer what's the use of a thing like this when death
itself cannot stop the movement.

(*Throws it against wall again.*)

FIRST ROMAN (*looking at it*). What! You refuse to shoulder the
burden of civilisation.

SECOND ROMAN. What has your civilisation ever produced to
equal this movement out from death?

This last line has a prophetic ring about it. Sinn Fein had risen
to power on the tide of reaction against the execution of the 1916
leaders. Now, in the next few years, each prison hanging or death
by hunger strike of a patriot was to strengthen the Movement and
gather about it many new adherents. One event which moved
Gogarty greatly was the death by hunger strike of Terence Mac-
Swiney, after a fast which lasted seventy-four days. MacSwiney's
self-imposed martyrdom drew the attention of the world to Ireland. On the night of October 25th, 1920, Gogarty woke Albert
Power, the sculptor, out of bed and made him catch the early
boat to London, to sculpt MacSwiney's death-mask. Gogarty
paid for both the journey and the execution of the mask.

Meanwhile the Dail proceeded to erect its administrative
machinery according to Griffith's plan. Arbitration Courts were
set up to decide on land disputes. Income tax was collected by the
Dail. Over £1,000,000 was raised in this way. Sinn Fein Courts
functioning at both magisterial and circuit court level were set up:
they gradually replaced the British courts in twenty-seven of the
thirty-two Irish counties. Hugh Martin in the *Daily News* noted
that 'even Unionists were astonished and pleased' with the efficiency and fairness of the courts.

However, 1920 and 1921 were terrible years for Ireland.
Grafton Street, with its fashionable parade of barristers and
gentry at four o'clock in the afternoon, had become, by 1921,
more like the Chicago of Al Capone. On each side of the street,

168

men in caps and trench-coats moved up and down, their hands on revolvers in their pockets. This was the Igoe Gang on the look-out for I.R.A. guerrilla leaders who might be visiting the city to contact G.H.Q. Sometimes, there was a rush from the street as the I.R.A. Active Service Unit moved in, summoned suddenly from their room in Dawson Street, to shoot up notorious Castle agents who had appeared in the street. A flurry of shots, a scamper down a side alley, and all that was left in the street would be a smoking body. Through the city, 'Black-and-Tans' and 'Auxiliaries' (hastily recruited into the police force) careered in lorries, with wire netting over them, to protect them from bombs and hand grenades that might be thrown in an ambush from a side street.

In the country-side, a reign of terror had been let loose. It is best described in the words of General Sir Hubert Gough:

> Law and order have given place to a bloody and brutal anarchy in which the armed agents of the Crown violate every law in aimless and vindictive and insolent savagery. England has departed further from her own standards, and further from the standards even of any nation in the world, not excepting the Turk and Zulu, than has ever been known in history before.

Between January and June 1920, fifteen reprisals on towns and villages had been carried out by Crown forces. Cork City was set on fire, and the incendiaries responsible encouraged by the authorities to display burnt corks in their caps as souvenirs of their deed of revenge. These activities were resolutely defended in Parliament by the Chief Secretary for Ireland, Sir Hamar Greenwood. Gogarty had no doubt as to which side he was on, during the conflict. He wrote, after he had been arrested by the Black-and-Tans at Clonee but released (since they missed when they searched him a cigarette case full of newspaper clippings, describing their own atrocities, which he kept in his pocket):

> I take my hat off to Dan Breen, who, single-handed, shot up a lorry load of ruffians such as these, and then, wounded, with his arm hanging useless, came back for more. And to Sean McKeon, who beat eighteen first-class soldiers with eighteen untrained men, and then beat eighty-four Auxiliaries the same evening.

There was this reflection for me: the best thing that happened for Ireland was that the Germans invaded Belgium. Whether Great Britain first broke the guarantee of neutrality by fortifying Belgium, as the Germans claim, matters not to the argument; but the self-righteous blather and skite about the rights of small nations which followed had bound more or less the upholders of the rights of small nations to practise what they preached. Great Britain hates to have her preachings cast in her teeth. She is loth to loosen her grip until her hand trembles. Well, her hands were trembling already in the persons of her representatives in Ireland for the rights of small nations, her Black-and-Tans. Her financiers were trembling about the terms of the American loan, and her sailors were trembling at the prospect of having to race the proposed naval expansion of the United States. Therefore it was of paramount importance to placate the feelings of the Greater Ireland which exists overseas in mighty America. And you do not placate popular feelings among nationals, by turning loose the offscourings of English ergastula on Irish fathers and mothers and sisters and brothers. Thus Greenwood was manufacturing rebels at the rate of thousands a day. I was the latest and enthusiastic recruit.*

Opposed to the British forces was an I.R.A. guerrilla force, operating in the country-side, and an Intelligence Corps in Dublin, which concentrated on breaking down the resources of the British Secret Service in Ireland.

A remarkable Irishman, Michael Collins, had become Director of Intelligence in the I.R.A. His plan was to put out 'the eyes of the Intelligence' in the country-side by attacks on police barracks, which would drive the constabulary into the towns and cities; then, by a series of carefully planned assassinations, he proceeded to eliminate, one by one, the key men in the Castle Secret Service.

They were out to get him; he got them first. By the middle of 1920, the Castle Intelligence knew they were in danger of losing their grip on the country completely. Something had to be done.

* It was typical of Gogarty that after his arrest by the Black-and-Tans he should have advised his captors to see his play *A Serious Thing* which was having a revival at the Abbey. Later that evening he went to the theatre and was amused to observe the individuals in question in the front row of the stalls, roaring with laughter and unaware that the work was a satire on their own activities.

What General Crozier (commandant of the Auxiliaries) has called 'a sub rosa murder gang' was formed among Intelligence and army officers. The methods employed were to lead to the events which took place in Dublin on Sunday, November 21st, 1920.*

On November 21st, 1920, small groups of young men were to be seen at eight o'clock Mass in various churches throughout Dublin. After Mass, they gathered together and then set out for different destinations in the city. The group which set out from University Church, across St Stephen's Green towards 28 Pembroke Street, was typical. A blond, bronzed, young man of twenty-five, named Flanagan, was their leader. The group included Albert Rutherford, George White, Charles Dalton, Martin Lavan and Andrew Cooney. Lavan and Cooney were students. They were not yet twenty. Anxiously the group waited on the landing of 28 Pembroke Street, watching their watches. Collins had told them not to begin 'business' before nine a.m., 'or not a minute after either', he had added. This was to be a precise job. On the stroke of nine, they opened fire. Eight British Intelligence agents were shot in their beds, some in front of their wives. In other parts of the city, there were similar shootings. The total killed reached fourteen. After they left Pembroke Street, Lavan and Rutherford cycled to Dolphin's Barn. There, they played a football match, while lorry-loads of police and troops whined by outside the ground. Flanagan, who had had personally to execute four of the Secret Service agents, was to end up in a lunatic asylum within five years. Four others of the group finished up their lives in mental homes.

What was the raison d'être of these terrible deeds? Collins,

* General Richard Mulcahy, chief-of-staff of the I.R.A., has been kind enough to draw up for the author a brief summary of the guerrilla campaign:

> The sequence passes from repression and resistance with the resultant spontaneous sparking-points, to the setting-up of a Government and the establishment for the people of an authoritative voice and an administrative hand, to the suppression of Government. 'Strategy' began after that. It involved, in so far as possible, the removal of the powers of control that the police barracks represented: the first move in a formal 'strategy' plan is represented by attacks on Carrigtwohill and Kilmurray, etc., Jan. 4th, 1920.
>
> Two things were emphasized as important elements in the strategy: (a) all possible avoidance of taking and loss of life; (b) normal 'innocence'-suggesting conduct of the next day's life. The Flying Columns resulted from the difficulty of mass training. The Column and mobile energy offensive gave you 'guerrilla dash'. Then the Tans came.

through his agents in the Castle, had discovered a plan to eliminate the political leaders of Sinn Fein, by 'secret murder'. The existence of this 'murder plan' is confirmed by General Crozier, who was in charge of the Auxiliaries. He states in his book *Ireland Forever* that he came to the conclusion, after investigation, 'that there was a "police plan" to do away with Sinn Fein leaders and put the blame on Sinn Fein.'

The Lord Mayor of Cork was murdered in his house on March 20th, 1920. In March of the following year Lord Mayor O'Callaghan of Limerick and ex-Lord Mayor Clancy were both shot in front of their wives on the same night. These last two murders were committed, as Richard Bennett, an English author, has recently proved with reasonable certainty, by Captain Nathan, a former non-commissioned officer in the Guards, who was then stationed in Limerick.

Arthur Griffith had also received threatening notes. Collins claimed he acted in the 'nick of time' to forestall further murders. General Mulcahy has assured the writer that those who were killed on November 21st 'were members of a spy organization that was a murder organization and that their murderous intent was directed against the effective members of the Government, as well as against the G.H.Q. and Staff of the Dublin Brigade.'

This was the day in which British rule in Ireland broke down. The Castle knew it was up against a new enemy – an Irishman with an Englishman's sense of precision and efficiency. That evening, Black-and-Tans machine-gunned a crowd at a football match at Croke Park, Dublin, killing twelve and wounding seventy before the army could stop them. It was the fury of impotency.

Michael Collins, who for two years rode round Dublin on a bicycle while he directed his Intelligence Service, became the most wanted man in the British Empire. One of his agents in the Castle, Eamon Broy, a G-man who risked his life to get secret information out to Collins, has said of him, to the biographer:

Collins was like a battery: he charged you just by looking at him. As a detective in the Castle, I had always wanted to work for Ireland. When I met Collins I knew that here was the man who could break the Castle machine. A contact, O'Hanrahan, introduced us at 5 Cabra Road. At first sight, Collins just seemed like any other Irishman, boisterous and full of good humour. Then one saw that he was also ruthlessly efficient. He had a pigeon-hole mind where he could secrete the most minute information and bring it out at a moment's notice. When he had to act quickly, it was like watching an automatic adding machine in action. After a few seconds' thought, instructions poured out right and left from him, which all fitted in to a carefully arranged plan his lightning brain constructed as he listened to his informant.

When he was 'on the run' Collins slept in different houses in the city, where he was sure of a friendly welcome. Those who sheltered him underwent considerable risk, for they would certainly have been arrested and perhaps shot had Collins been found in their house. Gogarty's house in Ely Place was always open to Collins, and he slept there on different occasions. Brenda, Gogarty's daughter, remembers seeing Collins in the drawing-room at Ely Place a number of times, and overhearing her parents express their concern as to whether she might blurt out at school that a strange man had been staying in the house. Collins actually used Gogarty's house from time to time as a depot for receiving important members of the I.R.A. whom he wished to contact. General Peadar MacMahon of General Headquarters Staff remembers visiting Collins at Ely Place on a number of occasions during the Black-and-Tan period.

Gogarty had the highest admiration for Collins. He was always ready to help the I.R.A. He operated on wounded volunteers. Once when Padraic O'Maille (later Senator O'Maille) was wanted in connection with the shooting of a policeman in Clifden, Gogarty drove him in disguise from Dublin to Connemara – O'Maille was dressed as a country gentleman in tweed suit and tweed cap, with a false moustache which he had fixed on with spirit gum in Gogarty's house. Young Noll Gogarty remembers sitting in the back of the car anxiously guarding a curiously shaped sock, in which was hidden O'Maille's gun in case of emergencies. On another occasion when Mario Esposito was going as a Sinn Fein agent to France, and it was feared he might be conscripted because of his Italian parentage, Gogarty forged a medical certificate for him.

Gogarty had no doubt on which side right lay.

Bernard Shaw wrote to me today [he wrote to Lady Leslie on October 25th, 1920] saying that he had seen Winston Churchill who said, 'Let the Sinn Feiners stop murdering and start arguing'; but that, as Larry O'Neill would say, 'takes us nowhere.'

He even assisted in a jail break in the summer of 1921, when Linda Kearns and a group of prisoners broke out from Mountjoy. Gogarty was waiting at Cross Guns Bridge with his Rolls Royce, in which he drove his charge to safety at rare speed. Dr 'Jammy' Clinch the famous footballer, who knew something of Gogarty's anti-Black-and-Tan activities at this time, refers to him as 'the most courageous bloody man I ever met'. General Richard Mulcahy, chief-of-staff of the Irish Republican Army, has pointed out that one of the chief services that Gogarty rendered the Sinn Fein cause was in providing a social milieu where Griffith could meet people of different political background from his own.

Gogarty's house was a valuable meeting ground for people of different beliefs and creeds. It was particularly valuable for Arthur Griffith who could meet there on terms of social inter-course, Unionists and landed gentry who differed from him in political principle but who had the common good of Ireland at heart.

Some time in 1921, the Provost of Trinity, Dr Bernard, who was no friend of Gogarty's, was overheard informing the Viceroy that 'Gogarty was the most dangerous intellect unapprehended in Ireland.'

Soon afterwards, raids began on his home and it became unsafe for I.R.A. men to go there. Gogarty had transferred the files of Sinn Fein to his own house for safety, just before the police raided Sinn Fein headquarters in 1919. Now, he had to clear his house of them, and send copies of the I.R.A. *War News* he had kept, for safe-keeping to his friend Shane Leslie at Glasslough Castle, County Monaghan.

In the midst of the terror, an extraordinary incident occurred, one perhaps which could only happen in Ireland. Lord Dunsany was arrested by the Black-and-Tans. As Dunsany was a staunch Unionist, and had a distinguished war record, he was not unnaturally furious at the treatment meted out to him. Gogarty gives an amusing account of the affair in a letter written to Lady Leslie on January 31st, 1921.

I spent last night at Dunsany comforting the peer. He had been snipe shooting in his demesne and some of those who form that senile asylum in Kildare Street [Biographer's note: The Kildare Street Club was the club for landed gentry.] got very envious, then spiteful and they got the military moving. On Saturday week back he was raided and a gun, rock-rifle 500 and 1,500 rounds for these, also some artillery the gamekeeper forgot to send in with the big game guns in 1916, were taken. On Monday, they raided him for a Sinn Fein permit which, of course, he had not got and he said so. So they took him out of bed on Wednesday but gave him time to dress and then off to Dunshaughlin prison. Whence he was bailed in a few hours. While he was up in Dublin seeing his lawyers the Black & Tans called at the Castle but only took a Malacca cane. As they were about to drive off in their lorry, Manders, the butler, asked unmoved: 'Whom shall I say called?'

What a picture it would make for Punch: only a doorway left from which the butler puts his query! But as they may make things serious for Dunsany with their outrageous talk of S.F. having anything to do with his snipe shooting, I wrote Seymour to explain things to W. The affair on paper looks like an armoury but he was quite secure from his own tenants, hence his keeping his gun and cartridges. This security has given rise to its tale of Sinn Fein connivance. His wages roll is £1,700 a year and it is not likely that they would drive him out. It is only the Government that believes in killing the goose in this Country. They will never rest until they set Sinn Feiners killing people who wear English clothes or buy English goods. The annual trade is £320,000,000 with this country and it may end in a boycott such as is acting on Belfast. What a pity some one does not see this and also what an engine for good the goodwill of 20,000,000 Irish would be. But race instinct must be at the bottom of it all for nothing else could be so irrational.

The matter turned out to be more serious than it seemed at

first. Dunsany found himself incarcerated in the Castle. He faced a serious charge and the affair was not helped by the rumour that his tenants were marching to Dublin to release him. He was a popular landlord, though his political opinions were known to be in stern opposition to that of Sinn Fein. Gogarty instantly got Seymour Leslie to write to his cousin, Winston Churchill, to do something about Dunsany's release. In the meantime, he comforted the peer by reminding him that if he were to be hanged, he would be hanged with a silken rope – a peer's privilege. He could not resist, however, adding that the silken cord is elastic and that, therefore, the person being hanged is liable to bob up and down like a yo-yo. Dunsany, who was feeling understandably tense, retorted:

> There are certain things which are not jokes, Gogarty, and one of them is my hanging.

Gogarty set himself out to use all the influence he could to secure the release of his friend. He was on close terms with James McMahon, an under-secretary of the Castle, and a Catholic with Nationalist sympathies. On February 3rd, Gogarty interviewed McMahon, and Alfred Cope, another under-secretary, on Dunsany's behalf. He put up all sorts of excuses for Dunsany, explaining that he was absent at the front, in America and England, when the ammunition might have been handed in. When McMahon, thinking to ease the situation with Cope, said that Dunsany was a poet and dreamer who wrote plays for the Abbey Theatre, Gogarty had to intervene.

> This, I could not allow to pass [he wrote to Dunsany], because apart altogether of the inaccuracy of plays for the Abbey Theatre, it might lead to identifying you with Sinn Fein, which was the aim of the malignant informer who caused all this trouble.

In the end, Dunsany was released. The whole affair is an indication of the confused state of Ireland at that time, when a person of Sinn Fein sympathies, like Gogarty, could intervene with Dublin Castle in order to secure the release of a well-known Unionist.

One of the outstanding facts about the Sinn Fein campaign was its propaganda machine conducted by Desmond Fitzgerald and

Erskine Childers. But the best propagandists for the Irish cause were courageous English journalists like C. P. Scott, H. W. Nevinson, Hugh Martin and others, who constantly placed the truth of what was happening in Ireland before their fellow countrymen.

In the end, liberal opinion in England began to gain the upper hand. Negotiations for a truce were begun and, on July 11th, 1921, a cease-fire was proclaimed between the British forces and the I.R.A.

Gogarty nearly played a small part in the peace negotiations. On the morning of July 5th, Arthur Griffith asked him to drive to Kingstown to meet the mail boat. General Smuts was coming to Dublin and Arthur Griffith wanted to speak to him before he got into the hands of the Castle officials. But Smuts hid in a life-boat for some time after the mail boat had docked, thus foiling Griffith's and Gogarty's search for him. Later, at the Mansion House, Smuts advised the Irish leaders not to try for a republic. 'I tried a Republic and it was a failure,' he said.

Curiously enough, though the truce brought great relief to the country as a whole, there were shouts of betrayal from the die-hards on both sides, Republican and Unionist. But the real betrayal of the period has been overlooked by history – the betrayal of those Irishmen who died in the Great War for the promise of Home Rule at the end of it. A deputation of survivors of all ranks went to Buckingham Palace in 1920 to make an appeal 'that Ireland be not robbed of her Treaty rights'.

The answer they got was the repeal of the Home Rule Bill, and the Black-and-Tans let loose in Ireland. England forgot about them. Sinn Fein ignored them. Tom Kettle, Gogarty's friend, was one of those who had laid down their lives. He had recruited enthusiastically in 1914 and then joined up himself. Of Kettle, Gogarty would never say an unkind word even in jest. The only others who enjoyed this exemption from his tongue were A.E. and Arthur Griffith. Gogarty wrote after Kettle's death: 'He died as it befitted his breed in battle, and he spent a great soul. When the news came of Tom Kettle's death, there were eyelashes, and not only women's, that were wet with tears.'

Kettle wrote his epitaph a few hours before he was killed at Ginchy in 1916: his words might serve for thousands of other Irishmen who fell in the Great War.

So here while the mad guns curse overhead,
  And tired men sigh with mud for couch and floor,
Know that we fools, now with the foolish dead,
  Died not for flag, nor King, nor Emperor –
But for a dream born in a herdsman's shed,
  And for the secret Scripture of the poor.

THIRTEEN

O N Tuesday, July 9th, 1921, a truce was declared between
the Irish Republican Army and the British forces in
Ireland. The announcement was greeted with relief by the
populace at large. For the Army, Michael Collins felt that further
resistance was proving increasingly difficult. Cracks had begun to
appear in his Intelligence system and he had begun to doubt
whether they could have held out for very much longer as an
effective force had the truce not been declared. Mr de Valera
began negotiations with Lloyd George, the British Prime Minister.
At length, after a series of exchanges, plenipotentiaries were dispatched from the Dail in September, 'with a view to ascertaining
how the association of Ireland with the community of Nations
known as the British Empire may be reconciled with Irish
National aspirations'.

The Irish plenipotentiaries were Arthur Griffith, Eamonn
Dugan, George Gavan Duffy, Robert Barton and Michael
Collins. Michael Collins felt that he was quite out of place in the
delegation and at first resisted all efforts to send him over. He
regarded himself as a soldier, not as a politician or as a statesman.
When Mr de Valera insisted, he obeyed his leader. A member of
the first Free State Cabinet has suggested to the writer that
De Valera sent Collins over to London 'in order to scalp him'.
What the speaker meant by this was that De Valera, jealous of
Collins's position and fame as leader of the physical force movement, had decided that if anything was to be lost in London it had
better be lost by Collins, and thus undermine his authority and
diminish the glory which he had acquired by his success during the
Anglo-Irish war.

The writer believes, however, that Mr de Valera sent Collins
over primarily for the purpose of using him as a symbol of the
physical force movement so that, if an agreement were arrived at,
it would be felt that Collins, representing the Army, had not conceded anything which a soldier would not have conceded in the
same circumstances. Mr de Valera himself has been criticized for
not going over to these negotiations. It seems, however, clear
enough now that his purpose in staying behind was to try and
establish some means of reconciling the extreme elements in the

Cabinet, with the minimum concessions which he felt he could get from the British Government. It must have been apparent to him at the time that there was no question of absolute Republican status being granted by Lloyd George to the Dail representatives. Mr de Valera himself was not a doctrinaire republican. On one occasion, he asked for some solution in order to get him out of 'the strait-jacket of the Republic'. But two members of the Cabinet, Cathal Brugha and Austin Stack, were both unprepared to accept any concession from Britain other than Republican status.

De Valera's problem then was how to reconcile the divergencies in his Cabinet and, as well, provide some form of compromise which would satisfy not only the Cabinet but the extreme element in the I.R.A. He succeeded in producing a proposed draft document which would associate Southern Ireland with the Commonwealth, while retaining the status of a republic. The king was to be recognized as head of the association and there was to be an oath of allegiance to him as such.

This draft was acceptable to both Brugha and Stack but it proved quite unacceptable to the British plenipotentiaries. They were concerned in a battle of symbols as much as the Irish were. Lloyd George and Churchill were old Home Rulers. There was no need to convince them of the righteousness of Ireland's claim to have self-government. But Birkenhead and Chamberlain represented the right wing of the Tory Party who were totally opposed to any form of settlement with the representatives of those whom they regarded as murderers. Sir Henry Wilson's comment to Lloyd George is typical: 'I do not speak to murderers. If I met de Valera, I would hand him over to the police.'

After some weeks of negotiation, an impasse seemed to have been reached. A letter from Gogarty to Shane Leslie in late October throws a valuable sidelight on the mood of the times in Ireland, indicating the pessimism with which the outcome of the negotiations was regarded in Dublin.

The P.M.'s [Prime Minister's] remarks on Collins are interesting, but only Griffith counts. Griffith is Ireland at present. The theories of the breakdown are various here; some say that possibly the Prime Minister thought he had taken the measure of the Delegates and, therefore, took steps to cajole them, and that Griffith interposed. Some say the North; but

Ulster was made in England, the Ulster difficulty is England's affair. It resolves itself into 20,000 hands from Workman and Clarks' yards, who are always available for disturbances. The last outbreak was staged in Derry so as not to interrupt business in Belfast, but after three days the Belfast visitors fell back in Belfast and have been troublesome ever since. If the Irish Bishops interfered now, surely it would only add colour to the objection that it was a case of Papacy-v-Protestantism and give Lloyd George a rallying point and cry. Of course, Civil War has always been a possible alternative of the Government to Civil liberty, but will it pay still longer to keep the best market a battlefield?

I think the Ports are not essential, provided they are not an excuse for a garrison of soldiers on land under the role of Marines. Personally, I cannot see Ireland free until after Egypt and India; yet a blaze of Irish gratitude would do more for the Empire just now than the retention of all these three. Meanwhile, even the graziers are saying 'that they don't hold much belief in the Conference, it will just be as easy to fight it out'. After all, they have the deaths of 1,000 Irishmen and the imprisonment of 5,000 others coming between the promises to Redmond and their fulfilment. Of course, a Japanese/American War would provide a 'divarsion' but it would only be for a while. There will be a War here in any case and it will take six months to meet it and more, and there will be a great loss of property in England at the same time and probably looting of the unemployed. We expect serious outbreaks in Belfast next month as a result of the boycott.

The problem facing the British delegation was how to find a solution which would satisfy the Tory diehards and, at the same time, offer the Irish delegates a substantial measure of freedom. At length, Griffith, according to Churchill, 'widely versed in the history and polity of nations', succeeded in converting Chamberlain to the principle of Irish self-determination. Collins brought Birkenhead round by a combination of personal charm and hard common sense. Eventually, on the morning of December 6th, agreement was reached. Ireland was to have full control of her own affairs: her status was to be in fact and theory equal to that of

Canada. Fiscal control was guaranteed. The British administration *en bloc* – army, civil service and judiciary – was to abdicate its powers in Ireland. An important reference in the Articles of Agreement was the phrase 'the Community of Nations known as the British Empire'. This implied a society of peoples bound together by common interest, and not under the dominance of a single imperial power. In the light of the times, it was an astonishing concession to have wrung from the British. The six counties of Ulster were to have the opportunity of opting out of the jurisdiction of the new Parliament, but, if they did so, a Boundary Commission was to be appointed to determine the area to be separated from the Free State 'in accordance with the wishes of the inhabitants'. Lloyd George and Churchill intended that this clause – Clause 12 of the Treaty – would give the Free State jurisdiction of Tyrone, Fermanagh and Derry City where there were predominantly Nationalist populations. As Ulster was one of the key points around which the debate revolved, this clause was a determining one in inducing the Irish delegates to sign.

Two days later, a majority of the Dail Cabinet approved the Treaty. The dissentients were Mr de Valera, Cathal Brugha and Austin Stack. These argued that the agreement should have been submitted to the Dail Cabinet before the plenipotentiaries signed. This was in accordance with paragraph 3 of their written instructions but there was an ambiguity here. The plenipotentiaries had full power to negotiate and conclude a Treaty as a result of their appointment by the Dail Eireann. This was in conflict with Mr de Valera's secret instructions. He should not have complained, therefore, if the representatives of the oldest parliament in the world, with centuries of diplomacy in their veins, had taken advantage of an ambiguity that was of his own making. The document that was signed was different in form from that submitted to and rejected by the Dail Cabinet on December 5th and, in Griffith's and Collins's view, the Treaty as concluded was in essence similar to the alternative draft Treaty that the delegation had been given a full warrant to pursue by Mr de Valera. Another factor which was not calculated to make for harmony among the Irish delegates was the fact that the Secretary of the delegation, Mr Erskine Childers, was in the habit of making telephone calls daily to Mr de Valera in Dublin. The nature of these calls was kept secret from the plenipotentiaries. I have this information from Judge Fionan Lynch, one of the assistant secretaries attached to the delegation.

The Treaty had to be submitted to the Dail for ratification. The debate began on December 14th, 1921. On January 7th, 1922, the Treaty was ratified by a majority in the Dail. From the perspective of forty years after the event, it is possible to state with a certain amount of emphasis one fact arising out of the debates: that history has shown that the interpretation which those who supported the Treaty placed on it was correct, while those who opposed it, because they read into its clauses other meanings, have been proved wrong.

'I do not recommend this Treaty,' said Michael Collins in the Dail, 'for more than it is; equally I do not recommend it for less than it is. In my opinion, it gives us freedom, not the ultimate freedom that all nations desire and develop to, but the freedom to achieve it.' Griffith said: 'This is no more a final settlement than we are the final generation on earth.'

Their prophecy was fulfilled when, after a series of constitutional evolutions, Ireland became a republic in 1948. The speech of Mr Erskine Childers, who, with Mr de Valera, was the most prominent of the anti-Treatyites, may be taken as an example of the failure of those who opposed the Treaty to interpret the issues before them on a realistic basis. Erskine Childers maintained that: (a) Ireland would not be given Dominion status; (b) there was nothing to prevent the British army, after evacuation, returning to Ireland with full legal authority and without the permission of the Irish Government; (c) that the commissions of the officers in the new Irish army would be signed by the King of England. None of these allegations turned out to be true. The last suggestion was particularly mischievous. For a soldier who had been fighting in the hills for two years in terror of torture or execution by the king's 'troops', which included the Black-and-Tans, the prospect of taking up a commission in the new army, which would have to bear the king's signature, was anathema. In fact, the commissions of the Free State Army officers would be signed by the President of the Executive Council, Mr W. T. Cosgrave.

Erskine Childers, a former clerk in the House of Commons and a nephew of Sir Hugh Childers – a former Chancellor of the Exchequer – was a close student of constitutional law who had produced a carefully thought-out work on Home Rule in 1912. Why should he have blundered in his interpretation of the meaning of the Treaty articles? His sincerity was unquestionable. But Childers was a late convert to Sinn Fein. Until 1918, he had been in the British army and had favoured Ireland's inclusion within the Empire. In three years he had undergone a radical change. By 1922, British imperialism had become for him the major evil the world had to contend with. To obliterate its influence became his life's aim. Ireland was merely to be a spearhead in the break-up of British influence everywhere.

Under the terms of the Treaty, a provisional government had to be set up pending the withdrawal of British troops from Ireland, and a general election, which would determine the new Irish Parliament, was to take place. Mr de Valera had resigned from the presidency on January 15th and was succeeded by Arthur Griffith who formed a provisional government from the pro-Treaty group, Mr de Valera and his supporters having refused to take part in government.

Between January and June, when the elections were finally held after many postponements, chaos and confusion obtained in the country. In some cases, British troops were fired on as they were in the process of evacuation. Soldiers of the new Irish army were attacked as they took over barracks in the cities and in the country-side, and there were many casualties. The Provisional Government was confronted with the problem that has become a familiar one in the pattern of political development of many modern states. How are revolutionary elements, who have helped a government to power, to be reconciled to democratic principles and the authority of parliament once peace has been established? The Irish situation was, however, in many ways unique and quite different from that of other countries who had faced or were to face the problem of control of revolutionary forces after peace has been established. In Ireland, for the two years of the Anglo-Irish War, there had been a parliament legally elected which had exercised judicial and administrative functions throughout the country. The army had been subject, in theory at least, to the control of Parliament. Had the Dail, from January onwards, shown a united front towards any tendency of the army to usurp its powers, it is probable that control would have been achieved and the civil war, which was to break out in June, would have been averted; but the anti-Treaty Party continually questioned the authority of the provisional government to exercise control over the country, and some of its leaders, tacitly or in fact, condoned the resistance of the revolutionary elements to parliamentary control.

Affairs reached their head on April 13th when Rory O'Connor, a former Director of Engineering in the I.R.A., assumed leadership of a group of army insurgents who took possession of the Four Courts and other buildings in Dublin City. When asked by newspaper men if he meant to declare a military dictatorship, O'Connor replied in the affirmative. Mr de Valera's actions during these dangerous months are worth scrutiny. He symbolized in his person, as a former 1916 Volunteer commandant and President of the Dail, the fusion between the physical force movement and the parliamentary programme of Sinn Fein. It seems clear enough that, during the treaty negotiations and during the debate in the Dail, his tactics and political manœuvres were directed towards preventing a break between the two wings of the Sinn Fein movement; but from January onwards, it is more and more the soldier in Mr de Valera who speaks out and not the democrat. 'The people', he said at a meeting on March 17th, 'have no right to do wrong.' In Dundalk, on April 2nd, he said: 'We made it impossible for a British Government to rule in Ireland – we can make it impossible for an Irish Government, working under a British Government, to rule in Ireland.' The following day, in Drogheda, he stated: 'Republicans maintain that there are rights which may be maintained by force by an armed minority, even against a majority.'

These statements are clearly inconsistent with democratic principles and, in fact, amount to a justification of military dictatorship. This writer believes that Mr de Valera did wish to avoid an armed conflict between the military and civil arm in Ireland; but his tactics were disastrous. Had he lent Arthur Griffith's Government his moral support; had he continued to assert the right of the people to decide the Treaty issue at the election and condemned the usurpation of civil power by the group in the Four Courts, the authority of the Dail would have been secure after the general election and the revolutionary wing of the army could have been dealt with, without involving a protracted civil war. Griffith realized all along that some conflict between the two elements in Sinn Fein was inevitable once the State was established. If it had been possible for him to act swiftly and with Mr de Valera's support, control might have been established in a matter of weeks.

It was during this period between the ratification of the Treaty by the Dail and the general election in June that Gogarty became friendly with Michael Collins. They had known each other during the Black-and-Tan War, when Collins often slept in Gogarty's house, but now a warm mutual friendship developed between them. Collins, who had a highly developed sense of humour, took a keen delight in Gogarty's company. Gogarty was fascinated by this man who had, single-handed, fought the British Intelligence with a precision and ruthlessness that made a wreck of the system in Ireland, but who had as well so many different sides to his character. He recognized that unlike some men of action 'he loved beautiful things and had a warm sympathy for Art', and this despite the fact that the only school he had been to was a primary one. 'He was', Gogarty wrote about him later, 'a smooth, burly man with his unlined face and beautiful womanly hands. His skin was like undiscoloured ivory; his body had the unroughened strength that a woman's limbs might have, or the body of those wrestlers, who are bred to incredible feats in Japan. I have seen such athletic limbs in a Spanish swimmer whose arms, when extended, were hardly dimpled at the elbows. A low forehead, but what was seen over the clear-cut brow was straight. The hair grew down and his head tilted forward as if his chin sought repose on his chest. Napoleonic: but a bigger and more comely specimen of manhood than Napoleon.'

On most afternoons of the week, Gogarty and Collins would drive out for tea to Beechpark, the house of Vice-President Cosgrave, which was situated at the foot of the Dublin hills in Templeogue. Here, for an hour or so, they could forget the atmosphere of doom that was gradually gathering about public life in the country during those fateful months. Collins would roar with laughter at Gogarty's sallies, particularly when Gogarty said something more than usually irreverent that caused a shadow to flit across the face of the Vice-President, who had a Dublin man's sense of humour but was inclined rather to piety.

'I often thought,' Mr Cosgrave has said to me with a twinkle in

186

his eye, 'that that pair of rascals took more delight in shocking me than in talking serious business when they came out to tea.'

He remembers too how Gogarty and Collins both liked to consume quantities of cake and sweet tea. 'You know,' continued Mr Cosgrave, turning to me, 'I believe now that Collins was the greatest Irishman who ever lived; greater than Parnell, Hugh O'Neill or Brian Boru. He was only on the threshold of his career. He died with so much of his greatness in him, we will never know what he could have achieved. He had courage, you see; so had Gogarty.'

Mr Cosgrave pronounced the word 'courage' with a special emphasis that made it clear that it was more than physical courage he was talking about. Later, he told me that it was his impression that, after the death of Collins and Griffith, Gogarty became slightly unbalanced for a short period. It broke his sensitive spirit and for a while brought on periods of deep depression.

On June 16th, 1922, the elections were held. Taking all the circumstances into account, it is clear now that the country voted in favour of the Treaty. The situation then amounted to this: the Treaty had been ratified by the Dail Cabinet, the Dail itself, and, finally, by the people. If democracy was to have any meaning, it was necessary for the Government to act and assert its control over the armed insurrectionists who were openly defying its authority.

Griffith said at the time:

If we were not prepared to fight and preserve the rights of the ordinary people, we should be looked on as the greatest set of poltroons that ever had the fate of Ireland in their hands.

On June 22nd, the Cabinet made a formal demand that Rory O'Connor and his insurgent forces evacuate the Four Courts. When this ultimatum was refused, Free State troops commenced shelling the building. After two days, the garrison surrendered and were taken as prisoners to Mountjoy. In the meantime, fighting had broken out in other parts of the city. Cathal Brugha was shot dead outside the Hammam Hotel in O'Connell Street. After a week, the fighting in Dublin stopped but the country-side was in open revolt. Within a few days, Mr de Valera had left Dublin to join a guerrilla force operating in the country.

Then, scarcely a month after its establishment, disaster struck at the foundations of the new State. On August 12th, 1922, worn out and exhausted, Arthur Griffith died. He was the spiritual father of the new state; his moral courage and strength of purpose would have been invaluable in dealing with the conditions of anarchy into which the country had been inexorably plunged; his loss was incalculable. For a week before, Gogarty had confined him to a room in St Vincent's Hospital. He noticed Griffith had tonsillitis: he suspected also a stroke of a sub-arachnoid nature; but he found it impossible to keep his patient quiet. As soon as Gogarty left the room, Griffith would be on the floor again, studying documents and papers which had just come in and which he could read upside-down – the result of his old training as a compositor. The tragedy of the civil war, as it unfolded day by day, contributed to his illness. Then, one afternoon, Gogarty received an urgent call to come along to St Vincent's Hospital. In the meantime, Surgeon Meade had been called to the room where he found Arthur Griffith dead. He and Jim McGuinness opened an artery in an endeavour to find out whether there was any life left in the body and it was in this condition that Griffith was when Gogarty entered the room.

President Griffith [Gogarty wrote], the man who believed in the Irish people, lay on his back: his left arm was outstretched from the body, and bloody. 'Take up that corpse at once,' I said, letting something of the bitterness of my spirit escape into that harsh word. A moment later, I regretted it. 'Take the President's body into the bedroom.' *I perish by this people which I made.*

They were the words put by Tennyson into the mouth of Griffith's namesake of the Round Table. Surgeon Meade remembers that Gogarty went over to the window and his eyes filled with tears as he murmured 'Poor Arthur, poor Arthur.' Yet, later that evening, after he had embalmed the body of his friend and laid him out in a pair of his own pyjamas, Gogarty was his gay, sparkling self again at a party attended by Kevin O'Shiel. Such was the armour with which Gogarty could invest himself, be it formed of irony or motley. Later, he was to write that the 'poison which slew Griffith, more deadly than prussic acid, was envy, jealousy and ingratitude', but in an article on his dead friend which he wrote in the August 19th edition of *The Free State*, his mood was of baffled grief rather than hatred or bitterness.

When I looked on the dead face with the straight lines on the forehead that Lavater knew to be the signs of genius and leadership, the marble features that were the clear hiero-glyphics of forcefulness and nobility of soul, the great strength of character in the jaw and the fine outline of it all, I felt with my memory full of their ingratitude and fickleness, inclined to ask if he had won for the Irish people a position in Europe beyond their deserts. Arthur Griffith justified Ireland. Now that his never comforted body, broken by the weight of raising and rebuilding the Nation, has been borne to its last resting place through the thronged City that he loved, now that the poor he lifted up and set on a road that leads from their poverty, have gazed at the tricoloured coffin surrounded by soldiers of his making and followed by the representatives of the Nation he renewed, have paid it the last tribute of reverence and awe; and now that his splendid soul glows with the splendour of God, it remains for Ireland to become worthy of Arthur Griffith.

> He shook from off him with a grand impatience,
> The flesh uncomforted,
> And passed among the captains in whom Nations,
> Live when these men are dead.

Ten days after Griffith's death, on August 22nd, Michael Collins was killed in an ambush in County Cork. His death had a traumatic effect on the mind of the nation. He was a son of the people, 'one of plain Irish stock whose principles had been burned into them'. Through natural ability alone, he had attained astonishing heights. In his person, he symbolized the claim of the Irish race to govern themselves. With all his boisterousness and good humour, there was majesty in Collins's presence. It is note-worthy that in Gogarty's poem on Collins, written just after his death, he refers to 'The battle-trooped host of the O'Coilean' (the Gaelic name for Collins), seeing Collins as a descendant of the Gaelic nobility who had been replaced by English settlers after the breakdown of the old order in the sixteenth and seventeenth centuries.

189

When the news of his death reached army barracks, soldiers broke down and wept; others leaned on one another's shoulders in silent grief. As the funeral cortège passed through Dublin, a young soldier turned to Senator Alice Stopford Green, in tears, and said: 'I can't bear it, ma'am.' Two days after Collins's death, Gogarty waited on the Dublin quays as a gunboat brought the body up the Liffey. It was impossible to bring it by road as communications between the South and Dublin had broken down. Women knelt in fur coats and the crowd chanted prayers into the murky sky as the body draped with the tricolour was brought off the gunboat. Next morning, Gogarty went out at four o'clock with Desmond Fitzgerald, the Minister for External Affairs, to the Royal College of Surgeons for the melancholy task of embalming the body of his dead friend. But in those days of fear and hate, even an errand of mercy was not sacrosanct. A bullet smacked into the wood above his head, as Gogarty knocked on the door of the College. Later that morning, he secured embalming instruments in Trinity College. With fine skill, he was able to hide the gaping wound in the back of the head and preserve in the dead man's face something of the nobility it bore in life. A tribute to Gogarty's technique in embalming is implied in Sir John Lavery's description of Collins as he saw him laid out after death.

He might have been Napoleon in marble as he lay in his uniform, covered by the Free State flag with a Crucifix on his breast.

At the graveyard next morning, the soldiers of the new state, in field-green uniforms, fired a fusillade over the grave of their dead commander-in-chief. In a speech delivered at the graveside, General Richard Mulcahy, Collins's successor, spoke finely in passages that he later claimed to the biographer were inspired by the pent-up atmosphere of grief that swept the nation after Collins's death.

'Prophecy,' said Peter, who was the great Rock, is a light shining in the darkness 'till the day dawns,' and surely our great Rock was our prophet and our prophecy a light held aloft along the road of hardship and bitter toil: and if our light is gone out, it is only as the paling of a candle in the dawn of its own prophecy. Men and women of Ireland, we are still mariners in the deep, bound for a Port, still seen only through storm and spray, sailing still on a sea full of dangers and hardships and bitter toil, but the great Sleeper lies smiling in the boat and we shall be filled with the spirit which will walk bravely upon the waves.

In a poem addressed to Collins, published in *The Free State* of August 29th, Gogarty wrote of 'his laughing face and unimpeded mind' and condemned bitterly the person responsible for his killing.

> Down the memorial ages, he shall have
> The fame of Judas who McMurrough clad,
> What alien schemer or deluded lout,
> What Cain has caught his country by the throat?

Deprived of their two outstanding figures, the provisional government were fortunate in finding leaders to replace them, as courageous and realistic as William T. Cosgrave, who became President, and Kevin O'Higgins, who became Vice-President. The Dail met on September 9th. On the 28th of the same month, a Bill was passed empowering military courts to pass sentence of death on persons found in possession of fire-arms. The Executive Council justified this proposal by reference to the state of the country. Law and order had vanished outside the cities. As can happen at such times, lawless elements had taken advantage of the confusion to indulge in orgies of crime. Banks and private houses were raided by persons singularly free from attachment to the Republic or Mr de la Valera's Document No. 2. Cattle-driving by land-hungry labourers was taking place in the south and there were actually Soviets established in parts of County Clare. Trigger-happy young men who had neither the discipline nor the morale of those they fought alongside, associated themselves with the revolutionary forces. These 'Trucilers', so called because they only took to arms after the Black-and-Tan War was ended, were often responsible for cowardly murders. Free State soldiers were shot in the back as they walked out with their girl-friends; non-combatants were shot in their own homes. Kevin O'Higgins's father and Mr W. T. Cosgrave's uncle were murdered in this fashion.

The most potent resistance was in the south. Though the Irish

Republican Brotherhood had declared for the Free State, a majority of the guerrilla force of the I.R.A. were in arms against the Government troops. Brave, intrepid men, such as Tom Barry, Frank Aiken, Liam Lynch, with the discipline of two years' fight against the Black-and-Tans behind them, were entrenched in an almost impregnable position throughout the south.

These were the fearful obstacles that confronted the Free State Government in the autumn of 1922. The Cabinet slept on camp-beds in Leinster House, sealed off like a fortress by barbed wire and armed guards. 'We were', Kevin O'Higgins said later, 'nine young men in the ruins of one Administration, with the foundations of another not yet laid, and with wild men screaming through the keyhole.'

On November 13th, a further threat to the existence of the Government arose. An order issued by Liam Lynch, head of the insurrectionary forces which had now brought themselves under the jurisdiction of Mr de Valera and a rebel 'Cabinet', stated that the following persons were to be shot at sight: members of the Cabinet, those in the Dail who had voted for the Army Powers Resolution Bill in September, High Court judges and aggressive Free State supporters. It was time for the Government to take decisive action to prevent the country slipping into 'chaos, anarchy and futility'.

On November 10th, Erskine Childers was captured: he was armed and had attempted to resist arrest before his gun was taken from him. Seeing himself perhaps as a sort of minor Lawrence of Arabia, he had been leading successful sorties through the south. He destroyed the Atlantic cable at Valentia Island. Tim Healy states in his memoirs, *Letters and Leaders of My Day*, that it was at Childers's behest that Mallow Viaduct, one of the main arteries of communication between Dublin and Cork, was destroyed. Unwittingly or not, Childers had become a symbol of the rebel resistance. For Kevin O'Higgins, he was that 'able Englishman striking ghoulishly at the heart of a Nation', though it was really unfair to call him an Englishman as his mother had been Irish, and he had other Irish ties. Gogarty called him 'that unsmiling Englishman' and was popularly supposed to have been the author of a sonnet which had appeared in *The Freeman's Journal* some months before, beginning:

Childers, thou shouldst be leaving at this hour,
England had need of thee beneath Big Ben.
Thy sword is stagnant, so should be thy pen.
Among thine own, intrigue will win thee power.

In his paper, *An Poblacht*, weeks before the General Election, Childers had printed: 'Why not execute the man who executed the Treaty.'

Now he himself was sentenced to execution under the Army Emergency Powers Resolution Bill, after facing a court-martial. He was superb in death, meeting the firing squad with composure and bravery. Had the court-martial not sentenced him, a section of the army had planned to ambush the prison van at the Mater Hospital and hang Childers publicly in the streets.

On December 7th, General Sean Hales and Mr Padraic O'Malley, both members of the Dail, were fired at on a local side-car outside the Ormond Hotel. General Hales died from his wounds. The following morning, four members of the Four Courts garrison, in prison in Mountjoy, were executed as a reprisal. This act by the Government was undoubtedly illegal. There had been no court-martial, as in Erskine Childers's case. In any event, it is doubtful whether an Act of Parliament passed in September would have been enforceable against men who had laid down arms more than a month before the Bill was passed and who were imprisoned at the time that it was given judicial force. The Cabinet justified their actions on the grounds that they were fighting for their lives and for the survival of democracy in the nation against a military dictatorship. That there was no vindictiveness in their action is indicated by the calibre of the men who were executed. Two of them were upright soldierly men with fine records in the Anglo-Irish War. Rory O'Connor, one of those executed, had been best man at Kevin O'Higgins's wedding only a year before. By a strange irony of fate, O'Connor, suspicious that he was to be deported to the Seychelles, had sewn ten golden guineas he had received as a present from O'Higgins, into the hem of his trousers before leaving his cell for execution. The quicklime of Mountjoy Prison still holds today those golden guineas.

If they were legally unjustifiable, the executions had a practical effect. Gogarty emphasized this in a letter to Shane Leslie written on November 15th.

I am sure Justice – protesting and confessing England must have been shocked at the execution of the four prisoners. In terms of Justice, of course, it cannot be defended: but inasmuch as Justice comes after order has been established and the humanities, this prescription for chaos was inevitable; and, when you think of the policy of assassination that confronted every member of Government, it is impossible to suggest any other remedy. As Mrs Wyse-Power says: 'I don't agree with it but, glory be to God, wasn't it wonderful.'

It stopped the murders anyway. Childers' execution was a different affair. I cannot see or excuse him from any standpoint, but that from which Savonarola was condemned. There was nothing mystical at all in Childers. He was one of those self-contained, unsmiling men whose doom seems to be written on their faces. He tried to kill the country's potentialities in the name of the ideal. After all, the ideal is to such men their own idea and little else.

Despite the disorder and chaotic conditions, the Government proceeded doggedly with its programme of setting up the new bodies for administration of the country. On December 9th, the Senate was convened. This was the Upper House of the Free State Parliament. The Senate was elected by the Dail and by popular vote. Forty seats were nominated by the Government. It had been agreed that a majority of these would be given to the Unionist minority, so that they could play their part in the government of the country. Gogarty and Yeats were included among the nominated members, though for quite different reasons than those which prompted the appointment of titled landowners. Gogarty had been an old Sinn Feiner, and Yeats a former member of the I.R.B. That there were certain hazards attendant on being a senator, Gogarty soon discovered. Senators had been included in the category of those who were to be shot at sight, in the order issued from the rebel headquarters by Liam Lynch on November 13th.

On January 20th, 1923, Gogarty was having a bath in his house after his day's work, when he felt a revolver being pressed into his ribs. Using a woman as a decoy, by pretending that she was a patient, armed men had gained entry to his house. They demanded that he should accompany them. As he was dressing, he glanced towards the chest of drawers where a revolver lay concealed, but calculated that the chances of getting it out in time before his captors shot him were negligible. He had better wait for his opportunity later on. As he got into the car, the revolver was pressed hard into his back. 'Isn't it a good thing to die in a flash, Senator?' one of the gunmen said, as they sped out along the Chapelizod road. Later, his captors would recollect how, despite the seriousness of the situation, Gogarty kept them amused with his constant flow of humour and wit. Alderman John McCann recalls that Peter White, one of the men who took part in the kidnapping, often told him, with admiration, of Gogarty's calmness and detachment in a desperate situation; and Brendan Considine, of the rebel G.H.Q. who organized the kidnapping, remembers that the report of Gogarty's conduct referred to him as 'confident and courageous'.

As they got out of the car, Gogarty made a typical remark: 'Are you not going to tip the driver?'

But how to escape before his captors shot him – that was his problem. Inside the house where they had taken him on the banks of the Liffey, near the Salmon Weir, his brain worked rapidly. He knew the layout of the house as he had been at an auction there not long before. 'I tried a number of ruses to get outside, as close to the Liffey banks as possible, but none of them worked.' Then, suddenly, pleading that his bowels were loosening with fright, Gogarty doubled up and asked to be assisted out. On a second occasion, he repeated his request, but kept his arms inside his fur-collared overcoat, ready to slip out in a second. As he took the coat off, he threw it over the heads of his captors, flinging himself recklessly into the swirling Liffey almost in the same movement. The Liffey was in flood and it was a night of extreme cold. For a man of forty-five to have survived the initial shock was in itself remarkable. Swept onwards by the flood, he thought he had had a heart attack; he found himself unable to breathe: some floating foam had entered his nostrils and prevented him drawing his breath. Sweeping the foam away, he struck out with a powerful trudgeon stroke. An overhanging branch enabled him to haul himself out of the racing torrent. Once on the bank, he staggered, a pale ghost-like figure, into the house of a Mr Butler. Not receiving a very cordial welcome there, he went out into the darkness, chattering and frozen with no feeling in his legs below the knee. Barely able to walk, he located the police barracks in the Phoenix Park. Incapable of speech, because of his experience, all he could do was to hiccup at the sentry. Finally, they admitted him, and the police surgeon, Dr Ellis, was brought to examine him. Gogarty merely said: 'I am Senator Oliver Gogarty.' Mrs Ellis recalls the incident vividly. Gogarty lay in a complete state of collapse while her husband gave him brandy to restore his circulation. As a souvenir, Gogarty gave Dr Ellis a gold cigarette case, before he left to be driven through the city in an armoured car to Government Buildings. Though a person of iron nerve, Gogarty was in a state of shock after his narrow escape; but, in the morning, he had recovered some of his natural good spirits and was able to return to his house under armed guard. That day, the Government troops recovered his coat where his captors had left it on the Liffey banks. In the evening he gave an interview to the press in which he laughingly told them he had been planning an 'Apologia for Cowards' during the two hours of his captivity.

On January 24th, he wrote to Lord Dunsany, apologizing for not keeping an appointment on the night of his capture:

> Instead of visiting you, I was visiting the bottom of the monstrous world. I have had fifteen minutes in the Liffey but I chose them instead of as many bullet holes which were in store for me, pending the execution of certain ruffians in Dundalk. Now I am hunting wild beast, and praying that I may have a sight of them. In short, I was kidnapped by six men and held as a hostage in an empty house near the Salmon Pool in the Islandbridge, from 8 'til 10 on Friday. I had a most lucky escape, due to the swiftness of the Liffey current and the swiftness with which terror winged my heels.

That the group which apprehended Gogarty included desperate gunmen is indicated by the fact that one of them, Denis O'Leary, may have been the assassin of an unarmed man, Mr Seamus O'Dwyer, who was shot a week later behind the counter of his shop in Rathmines. Mr O'Dwyer was a supporter of the Free State. This information was given to me by a member of the Free State Cabinet, but members of the anti-Treaty group deny that O'Leary was associated with the O'Dwyer shooting. Some days later, O'Leary himself was mown down by Free State soldiers outside Tranquilla Carmelite Convent in Rathmines. On the 29th, Gogarty wrote to Lady Leslie:

> The fellow who led the raid on me was found riddled with bullets outside the Tranquilla Convent in Rathmines, an appropriate place for a quietus.

The woman who acted as the decoy in entering Gogarty's house is said to have become a nun in the same Convent outside which, today, a plaque is erected to the memory of Gogarty's dead kidnapper.

Later, Gogarty was to fulfil a vow he had made while immersed in the swirling torrent, that he would present two swans to the Goddess of the River, in thanksgiving, if he reached the bank in safety.

But the whole affair had been a terrifying experience and he was not inclined to joke about it. When, as often with notable events in Dublin, a ballad appeared commemorating the escape, written in satiric vein, Gogarty was not at all pleased with it. The ballad, written by William Dawson, is amusing enough, and has a most effective tune. It was sung by its author at the Arts Club amid acclamation.

> Come all ye bould Free Staters now and listen to my lay,
> And pay a close attention, please, to what I've got to say,
> For 'tis the Tale of a Winter's Night last January year,
> When Oliver St John Gogarty swam down the Salmon Weir.

> As Oliver St John Gogarty one night sat in his house,
> A-writin' of prescriptions or composin' of a poem,
> Up rolled a gorgeous Rolls-Royce car and out a lady jumped,
> And at Oliver St John Gogarty's hall-door she loudly thumped.

> 'Oh, Oliver St John Gogarty, come let yourself be led'
> Cried a couple of masked ruff-i-ans, puttin' guns up to his head.
> 'I'm with you, boys,' cried he, 'but first, give me my big fur coat,
> And also let me have a scarf – my special care's the throat.'

> They shoved him in the Rolls-Royce car and swiftly sped away,
> What route they followed, Oliver St John Gogarty can't say.
> But they reached a house at Island Bridge and locked him in a
>   room,
> And said, 'Oliver St John Gogarty, prepare to meet yer doom.'

Said Oliver St John Gogarty, 'My coat I beg you hold,'
The half-bemoidered ruff-i-an then did as he was told.
Before he twigged what game was up, the coat was round his
  head,
And Oliver St John Gogarty into the night had fled.

The rain came down like bullets, and the bullets came down
  like rain,
As Oliver St John Gogarty the river bank did gain;
He plunged into the ragin' tide and swam with courage bold,
Like brave Horatius long ago in the fabled days of old.

He landed and proceeded through the famous Phaynix Park;
The night was bitter cold, and what was worse, extremely dark;
But Oliver St John Gogarty to this paid no regard,
Till he found himself a target for our gallant Civic Guard.

Cried Oliver St John Gogarty, 'A Senator am I!
The rebels I've tricked, the river I've swum, and sorra the
  word's a lie,'
As they clad and fed the hero bold, said the sergeant with a
  wink:
'Faith, thin, Oliver St John Gogarty, ye've too much bounce
  to sink.'

Could there have been a slight overtone of revenge in Dawson's
motive for writing this ballad? When he had been a student at
Trinity, Dawson once boasted that his father read *chapters* of
Sappho before going to bed. Gogarty had coined a derisive
quatrain, which played on the fact that only fragments of Sapphic
poetry remain today.

> No need to boast yourself well-read.
> The gift's hereditary rather.
> 'I read before I go to bed,
> Chapters of Sappho': thus your father.

It was obvious that a campaign of organized destruction was
being directed at members of the Oireachtas. In January and
February of 1923, the houses of thirty-seven senators were burnt
to the ground by anti-Treaty forces. Since many of these senators
were landed gentry, the loss of property was considerable and
objects of irreplaceable value were consumed in flames. On

February 29th, Renvyle, Gogarty's Connemara mansion, was burnt down. It is not difficult to understand the mood of bitterness that filled him after this event. Since his early years, he had been a member of Sinn Fein. He had maintained his association with the Party through its vicissitudes. Now, he found his life in danger and his property destroyed by men of his own race whose liberty, Gogarty believed, had been achieved by the statesmanship and sacrifice of the Sinn Fein leaders who had signed the Treaty.

Memories, nothing left now but memories, and in that house was lost my mother's first portrait, painted when she was a girl of sixteen. Her first attempt in oils; books, pictures, all consumed for what? Nothing left but a charred oak beam quenched in the well beneath the house; and ten tall chimneys stand bare on Europe's extreme verge.

Gogarty found it difficult to continue his practice in Dublin. Patients coming to visit him had to be examined by the eight Guards who guarded his consulting rooms. He disliked carrying a revolver, as he had been ordered to do by the Government: it was putting his suits out of shape; besides, busy with the composition of his poems, he was often inclined to forget the revolver, leaving it behind him in places like the lavatory of the Shelbourne Hotel, where a waiter came screaming after him with the forgotten weapon in his hand.

In May 1923, he moved for a while to England and began practice in 20 Grosvenor Square. Friends were anxious to help him and in a short time he had a nice practice in full swing. Each week, he returned to Ireland to attend meetings of the Senate. This was courageous of Gogarty, but typical. It was typical, too, of others who accepted the burden of establishing governmental authority in Ireland during those appalling months when the country seemed on the brink of anarchy. From the policemen of the new Civic Guard who took over their duties as an unarmed body, to the district justices, civil servants and members of the Dail and Senate, there is nowhere one does not encounter a sense of civic duty and a refusal to submit to the threat of the armed bully. The army, too, at a strength of almost 60,000, contained many volunteers whose purpose in joining up was to protect the country against the rule of the gun. On such a class does a nation depend in times of anarchy to fortify itself against destruction and to ensure the permanence of democratic institutions.

In the midst of the civil war, the Cabinet had gradually been setting up a new administration. Departments of the civil service had been reorganized. Courageous magistrates, selected by Kevin O'Higgins, were setting out into the country-side in the face of threats of assassination and had begun the administration of justice under the authority of the new State.

When the cease-fire order was promulgated in May, the damage done by the anti-Treaty forces in the country-side and cities had been considerable. They had, according to a pastoral of the Irish bishops, issued at the time, 'wrecked Ireland from beginning to end and caused more damage in three months than could be laid to the charges of British rule in so many decades.' But the foundations of the new State had been laid and, from the ruins, a new edifice slowly began to emerge. The Civil War had cost Ireland £23,000,000; it also had probably cost her the loss of the two counties of Ulster, Tyrone and Fermanagh, which it was intended under Clause 12 of the Treaty should pass to the Free State. In 1924, the Boundary Commission decided in favour of leaving the border in its existing state. This was another betrayal of Irish rights by an English government. But Sinn Fein had shown for the first time that it was possible, by the threat of armed force, to overcome the tendency of the British politicians to abandon Ireland when party claims conflicted with Irish national aspirations. That is why the Treaty of 1921 was superior to the Home Rule Bill. The Treaty was obtained at the point of the gun. What was obtained once could be obtained again. Had the army remained united under a strong Dail in 1922, there is no doubt that, by 1924, when the Boundary Commission was appointed, threats of a compellingly coercive nature could have been used to prevent Ulster breaking Clause 12 (as she did by refusing to appoint a representative to the Boundary Commission) and to ensure the appointment of a chairman more sympathetic to the Southern Ireland cause than Mr Justice Feetham proved to be.

Later, Gogarty was to state that Mr de Valera did more harm to the country than Cromwell. But this is a statement from one who had suffered as a result of Mr de Valera's actions. In considering Mr de Valera at this period, one has always got to see him against the background of Griffith's statement at the conclusion of the Treaty debates. 'There is scarcely a man I have ever met for whom I have more love and respect than Eamonn de Valera.' Sean Milroy records that Griffith would not tolerate criticism of Mr de Valera in his presence, even after the Treaty debates. 'To insult de Valera,' he would say, 'is to insult me.' Collins said about the same time: 'Mr de Valera holds the same place in my heart as he always did.'

In these utterances are revealed the personal charm, the gift of friendship and the sincerity that were patent in Mr de Valera's character to those who knew him. But he seems to have lacked, during this crisis, the realistic touch which is necessary for a statesman. Having conceived an abstract solution to the problem, he was incapable of bringing it down to earth and resolving it against the immediate difficulties that presented themselves. When his tactics misfired, he should have accepted the Treaty instead of harking back to an ideal which was now impossible of attainment. Looking back, it can be seen that circumstances may have made him reluctant to relinquish his leadership of Sinn Fein. In the minds of the Irish people, he had become a Messiah.

Arthur Griffith had hailed him as an Avatar in 1919. The people had made him into a myth. Now he himself came to believe in this myth and the aura of infallibility that accompanied it. When he found himself a punctured Messiah, it is possible that his judgment may have been set off balance. Meanwhile, in May 1923, he was arrested by Free State troops. Soon he had resigned himself to prison life with that fortitude and patience, qualities rare among the Irish, which, more than any others perhaps, have been the mainstay of his subsequent political success.

FOURTEEN

SHANE LESLIE, referring to Oliver Gogarty's success as a conversationalist during the London Season of 1924, says: 'His conversation was a nine-day wonder. All the leading hostesses vied to have him at their dinner-parties and "At Homes".'

Edward Shanks has written that Gogarty's conversation exemplified 'the ripe Dublin talk that astonished London when it was first heard on the lips of Wilde'. London, however, had had an opportunity of hearing 'ripe Dublin talk' before Wilde's era. Another Trinity man, Charles Lever, doctor and author, had kept up the city's reputation for the gift of gab in London in the 'seventies. 'Lever,' wrote a correspondent in the *Daily Telegraph*, March 1872, 'beguiled the London tables with an inexhaustible fund of anecdote and prodigality of fun.' Before Lever, there had been Tom Moore, with his special brand of song and charm, to enthral the London drawing-rooms; earlier still, Curran's reputation as a talker had been such that, when the great lawyer sat down to eat in the Coffee House of the Hotel Calais in London, crowds gathered nightly to hear his flow of conversation and wit. Thus, Gogarty had an advantage when he arrived in London. He was in the tradition of witty Dubliners who had enthralled the Saxon with their gift of words; but he had no literary reputation behind him as Wilde, Lever or Moore had, when they acquired their fame as conversationalists.

Gogarty's escape from the gunmen in Dublin, combined with his reputation as a skilful surgeon, had made him something of a celebrity. But this would not have been sufficient to launch him on London society in a single season, had it not been for the skilful tactics of two leading London hostesses, Lady Lavery and Lady Leslie, who saw to it that he was given the best opportunities possible to exercise his conversational powers. His success was rapid. The rumour went round that a successor to Oscar Wilde was to be heard at the best tables. Soon he was in demand. Lady Cunard had him to her dinner-parties. Lady Leconfield, Mrs Benjamin Guinness, Lady Colefax, Lady Ottoline Morell, were others at whose 'At Homes' he was lionized. Lady Islington and the Earl of Granard he knew from his Dublin days. Invitations to stay at country houses poured in. One spring evening at Garsington Manor, near Oxford, he walked behind Yeats and Lady Ottoline Morell, noting the stately figure of the poet, with his silver hair parting in the breeze, and his hostess in period lilac silk.

> My mind seeks beauty and it dwells on you,
> Under the elms – and all the air was Spring's
> A leaven of silence in the misty dew,
> Leavening the light, the shadow leavening,
> Your cloak, the tall feather, white under blue,
> Walking beside a poet in the evening.

He stayed for a while at Lytham Hall, Lancashire, with his friend Talbot Clifton, the squire of Lytham. His host's wife, Mrs Violet Clifton, recalls that while Gogarty was at Lytham he seemed at his best in the open air in the presence of natural beauty.

> To me Gogarty was most lovable when out of doors, he would suddenly break into verse, Herrick and Marvell, in an English garden. In the Hebrides he would come out with Robert Burns. The glory of the natural scene delighted him. Once I remember his delight in a rain-jewelled cobweb. Flowers as a table decoration he detested; a table so dressed reminded him of a coffin.

He wrote to Lady Leslie to tell her jokingly that he only felt safe sleeping in moated houses, and conjectured the possibility of putting a moat round Renvyle when it was restored.

Gogarty was now at the top of his form as a talker. The young iconoclast who had dazzled George Moore's gatherings twenty years before had matured considerably and could adapt himself to more varied types of audience. His choice of syntax and word was perfect, as if he had prepared his sentences the night before; yet all was uttered spontaneously. His speech was delivered with the speed, though not the sound, of a machine-gun. He had clear diction and a soft euphonious Dublin voice. Sometimes, ideas flowed from his brain to his tongue so fast that he had to make a grimace with his lips to get the words out in time. Often he made a clever remark in the middle of a torrent of words, that he had forgotten almost immediately he had made it. 'Did I say that?' he would say, in genuine wonder afterwards, when someone might recall to him something particularly amusing he had said.

Many of his sayings made the rounds of London afterwards. He once remarked about Lady Colefax, who was notorious for her efforts to secure famous guests at her receptions: 'Sybil is giving an "At Home" for the Widow of the Unknown Soldier. They say they were not married, but after all one must think imperially at Lady Colefax's.'

Another remark referred to a languid aristocrat who had recently been converted to Catholicism: 'If Evan gave *all* his reasons for joining the Church, he'd be excommunicated.'

There was something in his talk to charm all types of listener. Asquith and Balfour, invited to dinner at Lady Leslie's, were charmed by Gogarty's slyly-inserted classical references and quotations. Asquith told Violet Clifton afterwards that he thought Gogarty the wittiest man in London.

He was like a character from the Commedia del Arte. Gogarty could mimic perfectly when he was telling a story. Sometimes, he would even rise from the table to assume more perfectly the character he was impersonating in some anecdote. Lord Dunsany has left an account of Gogarty, telling the story of a stag-hunt in which he took part with Talbot Clifton in Scotland, in the autumn of 1923, and the tale formed a prominent part of Gogarty's repertoire.

> Suddenly Gogarty turned into a didactic Highland Laird, showing a novice how a stag ought to be stalked. The stalk was a very good one, advantage being taken of every scrap of cover provided by any chair that was met on the way. Indeed, after a short homily, in a whisper, the Laird was actually about to shoot when he noticed that his ghillie had neglected to bring his rifle. The oaths that then broke out from the thwarted sportsman, made one forget that a Dublin surgeon was talking in a smoking room.

It was not merely Gogarty's talk, mimicry or wit that enabled him to capture his audience at first impression. It was the effect of his whole personality. He exuded a gaiety that it was almost impossible to resist. When he cast his blue eyes round the room, he drew its occupants into his orbit with a power that had something of the mesmerist in it.*

* Anyone who has seen an Irish story-teller in action will recognize the source of this gift ;the subtle inflexion of voice, the lightning mobility of feature, the rapid change

In November, Gogarty wrote to Lady Leslie to tell her of his round of entertainment.

I had lunch with your friend, Miss Ogilvy, one day; Mrs Asquith was next me. Lady Bonham-Carter; Gardiner (a newspaper); Princess —— from Rome, dark, vivacious, crimson nails, just divorced him, endless talk was there; and some man whose office is in Sackville St. I never can catch names! No Mr Asquith. Mrs A. very engaged in politics, saw me twice during lunch. I sat on her left, she turned to breathe, 'but if that is the intention of the Beaverbrook clique' ... Whatever the 'intention' was, I cannot say. Hardly 'honourable', I can surmise.

And a few weeks later:

I dined at Chamberlain's. Present were:

> Sir Campbell Stuart of 'The Times'.
> Lady Elvery.
> Mrs Chamberlain. ⎱ for all time.
> Austen Chamberlain. ⎰

Did you notice? Of course you did: that is what alarmed you about me – my new drawing-room manners. Perfect repose? No wonder it looked as if I had committed or rather attempted Hari Kari or Majong.

Chamberlain captivated him; 'one of the grandest human beings I have ever met.' Gogarty was highly impressed with the manner in which Chamberlain spoke out against a current leader in *The Times*. The fact that Sir Campbell Stuart, a director of the paper, was present, did not deter him.

The grandeur of the man lifted all about him above pettiness. No need for Wellingtonian 'publish and be damned.' You are damned in your own estimation if you ever entertained the thought of taking an advantage of his expression of opinion.

from didactic to narrative in the tale combine to exercise a trance-like effect on the listener. This folk tradition, consciously or unconsciously, influenced Sheridan, Curran, Thomas Moore, Levy and Wilde. Louis Gillet has noticed how at times James Joyce would burst into a joyous narrative exemplifying what Gillet calls 'the gifts of the oldest story-telling race in Europe'.

Later, he met Lord Birkenhead, who had scarcely received sympathetic treatment in the old days from Griffith's Sinn Fein paper. But the Birkenhead that Gogarty met was quite different from the 'Galloper' Smith of the Carson treason trials. His contact with Griffith and Collins during the Treaty debates had altered his view on Ireland. He admired the achievement of the new Free State in restoring order: his affection for Collins had not dimmed with Collins's death. Gogarty admired Birkenhead's trim figure; the build of a natural athlete; he was impressed with his terse replies to bores at table, and noted that his pallor increased as he drank, as if it were a sign of the inward clarity of his mind. Birkenhead pleased him by remembering Mahaffy. 'Why should Mahaffy, with his wit and intellectual gifts, have chosen to remain in Dublin?' Birkenhead asked.

Gogarty replied: 'He was Provost. He was knighted. What Fellow in Oxford can be knighted without being benighted first?'

Only once did Gogarty meet his master in conversation while he was in London. This occurred in an encounter with his fellow-citizen, Bernard Shaw, who was invited to dinner, with Gogarty, at Lady Asquith's. Gogarty told me this story against himself. Knowing Shaw's ability as a talker, he had carefully prepared his opening so that he might be able to seize command of the conversation at the outset of the evening. He began:

I believe it was an attribute of great artists that their own immortality was apparent to them during their lifetime.

He was about to follow with a list of carefully-prepared examples, but Shaw interrupted instantly, with a devastating example of the assumption in reverse,

What about Marie Corelli gliding down the Avon in a gondola with her parasol?

The initiation was lost. The ludicrous picture conjured up by Shaw's quick imagination destroyed the effect of Gogarty's opening gambit and effectively torpedoed him as master of the evening's conversation.

One evening, Gogarty dined with the Duke of Connaught; the next evening, he dined with Lord Granard at Forbes House, where the King came to dinner twice monthly; a day or two later, he was deputed to amuse two Greek princesses. He began to worry if there was not something of the courtier, or even the flunkey, in his disposition. But a consideration of his countrymen's character satisfied him that he was acting according to the natural instinct of his race.

> Every Irishman loves an aristocrat. In all the sagas of Erin there is not the name of a commoner mentioned, even the charioteers were noblemen. Let my critics digest that. Anyway, I dearly love a Lord and I think I can analyse the reason: he stands for an established order of things; for a household of continuance with the obligations its tradition's concern. There is the knowledge that they, like Kings, seldom have any selfish or personal interest in mundane affairs. Their axes were ground long ago. They can be trusted not to lower others in order to gain height themselves. Long ago, 'they bared them right doughtily', and stock raisers as we are, we Irish believe in good blood.

A remark which Collins made to Gogarty shortly before his death seems to show that he shared Gogarty's views on this matter. The reference is in a letter Gogarty wrote to Lady Leslie, asking her to use her influence with her nephew, Winston Churchill, to stop a notorious money-lender from pressing his claim against the Duke of Leinster.

> Nonsense aside, you can do this with your cloud-compelling nephew. Ask him very kindly to make M.– D.– take his talons out of His Grace of Leinster. The Duke was at the funeral today and he represented the much-needed classes over here. He may be made a barrier against Bolshevism which, here, is tainted with patriotism: an awful blend. The Irregulars' idea of Ireland is a desert with a robbable Bank, but as poor Collins said when I discussed the Duke's joining the Free State Army: 'the Irish love Doureas', i.e., blue blood.

Even in London, Gogarty was not entirely safe from the depredations of the anti-Treaty forces. He received a threatening note demanding that he should resign from the Senate: if he did so, he would be allowed 'to resume his practice in Dublin'.

Gogarty's reaction was contained in his reply, issued through the Free State Publicity Department:

Information was conveyed to Dr. O. Gogarty that he could continue his practice on condition that he resigned from the Senate. To this impertinent message, Dr. O. Gogarty replied that he had no intention of betraying the Government, and that as for his practice, it could be continued when there was no longer a political party which approved the decoying of medical men in its resistance to civilization.

This aspect of his exile made him bitter. All his life, he had supported Sinn Fein, even in its most unpopular phases. Now, when British rule had ended in Ireland, it was unsafe for him to live in his own country.

His English colleagues generously helped by sending him patients to build up his practice at 20 Grosvenor Place. In London, he visited old Oxford friends like Compton Mackenzie, who was editing *The Gramophone Magazine*, and Christopher Stone, who lived in Horsham, Sussex, where Shelley was born.

While he made his living in the capital of Ireland's traditional enemy, he was able to note the customs of the country at close quarters. 'Make no mistake about it,' Tom Kettle had once said to him, 'the English have organisation.'

Gogarty was impressed by the atmosphere he found there.

Here was Freedom visibly being founded, apportioned and assured. The queues outside each theatre witnessed to this order as their humour and their patience witnessed to their goodwill. London is a University with ten million graduates qualified to live and let live.

He noted that the taxi-drivers painted their tyres white each day, even though they would inevitably be coal-black by evening. This was an exercise in citizenship. *England expects every man to invent a duty.* But he deplored the absence of village idiots. Without them, there was no way of knowing who was sane. In the biggest city in the world, there was little time for speculation. The 'metaphysical man' had no place. The English were as fond of gossip as the Irish, but their methods differed.

What constitutes an Englishman's silent strength? He is loath to say or waste a word on an outsider: he wants to keep them all for his Club: he won't let a foreigner in on it.

Presently, Gogarty began to develop nostalgia for Dublin. He began to dream of dinners at Larkey Waldron's, with the great host booming quotations down the table, while:

> Martialled by his genial roar,
> The servants, massed in order, pour;

and ice-cream served between the courses to divide the stomach into two hemispheres, making room for later additions; of saunters round the Green and encounters with genial priests who would discuss anything from the third Book of Rabelais to the fifth Book of the Pentateuch.

What, I ask myself, has Dublin to offer me in place of London? It has neither dignity, majesty, rank nor fashion, yet how I love the old town where every man is a potential idler, poet or friend. I love the old town where sock suspenders are less important than poems, and directions depend on Inns 'up by the Yellow House where Robert Emmet hid, to the Lamb Doyle's'.

A visit to Bristol decided him. The masts of the ships showing through the houses in the middle of the city brought an echo of his own city to him. In February 1924, he closed his English practice and returned to 15 Ely Place in Dublin. As he got off the boat at the North Wall, a sailor approached him: 'Excuse me, Senator,' he said, 'there's a few stanzas in me pocket I'd like you to look over some time.'

He was back in Dublin.

FIFTEEN

B Y a curious chance, Gogarty's first year on his return to Dublin was to bring him the biggest professional awards of his career. Normally, it is fatal for a professional man to absent himself from his profession for any length of time. But Gogarty made more money out of medicine in the years 1924–5 than he had ever made before, or was to make again in the future.

It was an unusually busy year for him. His Senate activities took up a large part of his time. In May, he published his first book of poems, *An Offering of Swans*. The title of the book was inspired by a ceremony which had taken place in March when he presented two swans to the Liffey, as he had vowed to do, when swept along in its icy flood.

He was engaged also, that spring, in the organization of the Taillteann Games. These were intended as a revival of an ancient sporting festival held by King Lugha, in honour of Queen Taillte, at Telltown on the plains of Meath. The competitions were open to athletes of Irish ancestry and it was hoped to attract entries from among the competitors who would be competing that year at the Paris Olympiad in July. Gogarty had been given charge of the committee dealing with the invitations of distinguished visitors of the Taillteann Games. He had decided to ask only 'Worthies'. His definition of a 'Worthy' was a person of personality. He wrote to his friend, Ernest Boyd, an Irish writer living in New York, in March, outlining his plans.

News item. Yeats is Chairman of my Committee for inviting Notables from all parts of the world to Jones' Road, that is to the Taillteann Games in August. As we have decided to ask the Worthies during Horse Show week, we may carry it off. We have old ladies offering large country houses already. I thought of inviting D'Annunzio with Sigmund Freud – 'Attaboy Sigmund' and of starting him on D'Annunzio, but he may go to Yeats. The rest of the Committee is Sir Henry McLaughlin, Sir Simon Maddock and the Marvellous Marquis MacSwiney for foreign correspondence.

In another letter to Lady Leslie, he tells her who the honoured guests are to be.

Mizra Riza Khan, the Persian Prince whose absence from Persia assures his successor of supersession, is one. Brazil sends another: Poland, and we hope D'Annunzio, but Lady Lavery might be carried off – her feet. That is, of course, figuratively speaking.

Chesterton, Compton Mackenzie, Talbot Clifton, Augustus John and the charming Mrs Fleming will be over. Mrs Fleming just for a motor tour. Lutyens and Baring are also Distinguished Visitors.

Lady Conyngham is giving them all lunch at Slane for a visit to Newgrange, which is described as a pre-Christian cemetery, but this would be misleading except to us who know that the suggestion of subsequent Christianity is unfounded.

D'Annunzio was unable to come, but His Royal Highness, Prince Ranjitsinhji, the Indian cricketer, with his secretary, C. B. Fry, were added to the list of guests. The social side of the Games, under Gogarty's expert management, was a great success. A photograph taken during a garden party at Gogarty's house, on Friday, August 6th, shows Lutyens, Compton Mackenzie, Augustus John, James Stephens, G. K. Chesterton and Lennox Robinson, in one group. In such company, brilliance was assured.

Tim Healy's witticisms when he spoke, as Governor-General, at the banquet to welcome the guests, set the tone of the gathering. He was particularly glad to welcome Prince Ranjitsinhji, Tim said, who might have cast a fly on the mighty waters of the Tigris, or the giant expanses of the Euphrates, but had chosen instead the tiny streams in Ballinahinch. (Ranjitsinhji had lately bought Ballinahinch Castle.) Tim's final sentence had a note of earnestness in it:

After the tug of War, let us celebrate the tug of Peace; when our eyes can bear the sunlight of liberty, all of us will join in celebrating a united Ireland.

C. B. Fry's observation on the first day pleased the Dublin public. He commented that the gymnastic display of the Artane Industrial School boys was the best he had seen. From an Englishman who had held the world long-jump record, played football for England and was perhaps the best amateur cricketer of all time, this was notable comment.

Compton Mackenzie remembers it as a *'real* festival'. The guests seldom got to bed before six. Most mornings after the night's celebration, Gogarty led the distinguished guests up the mountains in cars, to watch the sun rise out of the Irish Sea over Howth. Anything could happen in Gogarty's company. One morning, Ranjitsinhji, who was something of a Hellenist, was astonished to hear the butler at the Viceregal Lodge addressing him in Greek. Gogarty had been giving the butler a little private tuition. On another occasion, he played a joke on Augustus John. Compton Mackenzie recalls what happened.

G.K. and I were at the Viceregal Lodge, the old Viceregal Lodge, with the Governor-General. Augustus John, he put up with Dunsany, and there, a typical practical joke, let me say, was played by Gogarty. He told Dunsany that Augustus John was a passionate teetotaller and couldn't bear the thought of liquor in any form. He also told Augustus John, 'now for God's sake, Augustus, don't ask for a drink because it upsets Dunsany; you'll only be there for two or three nights, you'll come and be staying with me then in Ely Place and for goodness' sake don't do this.' All right, this is what happened. Augustus stood it for a bit until finally Dunsany tried to teach him how to play the great Irish harp. This was too much for John without a drink, don't forget, without even the mention of a drink, so he climbed over the wall at Dunsany Park and walked fourteen miles to Dublin.

On the Friday evening of the first week, a musical entertainment for the guests was given at the Theatre Royal. A massed choir sang Gogarty's Taillteann Ode, which had been written at the request of the Irish Government. The music was composed by Louis O'Brien, and Joseph O'Mara, a well-known Irish operatic tenor, sang the solo parts.

The ode was in three parts. The first recalled the ancient contests at Tara.

> Empyrean is the source
> Of indomitable will.
> God the runner to his course
> Holds, and urges on until
> Lips and face of blood are drained,

And the fainting limbs are numb:
Till the heart, by God sustained,
Bravely to the end is come.

Where are they who ran before
Under Tara's wide-eyed steep;
And the chariots that tore
Parallel the ridges deep?
Where are noble man and horse?
Ah, they both have lost the rein,
They have circled in a course
Tara shall not see again!

King Leary welcomes the kings of the South and the West in the second section of the Ode, and their Majesties make suitable reply. In the final section, the poet reminds the athletes that were it not for his song, their feats of courage and endeavour would remain uncommemorated for posterity.

What should follow Sport but Song,
And the victor but renown?
Many men are brave and strong,
But if Courage strive unknown
And no poet make it sweet
With the words that rouse the deed,
Even better were defeat:
Who will men forgotten heed?

Where the blue eye beams with light,
Where there is the open hand,
Where the mood is dark and bright
There is also Ireland.
Welcome, Brothers, and well met
In the Land that bids you hail;
Far apart though we be set,
Gael does not forget the Gael.

In the athletic contests the standard was high. A gratifying number of American athletes from the U.S.A. Olympic team had unearthed Irish ancestries, which enabled them to compete in the competitions at Dublin. Scholz, the American sprinter, actually ran a fifth of a second faster in the Taillteann 220-yards championship than he had returned when winning the Olympic title in

Paris. Osborn, the Olympic high-jump record holder, demonstrated his famous 'Western Roll' in winning his event. LeGendre, the American, who had broken the world long-jump record at Paris, was another competitor. Pickard of Canada, the pole vaulter, and Atkinson of South Africa, the hurdler, were other notable athletes who competed at these Irish Games. Actually, the organizers were not over-scrupulous in interpreting the 'ancestry' rule. At the following Taillteann in 1928, a coal-black negro won the 800 metres, to encouraging shouts of 'Come on Murphy' from cynical Dubliners in the crowd. Boxing, swimming, tennis, golf, yachting, motor racing and archery competitions were also held.

Gogarty had a dual success at the Games. He came third in the archery competition to H. A. Cox and Cecil Baring. This was one of his recently adopted sports. As well, he won the Taillteann gold medal for poetry, for his book *An Offering of Swans*. The week following the Games, Yeats crowned Gogarty with a wreath of bay leaves at a meeting of the Royal Irish Academy, in recognition of his feat in winning the Taillteann poetry medal. Yeats said, at this ceremony:

> The great Victorian poets wrote long poems and touched upon many topics, and though they wrote many beautiful lyrics, these seemed almost an accident, something apart from the ambition of their lives. That was so, too, to an even greater extent with the great Elizabethans and, just as the latter age was followed by the Jacobean with its lyricism, the Victorian was followed by the poetical age in which we live. During the last twenty years, poems have grown very short, and, instead of touching upon many topics, poets have celebrated life at its crisis when it seems caught up with what Patmore calls the integrity of fire.
>
> Irish poets had felt the general movement and, for the last three years, they had suddenly freed themselves from historical prepossession and written only out of themselves. It may prove in the end that they are not the less Irish because not obviously Irish at all. One book seemed at once pre-eminent, *An Offering of Swans* by Dr Gogarty, who, like Henry James, discovered his genius in contemplating with the eyes of a stranger, and so with clear eyes, what seemed most beautiful in the life of England, a beauty of great houses, and this

beauty once seen, he discovered Rome and the nobility that is inseparable from power. In the midst of the Civil War, he created style and music and became a poet. His genius reminds us that God came to Danae in a shower of gold, and yet it can sing finely of death.

Strictly, *An Offering of Swans* was not the first book of poetry that Gogarty published. *Hyperthuleana* had appeared in 1916. There were only five copies of this work printed, part of which was Rabelaisian in quality. In 1919, he published a pamphlet of eight poems called *The Ship* with drawings by Jack Yeats, the poet's brother.

But *An Offering of Swans* was the first book of Gogarty's poems to reach the general public. That the book did make an impression is evident from the fact that, a few years later, two poems from it were included in the revised edition of *The Oxford Book of English Verse* edited by Sir Arthur Quiller-Couch. George Moore was delighted with the poems in *An Offering of Swans*.

I like extremely [he wrote] the poems you sent me. They are the best you have done and they encourage me to believe you have come into your complete talent at last. I had to wait longer.

When the Irish edition of the book appeared in May, published by Cuala Press, John Eglinton wrote in *The Irish Statesman*:

There is a lightness and transparency about Senator Gogarty's lyrics as if they were carven out of compressed air. Senator Gogarty's muse long since sowed its wild oats, haunting the mythical taverns around Parnassus, the taverns once haunted by Villon and Rabelais; but the Senator's muse was never truly dissipated, being rather the artist of a perfect sobriety seeking literary adventures, than a fallen angel of song. How little it was affected, appears by these lyrics, which move with the delight of perfect poetic health as if they never had a headache or a heart-ache to look back on.

Later, A.E., reviewing the English edition of the book, wrote in the same journal:

The wit that used to delight his friends is here carved and polished more delicately and given a soul of bravery or light melancholy.

An Offering of Swans contains eighty-one poems. It is a slim volume. The majority of the poems are short; but the selection exemplifies the different aspects of Gogarty's work – lyrical, classical, metaphysical.

'My Love is Dark', 'Golden Stockings', 'To Maids not to Walk in the Wind', which have been quoted elsewhere in these pages, are representative of his lyrical side. The classical note, however, is the dominant one. 'Non Dolet', 'To Death', 'Dedication', also quoted in earlier chapters, are included. Another poem in the classical mode, unquoted so far, takes its mood from a line of Catullus, 'Sunt apud Infernos tot Milia Formosarum'.

> I, as the Wise Ones held of old,
>   Hold there's an Underworld to this;
> And do not fear to be enrolled
>   In Death's kind metamorphosis.
>
> More wonderful than China's halls
>   To Polo; more than all the West
> That shone through the confining walls
>   When great Magellan made the quest.
>
> Enlarged and free, the wings of Rhyme
>   Cannot outreach its purple air;
> The generations of all Time
>   And all the lovely Dead are there.

Yeats states in his preface to *An Offering of Swans* that it was the atmosphere of English county homes that had enabled Gogarty to escape from himself and 'discover the rhythms of Herrick and Fletcher'. But the poems which echo most, the rhythms of Caroline verse, were written many years before Gogarty's enforced exile among England's stately homes. The English influences in some of his later poems are of a different period than that of Herrick or Fletcher. 'Excommunication', for instance, has a Tennysonian touch.

> Go to the fields of purple and gold;
>   With lovers and young Queens remain
> Blossoms and battlements of old,
>   Far in the background of my brain,
> Rest with them there, but stand apart,
>   Although you equal those who died;

> For no one enters in my heart
> By Death or Love undeified.

The book contains a number of epigrams – the most famous is 'To Petronius Arbiter'.

> Proconsul of Bithynia,
> Who loved to turn the night to day,
> Yet for your ease had more to show
> Than others for their push and go,
> Teach us to save the Spirit's expense,
> And win to Fame through indolence.

Sometimes even among the intimations of decay, the poet replaced the physician in the perception of beauty.

> But I by bed and in the lazar-house
> Where misery the Feast of Life derides
> And Death confuses Autumn with the Spring,
> Can sometimes, though I see not Beauty's brows
> Catch the uncertain syllable that bids
> The blackbird leap from his dark hedge and sing.

'The Old Goose' is interesting intrinsically and because it is written in mock-heroic mood, which was to become a notable characteristic of Gogarty's verse later on. He was to use this style, with great effect, in classical poems like 'Europa and the Bull' and 'Leda and the Swan'. In 'The Old Goose', he imagines a ranging past for this humble farmyard creature:

> Soon you will cross the loam,
> And walk the pathway home
> Before the faint stars come,
>   And seek your stable.
> Your old wild life exchanged
> For comfort: all is changed;
> For rime-white deserts ranged,
>   A white-washed gable!
>
> Oh, have you quite forgot,
> The flights outbreasting thought
> Before this homely lot
>   Half tamed your pinions?

217

The mountains and the stars
Were once your only bars,
And where the north wind soars
    Were your dominions.

The wild geese flying over Ireland have romantic associations
in Irish patriotic literature. Gogarty sees them flying towards the
Hero-Isles, the Irish Valhalla, the Land under the Wave.

Islands that gleam and float
Untouched by voyaging boat,
Withheld but not remote,
    Where wave breaks slowly
Till all the beach is green,
Where the great lords are seen
Who fought and loved a Queen,
    Armed, amorous, and holy.

Easy to put life by
When friend and foe were nigh;
Easy for them to die
    Armed and elated!
And well they died in sooth,
Who found, in fighting, truth,
Before old age had youth
    Repudiated.

The last verse recaptures the theme of the poem, that old age is
redeemed by a 'ranging youth'.

Love life and use it well:
That is the tale they tell,
Who broke it like a shell,
    And won great glory.
But you and I are both
Inglorious in sloth,
Unless our ranging youth
    Redeem our story.

'The Ship' is a simple poem. It formed the title piece of
Gogarty's first little collection of verse. It tells of the longing for
distant, sunny lands, inherent in the northern soul:

A ship from Valparaiso came
 And in the Bay her sails were furled;
She brought the wonder of her name,
 And tidings from a sunnier world.

O you must voyage far if you
 Would sail away from gloom and wet,
And see beneath the Andes blue
 Our white, umbrageous city set.

But I was young and would not go;
 For I believed when I was young
That somehow life in time would show
 All that was ever said or sung.

Over the golden pools of sleep
 She went long since with gilded spars;
Into the night-empurpled deep,
 And traced her legend on the stars.

But she will come for me once more,
 And I shall see that city set,
The mountainous, Pacific shore –
 By God, I half believe it yet!

In his preface to *An Offering of Swans,* Yeats has related how Gogarty rang him up in the Saville Club in London one evening and asked him where he could buy a pair of swans. Yeats was surprised at the request, but made inquiries. Gogarty was having more difficulty obtaining the birds than he had anticipated. He wrote to Shane Leslie in December 1923, explaining how even the simplest of projects can become complicated in Ireland.

> Have you any spare cygnets at Glaslough? [Leslie's residence.] If you have, could you spare me two. The swans Colonel Crighton was to give me were to be given by the King; this I could not accept as I intended them for political purposes, so I am at a loss for birds to present to the Liffey.

Eventually, two swans were secured from Lady Leconfield's lake in Petworth House, Sussex. Gogarty now proposed to fulfil the vow he had made when up to his neck in Liffey water, that he would present swans to the goddess of the river if his life were saved. The presentation ceremony furnished him with a title for his book of poems. He decided to stage the presentation ceremony from the Trinity Boat Club House, opposite the Salmon Weir where he had climbed from the river. T. H. Dagg, who had charge of such matters in the University, readily gave permission.

On March 24th, 1924, after a champagne lunch in the Shelbourne, the party proceeded to the Zoo, where the swans were lodged pending their launching. Mr W. T. Cosgrave, the President of the Irish Free State, W. B. Yeats, Mrs Gogarty, Lennox and Mrs Robinson, and Gogarty's sons, Noll and Dermot, and his daughter, Brenda, were present at the ceremony. A photograph taken at the time shows Yeats and Gogarty striding in the gateway of the Boat House. Yeats's face bears the solemn look he assumed for ceremonious occasions, but Gogarty is bubbling over with zest. It is the mask of a Dubliner on the brink of gesture: about to perpetrate a deed that will pass into the legend of the city, like the extravagances of the 'Bucks' of old. It was to do so, for Dubliners today will tell you, rightly or wrongly, that there were no swans on the Liffey before 1924, and that the flotillas of birds that pass up and down the river nowadays are descendants of Gogarty's pair.

The swans were confined in a wooden box. When the box had been prised open with some difficulty, a problem presented itself. The ceremony had begun but the birds seemed unwilling to emerge of their own accord. Yeats, meanwhile, was chanting some verse of his own. When he was told that the swans would not come out he became perturbed. An unfulfilled vow would have most serious consequences, he thought. But to pull the birds out by the neck might be to strangle them, and to pull them out by any other part of their anatomy, could have dire results for the person engaged.

Eventually, Gogarty solved the problem in typical fashion by delivering a hefty kick to the back of the box, whereupon the swans emerged like torpedoes and sped up the bed of their chosen river. The ceremony was over. It was typical that Mr Cosgrave should have honoured the occasion by his presence. A Dubliner, like Gogarty, he shared his delight in gesture, and was not above taking part in a little myth-making.

For the rest of his life, Gogarty seemed to have a curious attraction for swans. It is said that, on occasions, these birds would come out of the Canal and walk across the road to him.

To commemorate the Liffey ceremony, Gogarty wrote a poem, 'To the Liffey with Swans'. In it, he links two swan-legends of Greek and Gael.

> Keep you these calm and lovely things,
>   And float them on your clearest water;
> For one would not disgrace a King's
>   Transformed beloved and buoyant daughter.
>
> And with her goes this sprightly swan,
>   A bird of more than royal feather,
> With alban beauty clothed upon:
>   O keep them fair and well together!
>
> As fair as was that doubled Bird,
>   By love of Leda so besotten,
> That she was all with wonder stirred,
>   And the Twin Sportsmen were begotten!

The 'doubled Bird' is, of course, Zeus, whose encounter in the form of a swan with Leda resulted in the birth of Castor and Pollux. The 'transformed, beloved and buoyant daughter' is Fionnula, the daughter of Lir, King of Ireland, who was changed by her jealous stepmother into a swan, and condemned to roam around Ireland for nine hundred years.

Professor Giorgio Melchiori in his book *The Whole Mystery of Art* has suggested that the impulse for Yeats's famous sonnet, 'Leda and the Swan', was inspired by the incidents surrounding Gogarty's Liffey adventure. But in his poem 'The Phoenix', written in 1915, Yeats spoke of 'that sprightly girl trodden by a bird'. And a perceptive essay in July 1962 in *The Times Literary Supplement* has established with reasonable certainty that it was from a Greek statue, which he would have seen in London in the 'nineties, that Yeats derived the specific image for his poem. But as is evident from Gogarty's poem, 'Elegy on the Death of the Arch Poet', the Leda legend was a favourite conversational theme between him and Yeats, and the Liffey incident must have led them to explore the fantasies of the tale with renewed interest.

Gogarty had christened the Viceregal Lodge 'Uncle Tim's Cabin', now that Tim Healy was installed there. He had got the post of Governor-General in spite of Griffith's prejudice against him. The latter used to say 'He betrayed Parnell,' but when the matter finally came up for decision, Griffith was no longer a member of the Executive Council. Healy had had powerful backers in England, the chief among them being Lord Beaverbrook. He had started life as the penniless son of a small farmer, and risen to the top of the English Bar and to a position of distinction in the House of Commons. He had a remarkable forensic brain, a superb wit and a voice of deep melodious quality that had made him an outstanding orator at Westminster. Yet for the greater part of his parliamentary career he was a lone figure, without attaching himself to any Party. With a single vicious phrase, he had exploded Parnell's influence in the Irish Party.

In the famous meeting in Room 15, held after divorce proceedings had been commenced against Parnell, Parnell had silenced rumblings of discontent with: 'I am the master of this Party,' delivered in his usual cold-featured manner with the unimpassioned voice of authority.

'Who's the mistress?' Tim Healy had hissed. With this single vicious phrase he had exploded Parnell's influence in the Irish Party.

Later, Healy refused to join the revived Irish Party under John Redmond. In 1916, he condemned with vigour the executions of the leaders of the Rebellion. During the Black-and-Tan War, he had made no secret of his disgust for Castle methods and defended I.R.A. prisoners on capital charges, without fee.

Thus, in the evening of his life, with a rare adroitness, he had captured the job of the King's representative in Ireland, under a Sinn Fein Government.

As a realist, he recognized that his function was to try and bring the old and new society of the country together. For the Anglo-Irish gentry, the Viceregal Lodge had been for generations the centre of their social world. They ruled there with a convention as rigid and an exclusiveness as select as that of the Courts of the Kaiser or the Tsar. Now, with a governor-general installed instead of a viceroy, would Anglo-Irish society mingle with the conglomeration of Free State ministers in top hats and morning suits, officials of the Dublin Corporation, civil servants, professors of the National University, officers of the Free State Army, and others who formed the bulk of those attending State functions at the Viceregal Lodge in the middle 'twenties? What protocol was to be followed? Were the ladies to curtsy to the Governor-General, as he watched them cynically with his dark black eyes in his Rabbi-like face? It was to Healy's credit that he managed to bring the two classes together to the extent that he did, with a minimum of formality and a maximum of common sense. Gogarty was one of his chief adjutants in this achievement. He had a foot in every camp, and there were few people whom he had not some acquaintance with in the different grades of Irish society. Once, Tim deputed him to secure Yeats's attendance at the Horse Show, in a top hat. Yeats had refused at first to support 'this mock Court held by a Babu barrister', but Gogarty got round his objections by reminding him of the Rabelaisian ballads that he might hear sung by the farm girls, churning butter in their milk cans at the Horse Show.

Certain titled Anglo-Irish women like Lady Mayo and the Countess of Fingall, a favourite of King Edward's social circle in pre-war days, set out to make the viceregal functions as pleasant as possible. Lady Lavery came over from London occasionally to act as Vicereine, Tim Healy's wife having died some years before. When distinguished visitors from the Continent or England were in Dublin for some special occasion, such as the Horse Show, Gogarty was usually summoned by Tim to entertain with his stories and conversation.

On this basis of pleasant social intercourse, a gradual mingling of two classes, who had kept apart for centuries, began to take place. Some, at least, of the old animosities were broken down at garden parties held on the viceregal lawns.

But Tim and Oliver were too old hands not to smile in private at the incongruities that occurred, though, in public, they preserved the serious demeanour appropriate to official occasions. During the Taillteann Games, a member of the new ruling classes, with Gaelophile tendencies, arrived at the official banquet clad in a tweed suit with a bow tie in the Irish national colours, green, white and orange. 'Baldy Doody's pig has not died in vain,' Tim whispered to Gogarty, when he saw this walking parody of nationalism coming up the stairs. A sow, with a litter of fourteen, belonging to one Baldy Doody of Skibbereen, had been shot by the Black-and-Tans during the Troubles, and the incident furnished Gogarty with one of his best stories.

Gogarty, referring to the period between the end of the First World War and the signing of the truce, had said of the Viceregal Lodge:

The only thing regal left in the Viceregal Lodge is the vice.

But under Healy's adroit management, he saw it now fulfilling once more a useful function in the evolution of society in the new State.

SIXTEEN

In October 1925, Gogarty went on what was an unusual journey for him – a pilgrimage to Rome, headed by President Cosgrave. Gogarty's friend and admirer, the Most Reverend Dr Fogarty, Bishop of Killaloe, accompanied the group. There is a photograph extant of Gogarty in the forefront of the group of pilgrims, looking remarkably sedate in a morning suit. Frank Flanagan, a fellow pilgrim, remembers that Gogarty would insist on calling a taxi for Irish nuns on the pilgrimage, if he met them walking in the street.

But his irrepressible good spirits broke out on a number of occasions. He reported home:

> His Holiness, the Pope yesterday received The Most Reverend
> Dr Fogarty and the most irreverent Dr Gogarty.

The leading members of the group received medals from His Holiness. When it was found that Gogarty had received the medal intended for President Cosgrave, with mock seriousness, he refused to part with it. 'Do you question the Pope's infallibility?' he asked.

It was typical of Gogarty that he could mingle with a group of pilgrims and make himself a popular member of the party. Bishop Fogarty was a close friend and admirer of Gogarty's; he delighted in his company; his face would crease in laughter and his voice break into involuntary chuckles in anticipation of the fun to follow, as soon as Gogarty entered the room. Mr Cosgrave was another friend, of pious instinct, who was nevertheless susceptible to the wit inherent in Gogartian irreverences.

Gogarty's vitality in these years seemed inexhaustible. He bounded in for lunch one day to meet Will Rogers, the famous American entertainer and wit, spoke continually throughout the meal, then rushed off to his surgery, leaving Rogers breathless with astonishment. 'I have never met such a man,' was Rogers's comment to Frank Flanagan, one of Gogarty's friends.

Gogarty used his lunch periods in between surgical work in the operating theatre and his consulting hours in the afternoon, as an opportunity for social intercourse. Once a week, he gave a lunch at Ely Place to which notable personages who were visiting Ireland at that time were invited. Gene Tunney (the heavyweight boxing champion), Colonel Roosevelt, Anna May Wong, Clarence Darrow, Harold Macmillan, Hugh McDiarmid, Roy Campbell, Sir Ronald Storrs, Charles Kingsford Smith, Jim Mollison, Amy Johnson, Sir Alan Cobham, the Marchioness of Londonderry and Ruth Draper were some of those who came to lunch or tea at Ely Place in this period. At a lunch to Gene Tunney, Gogarty said:

> There was one thing that proved that their guest was Celtic and that was his taste for literature. It showed he had a soul as well as a body. He showed sense by leaving the ring in his heyday, unlike the protagonists in present-day politics.

Gogarty's Friday nights were set aside for regular callers. James Stephens was usually to be found there sitting cross-legged on the sofa, for he was double-jointed. He had been Irish rope-climbing champion. Often he spoke of encounters with centaurs and fauns in the Dublin hills, and few disbelieved him when he spoke in this way: Walter Starkie remembers him as a Dublin Demeter, the half-mortal nursling of Demephon the Goddess of Nature. A.E. would arrive after dinner about eight-thirty p.m. Then, within an hour or so, Yeats would come. A.E. spoke continually till Yeats came, and then would retire into his shell as Yeats held the floor. After Yeats had left Gogarty would sometimes give an impersonation of his departed guest. Yeats knew this was going on, and was not in the least annoyed by it. Another distinguished visitor was not so pleased. As Count John McCormack, the famous tenor, was leaving the hall of Ely Place one night, he remarked to Walter Starkie, 'Gogarty's a wonderful mimic, isn't he?' Starkie replied, 'I'll bet a pound he's mimicking you just now.' They slipped up the stairs again, where Starkie collected his pound; but McCormack was not at all pleased at the impersonation of himself, with which he found Gogarty entertaining the crowd.

Gogarty had invented a little charade of Yeats receiving the Nobel Prize, which was especially entertaining. He would depict the poet receiving the award with lordly disinterest, his head in the air lost in dreams. As soon as he moved away from the audience, however, the poet could be seen examining the cheque with a careful scrutiny to make sure it was made out for the right amount.

This constant round of entertainment made demands on

Gogarty's time. But he was fortunate in that his wife had a flair for household organization and was able to run the many luncheons, teas, and dinners with flawless precision. Gogarty was still in his forties and believed in keeping his body fit by constant physical exercise. For a while, horse-riding absorbed him. He would rise at six o'clock in the morning and ride out on his horse to Sandymount Strand, which is little more than a mile from Ely Place. Once out on the sands, he could gallop to his heart's content in the early morning air, with the scene he loved so well surrounding him: Howth 'amethystine' on the left, and on the right the Golden Spears and Shanagolden, the sweetly-named Dublin hills which he never tired of gazing at, especially when burnished by the light of the morning sun. Replenished by this prospect of beauty, he would ride back to breakfast and then proceed to his operating theatre at the Meath Hospital. In summertime, he would sometimes drive to Portmarnock beach on the other side of the city, eight miles of unflawed silver strand. With a few friends he would run along the sand after his swim before coming back for breakfast. Walter Starkie, Mahaffy's godson, one of the younger Fellows of Trinity, Harry Ericsonn, the Swedish Consul, and André Le Prévost, the French writer (whose pseudonym was André Malvil) were usually his companions on these early morning runs. Starkie was small and inclined towards stoutness, so he had to move his short legs rather faster and exert more energy to keep up with the others. On one occasion, a passer-by took the group to be lunatics from the near-by asylum and surmised that the two taller men were trying to run Starkie off his feet. 'The little fellow is doing well to keep up with them,' was his audible comment.

In January of 1925 Gogarty went to St Moritz for winter sports. There he met his friend, Lady Ribblesdale, who held a record for the Cresta run. Gogarty himself took part in a race down the Cresta, in which his son Noll took second place. He was constantly seeking outlets for his physical energy. As he tired of one activity he would adopt another with renewed enthusiasm, in his ceaseless pursuit of 'movement the ritual and recognition of the Divine nature of our substance, which directs our bodies towards the All-Mover, the PRIMUM MOBILE, whose glory thrills and penetrates the Universe.'

Occasionally before breakfast, Gogarty would sample the

pleasures of sky as well as land. After riding on Sandymount Strand, he would drive to Baldonnel Aerodrome, the headquarters of the army air force, at the foot of the Dublin hills, on the south side of the city. There, he would take off in an army plane and spend a half an hour flying before coming down for breakfast, and out again to his practice at the Meath Hospital.

On his return from England, he had added flying seriously to his list of activities. A friend whom he had met in London, Captain Cyril Unwin, a famous test pilot, had shown him over the works of the Bristol Aircraft Company. Gogarty was fascinated by what he saw, the rows of truncated cones, the shining cylinders, the superbly cut propellers. Like the true creative artist, he was a child of his age. Here were instruments which could provide a pathway to a new and exciting experience. He saw in the inventors who were working in the factory 'the Beaumonts and Fletchers of the air, poets who have not only Muses of fire by which they ascended the highest heaven of invention, but an orchestra of 1,500 men to materialise their dreams'.

It was typical of him that he saw no conflict between the artist and the inventor. For him, the inventor was brother to the poet.

Invention needs the same spark from Heaven, for the man who can bend faith by rhythm, as it does for the man who can transcend the limitations of time and space.

He determined, as soon as he got back to Dublin, to learn more about this exciting sport. He took flying lessons at Baldonnel airport. At that time, the members of the Irish Air Force were a convivial crowd of young men – most of them ex-officers of the Royal Flying Corps. It was a small force, with few officers and fewer planes. One of the pilots, Major Fitzmaurice, had been the first man to make a night flight across the Channel during the First World War. Later, in company with two German airmen, Von Huenfeld and Köhl, he flew the first aeroplane across the Atlantic from East to West. Another friend of Gogarty's in the Irish Air Force was Colonel Charles Russell, a tall, good-looking, white-faced adventurer, with flaming red hair, also a former R.F.C. pilot, who had a keen brain and was a fine raconteur. In such company, Gogarty found himself very much at home. He seems to have had little difficulty in obtaining the use of army planes whenever he wanted to go up for a spin with his officer friends. When I asked someone who was stationed at Baldonnel at the time how this was so, he replied: 'Ah, St John could get anything he wanted. You couldn't refuse him.'

Soon Gogarty began to fly across the Channel to perform operations in London hospitals. He found that the fees paid amply compensated him for the money expended in hiring army planes and, in addition, there was the thrill and interest of the flight. He could save time by flying and yet get back to Dublin the same day, or, at latest, by the midday following.

On one occasion, as Johnny Maher, of the Free State Air Force, was taking him over Howth to London, Gogarty's parachute opened while he was still in the cockpit and almost blew him out into the sea. Eventually, after a rather hazardous crossing, they had to land at Chester, where Gogarty spent the night in the pubs looking for Irish labourers, whom he felt might amuse the two airmen who had flown him over, with their picturesque language, though the language of the labourers could hardly have been more picturesque than Johnny Maher's when he discovered what had happened to Gogarty on the flight over Howth.

In 1928, when a pupil of Rodin offered to do a sculpture of him, Gogarty flew to Paris at four one afternoon, sat for the artist until midnight and left next morning at four-thirty, and was back at ten-thirty ready to receive his patients.

Needless to say, he was enthusiastic about his new hobby and tried to induce his friends to take part in it. Yeats was taken up in an aeroplane and so was A.E. A problem was, would A.E.'s beard have to fit inside or outside his air helmet? Loyally, Gogarty never revealed the precise fate of his friend's whiskers when subjected to the hazards of flying gear. He tried to get Sara Purser to come up but she refused. He felt that flying actually had a health-giving effect on those who took part in it.

No one has advocated flying for its exhilaration effect and the nervous tone it produces. The element of danger is absolutely necessary for this tonic effect. Even though the danger of flying is becoming more and more illusionary every day, I would prescribe it for many kinds of nervous cases, or rather cases of nerves. I am glad to see that women are rushing to learn. Every middle-aged and elderly man should go into the air. The effect is marvellously rejuvenating. And as for that crystallisation with which all people are threatened as they become old, the condition for which Plato advocated travel, what travel is there to be compared with this?

It would not have been Gogarty if his flying activities had not brought him, somehow or other, into the public eye. On one occasion in the 'thirties, he landed and killed a sheep. The event was reported in *The Times*. Writing to Lady Londonderry, Gogarty described what happened. 'I hit an unsaleable sheep. I said "the Government's policy is right". Then I knew I had concussions of the brain.' The government Gogarty was referring to was Mr de Valera's Government, which had just come to power.

On another occasion in September 1928, he and Lady Heath, a well-known woman pilot, set off from Renvyle to Tullabawn Strand, some miles away, to have a swim, and then fly back to Dublin, but they got stuck on soft sand and were unable to take off again. The result was that they had to be rowed back to an island. Gogarty returned to Renvyle with a lobster in each hand, having been received hospitably by the islanders, but Lady Heath stayed on for a few days in one of the cottages, until a new propeller with a fuller pitch could be flown down from Dublin and the plane was able to take off and fly again.

Lady Heath was a famous airwoman. As Mrs Elliott Lynn, she had won many flying trophies, including the Grosvenor Cup. She was also the first woman pilot in Britain to hold a commercial flying licence. A handsome woman of daring and resource, she fitted very well into the loosely constructed, easy-going Irish society of the 'twenties. Gogarty and she were firm friends. In a letter to Harriett Weaver, James Joyce refers to the incident on Tullabawn Strand, having read of it in a local newspaper, but he adds kindly: 'I am glad to see that Buck Mulligan was unhurt,' an indication of the fact that by this time his feelings towards Gogarty had mellowed.

Major-General Emmet Dalton, a close friend of Collins, who was with him when he died and carried his comrade's dead body across the fields to the city of Cork, has related to the author an incident which indicates the extent to which Gogarty mixed his medical practice and outdoor activities at this period. One day, Dalton was suffering from a particularly heavy hang-over. He met Gogarty in Talbot Street, outside Moran's Hotel. Gogarty took one look at him and said: 'What you need, me dear fellow, is a flip.'

Dalton thought that Gogarty meant an egg-flip and weakly allowed himself to be led along to Gogarty's suggested destination. The net result of his agreement to follow out Gogarty's medical advice was that he found himself with Gogarty in a Puss Moth plane, high over Howth, being violently ill and screaming to be let down. However, when they got down after a somewhat bumpy landing, Dalton certainly felt much better. It was then that he noticed that Gogarty was not quite himself either; in fact, he had been in attendance all night on a member of the Earl of Granard's family and had been drinking sherry to keep himself awake on the journey home.

> However [says Dalton], we both felt great after our adventure and Gogarty suggested, as it was now 10.30 in the morning, that we should proceed towards The Lamb Doyle's on the other side of the hills in the Dublin mountains. Having reached this famous pub, we ordered four ponies of stout to cap the cure we had just undergone. It was then that Gogarty produced a typical flourish. *All he had on him was a hundred pound note* – his fee for his attendance at Lord Granard's. However, Lamb Doyle was equal to the occasion and gave Gogarty his change in crisp tenners. We then repaired to the town, fully restored in soul and body.

As a matter of fact, Gogarty was quite a good pilot and was able to do a number of small stunts when he had learnt to fly. He wrote to Montgomery Hyde in 1934, promising to come up for an air display over Ards airport on November 28th. The tone of the letter is rather like a travelling actor advertising his repertoire.

> I'm rather limited in my stunts, but if you see a Moth plane, blue IU, coming from the South, along the west border of Strangford Lough at 4,000 feet, it will be mine. All I can do is to lose height by half a dozen spins, a loop or two, and a landing (this last, I hope, shall not be exceptional).

Oliver Gogarty had a curious gift with engines: while not particularly mechanically minded, he could often achieve by unorthodox methods the same results as a skilled mechanic. Of course, he had a fair knowledge from his experience with motor-cars. In a car, he could often get an engine running in a few seconds, which might have taken a mechanic hours to get into action again.

In America, he took every opportunity he could, when on lecture tours, of flying from place to place. He was enchanted to find, when he was there in 1932, that he could fly from Los Angeles to San Francisco, which is a distance of 400 miles, in just under two hours. This meant going at 200 miles an hour – an enthralling thrill for Gogarty. He was allowed, during these flights – and this speaks well for his skill as a pilot – to take over control even on night flights conducted along a radio beam about 200 yards wide. Below him at intervals of ten miles, red beacons flashed, to indicate a possible landing place in an emergency.

He had great admiration for American aircraft: 'At present,' he wrote to Lady Londonderry, 'America rules the air, and may go on doing so, if the over-weaning confidence of her Admirals does not end in dashing the whole of our civilization against the shores of Japan, and that was their intention last March, in San Francisco.'

On August 16th, 1928, Gogarty proposed the formation of an Irish Aero Club. In fact, this was to be an important date in Irish aviation history. The Irish Aero Club helped to lay the foundations for the formation of the Aer Lingus Company which began operations in 1936. As a commercial airline, Aer Lingus has had a remarkable record and is perhaps the most successful of all the public enterprises undertaken in Ireland since the founding of the State. On the same occasion as he proposed the formation of the Aero Club, Gogarty forecast that Ireland would become a natural stopping-off place when commercial airlines began to operate Atlantic services. In fact, his forecast came true in the period after the Second World War, when Shannon became Europe's No. 1 refuelling centre for Atlantic air traffic.

The Irish Aero Club was largely composed of professional men. It has had an interesting history. One member who owned his own plane was Sir Osmonde Grattan-Esmonde, a member of the Dail and a direct descendant of Henry Grattan. Starting with two Avian planes, the Club eventually acquired a number of machines for the use of its members.

In an essay which appeared in A.E.'s *Irish Statesman* in the 'twenties, Gogarty left an interesting account of his reaction to one of his first flights, made in Bristol, in one of Unwin's aeroplanes. We can see from this description how these ventures into the clouds opened new vistas of the imagination for him.

The engine is already running. We are blown by the slipstream as we climb into the cockpit, which is the portal of the blue sky. The seat is so far down that we are up to our neck and feel secure without a belt as with one. But we put the belt on. It steadies the midriff, and, like that whiskey mentioned by Hollinshead, it prevents 'the belly from wambling the stomach from wurching: it puffeth away all ventosities.' And here is a 'ventosity', a true air adventure! What if we crash! I notice that the young men around us have no time to dally with the idea of death and, anyway, all one wants to face death with, is good company. It is not dying, but flying we are engaged in now. The roar of the engine increases, and increases your assurance. I find that my courage such as it is, is largely a matter of horse-power. If you put your face outside, the little windscreen may blow open or your lips may be blown across your teeth. This is the reason for the telephones. Without them it would be impossible for the pilot to speak to the pupil. The men leaning against the wings and the man who leans on the tail, leave go. The wedges are pulled from under the wheels. Our speed increases. It is growing over 60 miles an hour. The seat which slanted back is level now. Our tail is up. Vibration is intermittent. Now there is none at all. We are flying. The air speed rises to 100 miles per hour. Up we go, climbing almost vertically, as few machines can climb. The air speed lessens the more vertical we are. But now another indicator tells us that we are 2,500 feet above the earth, 'the deck' the young men call it, the same young men who christened the cockpit with its array of instruments 'the office' – young men remembering, perhaps, the sanctum of some rheumatic uncle, merchant or stockbroker with its barometer, thermometer and clocks. But this 'office' is a magic room, your relations to the sides of which have but little to do with your relations to the world outside. You may be upside down and you would hardly notice it. Presently the floor seems to be surging upwards. Our head bends forwards towards our knees. 'Put your head back,' says the

telephone. And on putting it back we see two horizons simultaneously. What phenomenon is this? We are upside down.
We are looping the loop. There is a slight vibration again. It
is our own airy wake we are in; we have struck our own slipstream. A proof of how perfectly the pilot can loop. We are
climbing again – 3,000 feet, 3,500 feet now. 'You have control,' says the telephone. Good Lord! *I* have control! Steady!
Perhaps it would be as well to begin with a little self-control.
Steady now, O son of Daedalus! Let me see! That cross-bar
at my heels is the rudder – dual control. This black, rubber-
covered, vertical lever is 'the stick' – also dual control. We
remember fragments of conversation. 'If you put too much
rudder without bank you will get into a flat spin.' 'If you
give her too much bank without rudder her nose will come
down.' But the machine seems to be flying all right. Unfortunately, the pilot knows that it flies automatically, otherwise
he might give me credit ... I really must do something to ...
make it wobble even. That brown canal down there with the
waves like those in Botticelli's Birth of Venus is the Bristol
Channel. 'Look at your left wing.' Ah, yes, it is dropping.
I lean my thumb ever so gently against the tremulous 'stick'.
'You are flying level now.' So I had control even though I
didn't do much with it.

No silence on earth is equal to it. It falls on the spirit softer
than sleep. I can understand the trance that fell on Aucassin,
though he was in mid-battle, a trance which made him
oblivious of danger, in which he became lost to everything
but love.

Even from that, at this altitude, there is peace. Here, I may
take mine ease in mine ether. This is better than the Immense
Void in the Zodiac which the Chinese found so repellent, but
in which I thought of sojourning after death for the sake of
a little privacy. It lies between the Great Splendour and the
Fire of the Phoenix, but up here one can 'achieve the Term'
and live in Nirvana just as well without the absenteeism of
death. *Si quis piorum animum locus*, I have found it, this must be
it, the place for pious souls. Here the spirit rests like the
younger Julia in her bath on whom Ovid spied:

> 'She lay at length like an immortal soul
> In endless bliss in blest Elysium.'

When Professor Mario Rossi visited Gogarty in 1933, at Renvyle, he saw him as a Renaissance prince, the great host, the all-round man – aviator, surgeon, poet, conversationalist, senator, playwright. After he had written this description of Gogarty in a book about Ireland, the professor received a typical letter from him: He was pleased, Gogarty said, to have this compliment paid to him. But alas, he could not induce his bank manager to consider him in the same princely context.

SEVENTEEN

O^N December 12th, 1922, the new Irish Parliament assembled for the first time. The Senate and the Dail met in Leinster House, formerly the palace of the Dukes of Leinster.

Gogarty had been nominated a member of the Senate by President Cosgrave. There were twenty-nine other nominees out of a total membership of sixty. Among these nominees of the government were four earls, one marquis, one peer and three baronets. The most notable were the Earl of Dunraven, Sir Thomas Grattan-Esmonde, Bt., a direct descendant of Henry Grattan, General Sir Bryan Mahon, who commanded the British forces in Ireland from 1917 until 1919, Sir Horace Plunkett and Lord Granard, the Master of the King's Horse. Andrew Jameson, former chairman of the Unionist Party, was a member; so was Lord Glenavy, a prominent Southern Unionist who had supported Carson.

The appointment of landed gentry and Unionist senators had been provided for in an assurance given by Arthur Griffith to the British Government during the Treaty negotiations that the minority would have a share in the government of the new State. In fact, the arrangement turned out to be an excellent one. Some of the Government nominees were owners of big industrial concerns in Ireland. Others had had experience of administration in public affairs under British rule. They understood the machinery of legislation. Their background proved invaluable to the new Free State Cabinet who had been thrust straight into the responsibilities of office, with hardly any previous experience of executive administration.

The main function of the first Senate was reviewing Bills placed before it by the Lower House. The Senate had a delaying power of 270 days; after that, a Bill became law nine months after its initiation in the Dail. The Senate could also initiate its own Bills. How far the Senate influenced the course of affairs in the young state is indicated by the fact that, during the first three years of their existence, the Senate considered 130 Bills and amended one-third of those submitted to them. Of the 500 amendments, all but a dozen were accepted by the Dail.

The first Free State Senate has been accused of being reactionary. In fact, it was the Unionist element in the Senate which fought most fiercely for the preservation of fundamental democratic rights. When Kevin O'Higgins tried to introduce a somewhat extreme Public Safety Bill in June 1923, it went back to the Lower House, despite protests on his part, with fourteen amendments.

In retrospect, and seen against the backgrounds of the emergence of other new states in this century, the first Free State Senate was a unique experiment. Here was a Left-Wing Party, come to power on the tide of a revolutionary movement, handing over a share in the government to those whom they had dispossessed. The Southern Unionists, too, must take credit for the adjustments which they made. They were asked to collaborate with a class who, twenty years before, they could not have considered in their wildest dreams as a governing elite. That each side collaborated so loyally with the other is a tribute to the common sense of both.

Donal O'Sullivan, who was Clerk of the Senate, a Catholic and a Nationalist, has written:

> The principal achievement of the Senate lay in the proof it afforded, that Nationalists and Unionists could work harmoniously together in Parliament for the good of their common Country. The Unionists unreservedly accepted the new order and I never found that they held corporate views which ran counter to the national interest. I never knew one who was not, in the most genuine sense, a lover of Ireland, or who regarded Ireland as other than his own country.

All this, in a very particular way, fulfilled the dream of Yeats and A.E., that the two classes in Ireland would some time fuse into a 'new Nation'. Yeats, indeed, wrote about this time, on his favourite theme: 'Preserve that which is living; help the two Irelands, Gaelic Ireland and Anglo-Ireland, so to unite that neither shall shed its pride.' Yeats himself had been made a senator largely through Gogarty's efforts on his behalf. A.E. had also been offered the honour but according to the President's emissary he retired to consult his gods: when however he came back, the emissary, unimpressed by what he considered to be the seer's manœuvres, had returned to the Executive with a negative

237

reply. When he learnt that his efforts on Yeats's behalf were successful, Gogarty rushed along to 82 Merrion Square to let the poet know the good news. Finding neither Yeats nor Mrs Yeats at home, Gogarty simply wrote in chalk on the door: 'Senator W. B. Yeats'.

This was the first intimation the poet had of the honour conferred upon him. Later, Gogarty confided to Yeats that what had turned the Committee in his favour was that many years before he had been a member of the I.R.B., the secret physical force organization that had backed the rising and had played an important part in the Anglo-Irish War. When Mrs Yeats heard this, she remarked: 'That's one secret he kept from me.'

In January 1923, Lord Glenavy was elected chairman of the Senate. A former Lord Chief Justice of Ireland, his forensic experience and knowledge of procedure were to prove invaluable to the body over which he presided for the next six years. After his election, Gogarty congratulated the chairman on electing to stay with his countrymen in the Southern Parliament, while Glenavy's former colleague, Carson:

> that sink of acidity whom Belfast owes a grudge for not supporting in Dublin, and whose spiritual life has been exaggerated by a chronic attack of mental gallstones, has used the enemies of Ireland as a springboard and is now safely deposited on the English Woolsack.

Though this may be said to be fairly typical Gogarty, it was not typical at all of his utterances in the Senate. Two Free State Cabinet Ministers have spoken to the biographer in the highest terms of Gogarty's contribution to the working of the Upper House in its early years. His long association with Sinn Fein and his acquaintance with Griffith's plans for a free Ireland, had made Gogarty keenly aware of many of the problems that confronted the new State. Even before the Senate was constituted, he had begun publicizing one of Griffith's favourite policies, the re-afforestation of Ireland.

During his term in the Senate, whenever he got an opportunity, he would turn to this theme. In March 1926, during a debate on taxation, he managed to make afforestation relevant by suggesting that if the demand on public funds became too great, trees might be grown on a commercial basis in the congested districts.

Gogarty was also a loyal supporter of the Shannon Scheme. This project, for rural electrification by means of a hydro-electric plant on the Shannon, was received with scepticism by the public and met with scornful opposition in the newspapers. The scheme turned out, in fact, to be a complete success.

Some of Gogarty's proposals in the Senate were remarkably far-seeing, even prophetic. The trend in present-day transport development in Ireland has been towards an increase in road traffic and a decline in rail transport. In March 1926, speaking to a Road Maintenance Bill, Gogarty said that:

> I see a rivalry between road and railway, we have a dying industry in railway and a growing form of traffic on the roads, but the roads at present are inadequate for it.

He advocated a mercantile marine for Ireland in March 1926. Fourteen years later, the war forced the establishment of such an organization on the Government. Today, there is a small, but flourishing, merchant navy operating under the Irish flag.

He never forgot the frightful horror of the Dublin slums. At every opportunity, he reminded the Senate of the housing conditions under which a large percentage of the working-class people were living. Foreseeing that the advance in motor transport would provide easy access to the green fields just outside the city, he advocated building working-class dwellings in such areas as Killester, Ticknock and Dundrum.

When the housing projects began in the late 'thirties, this was the precise policy which was followed out. Speaking on the second stage of the Housing Bill, on November 8th, 1928, Gogarty said:

> I have seen a house eight feet below the level of the road, and which you could not distinguish from a manure heap. I asked why it was not condemned and I was told it was condemned by an inspector but that such houses must continue to exist as men could not be put out on the mountain-side. The labourer is the cause of the slum problem in Dublin. One thing that could be controlled by the Labour Party is the auctionings of labour on the quays. That you have on the quays three times as many men as you can get employment for, is one of the causes of the slum problem. As long as the old filthy houses are there waiting for new tenants, the slum

problem will continue. The tenement houses that are unfit to live in should not be allowed to be occupied again after they have been emptied. The health condition in Dublin is low. It is not as healthy as some of the cities in Great Britain according to the death-rate returns. Money is wasted in the attempt to cure tuberculosis. If the money were spent on providing housing for the dwellers, better results would be obtained. If you got a case of tuberculosis in an Irish village, that victim is removed and put into a windy house in some other place in order to try and effect a cure ... Some of the slum areas in Dublin, like Summerhill, are a disgrace to civilization and for that you cannot definitely bring the blame home to anyone's door. *Owing to the extraordinary use of modern transport, satellite towns could easily be built up around Dublin.*

His enthusiasm for the 'satellite towns' broke out in his verse:

> Break down the tenement
> Walls that surround them;
> Lead out from festering
> Lane and back garden
> The heirs to the Kingdom,
> To sunlight, to highland,
> To winds blowing over
> Greenfields; and restore to
> The sons of a city,
> By seafarers founded,
> The sight of white clouds on
> An open horizon ...
>
> Build not in lanes,
> Where the thought of an angel
> Is one with a tombstone;
> But out where Raheny
> Gives on to Howth Head
> And the winds from Portmarnock;
> Or build where Dundrum,
> With its foot set in granite,
> Begins the long climb
> To the hill which O'Donnell
> Crossed ages ago
> In his flight from the city.

When the occasion demanded it, Gogarty could deliver cutting remarks in the Senate. Of a proposal to close the public houses on St Patrick's Day, he said: 'I put myself in the position of St Patrick. What would he say to it? When he visited Ireland, there was no word in the Irish language to express sobriety.'

He had no love for the legal profession. Perhaps he had suffered from it. During the debate on the 1924 Courts of Justice Act, he recalled the position under British rule, that preference at the Bar depended largely on Court patronage. 'At that time, the legal profession was able to trim its sails in a manner creditable to Sir Thomas Lipton's skipper, whenever there was talk of a new Lord Lieutenant.'

On another occasion, criticizing the rather vague phrasing in Article 30 of the Constitution, which provided that 'Senators shall be nominated if, by reason of their achievements or special qualifications, they represent important aspects of the Nation's life.' Gogarty remarked: 'A man with St Vitus' Dance might be said to represent a separate and salient movement in the life of the country.'

Gogarty was regarded by the Free State Cabinet as one of their strong men in the Senate. He proposed the introduction of two Public Safety Bills, giving the Government peremptory power to deal with armed terrorists, the first in 1926 and the second on August 10th, 1927, after the murder of Kevin O'Higgins.

O'Higgins was the iron man of the Free State Cabinet. Under the shrewd leadership of W. T. Cosgrave, who was able to curb his occasional impetuosities, he had emerged in a few years as a minister with statesmanlike vision. He was Cato-like in his detachment from the emotions of the mob. Yet there was no doctrine to which he clung more closely than that of the right of the people to have their will given effect to by the Government. Behind his outer mask, there was a passionate and sensitive temperament; yet he never allowed sentiment to influence his public actions. Regarded by some as having authoritarian tendencies, he was, in fact, a true democrat: he recognized the right of the people to do wrong. In many ways he was the inheritor of Griffith's mantle. He had plans to revive Griffith's theory of the dual monarchy, making it possible for Ulster to find a rapprochement with the Free State. His outstanding contribution to international politics was at the Imperial Conference in 1926, where he was largely responsible for the drafting of the Statute of Westminster. This Act, which took effect in 1931, makes it possible for Dominion parliaments to enact their own laws independent of the Imperial Parliament, and is the keystone in the subsequent evolution of Commonwealth relations.

'We saw,' says Senator Jameson, after O'Higgins's death, 'his great moral bravery and we recognised above all things that what he said he would do, he would do, no matter what it cost when it came to the doing.'

He met his death in a fashion that, even thirty-five years afterwards, is abhorrent for Irishmen to recall. He was shot in the back by five men on his way to Mass. Churchill, who described O'Higgins as 'a figure from the Antique, cast in bronze,' was later to say to a Free State Minister: 'The nation which will not bring to boot the murderers of a man of O'Higgins' calibre is not worthy of its status.'

Gogarty had no compunction in proposing the Public Safety Bill after O'Higgins's death, although, four years earlier, he himself had nearly been the victim of a similar plot by armed assassins. On August 12th, two days after the murder, speaking in the debate on the Public Safety Bill, he said:

> It comes shortly to this: that clemency where it is not required, as in this instance, is conspiracy; and the sooner that the Bill is made law, the sooner the enemies who are now in line with 'Buckshot Foster' and 'Bloody Balfour', and who are trying to deprive people of their rights, will be controlled.

In 1929, two Bills came before the Senate, which dealt with the censorship of films and books. At the outset, Gogarty does not seem to have opposed the censorship of books with much force. He felt that censorship might lend strength to authorship, by keeping writers who relied on sex for their sales out of competition with true creative authors. But as the Bill progressed, he saw that it might provide an opportunity for people to exploit 'a lay vocation at the expense of their neighbours' and would lead to the situation of eighteenth-century Scotland: 'a Holy Willie in every Parish'. He therefore turned against its provisions. His last fling at the Bill was:

> It is high time the people of this country found some other way of loving God, than by hating women.

In fact, the Censorship Board was to take the pattern which most liberal-minded people prophesied at the time that it would. A few cranks secured a monopoly of the Board and almost every notable contemporary author, including Gogarty, was at one time or another included in its list of 'banned' books. Reconstituted today, it is operating with good sense and with regard to the explicit provisions of the Act itself, which had been grossly misinterpreted by the predecessors of the present Board.

Gogarty was in favour of film censorship for an unusual reason. He felt that talking films, with their flow of Americanisms, would corrupt the spoken English of the younger generation; he objected also to 'Christ being made a colleague of Charlie Chaplin' – a reference to a recent Hollywood film on the life of Christ.

One of his privileges as senator was that he was able to propose votes of congratulations to Irish citizens who had made outstanding contributions to the nation. In November 1923, he proposed a vote of congratulation to Yeats who had been awarded the Nobel Prize for Literature.

> What is the meaning of outstanding names in the history of civilization? The meaning is that it is by such men as they, that our civilization is assessed. Our civilization will be assessed on the name of Senator Yeats. Coming at a time when there was a regular wave of destruction, hatred of beauty, a crushing out of perfection and blindness to the national ideal in this country, it was a very happy and welcome thing.

After Commandant Fitzmaurice had made the first successful East–West flight across the Atlantic, Gogarty, in the course of proposing a vote of congratulations in the Senate, said:

> The honours in this country's gift are limited. Major Fitzmaurice cannot be made by our country a colleague of that coloured king, Sir Ofori Atta, or be given a seat in the House of Lords with Lord Terrington, or be given a title like Sir Alfred Mond, but he can be noticed by the Seanad, and it should be put on record that the Seanad of Ireland did for an Irishman what the Senate of France did for the two people who fell into the Atlantic.

In the first decade of the Senate's history, Gogarty took his political duties seriously. Beside the two Free State ministers mentioned above, other members of the Senate, including Senator O'Farrell, one of the Labour members in opposition to the Cumann na nGaedheal, have spoken of his contributions as being noteworthy and worth while. When the Cumann na nGaedheal Government fell from power in 1931, Gogarty's interest in public affairs underwent a gradual decline, the reasons for which we shall see in the next chapter.

In the elections of March 1932, the Cumann na nGaedheal Party were defeated and Mr de Valera's Party came to power. Mr de Valera had broken with the physical force movement in 1924–5 and formed a new organization called Fianna Fail, which, translated into English, means 'Soldiers of Destiny'. Fianna Fail proposed to enter the Dail and to abolish certain institutions which Mr de Valera felt resulted from 'the paralysing dilemma of the Treaty'.

One obstacle was the oath of allegiance which Mr de Valera declared was a bar to any Republican accepting the authority of the Dail. Two years later, he appears to have changed his mind for, after the Elections of 1926, he and his Party entered the Dail despite the fact that the oath of allegiance was still in existence. Mr de Valera explained his action by stating that: 'I signed the Oath the same way as I sign an autograph for a newspaper.'

The Fianna Fail Party had a brilliant organizer in Sean Lemass and their election to government was inevitable at some stage. The country had had ten years of Cumann na nGaedheal government. There had been a record of outstanding achievement during that period but a popular vote will normally swing away from the party in power, over a period of years, and there had been some serious mistakes by certain Cumann na nGaedheal Cabinet Ministers in the years preceding the election, which hastened the change in government.

When he formed his Cabinet after the general election, Mr de Valera proposed to abolish the oath of allegiance, the right of appeal to the Privy Council, the post of Governor-General, the Senate and, finally, to withhold payment of the land annuities to England. He regarded these institutions and obligations as survivals of the British connection and, therefore, repugnant to the majority of the people. In this surmise, he was probably right. Cumann na nGaedheal, on the other hand, followed the policy of

Griffith and O'Higgins; though they had no inherent love for British institutions, they felt that these provided a bridge between north and south for an eventual settlement with the separated Ulster counties. It has been said that Mr Cosgrave seemed more enthusiastic for the retention of the oath than the British Government themselves were. If this was so, it was for the reasons given above.

Gogarty regarded Mr de Valera as responsible for the civil war and considered his coming to power as a tragedy for the nation. It cannot be denied that some of Gogarty's opposition to Mr de Valera was activated by personal bitterness. He could never obliterate from his memory the death of Collins and Griffith. He saw in Mr de Valera the man who had associated himself with the attempt to destroy the Free State Parliament by armed force and who was now taking his place as Prime Minister in that very Parliament. He watched him remove, one by one, articles of the Treaty, empowered to do so by the provisions of the Statute of Westminster, which owed its inception to the statesmanship of the murdered Kevin O'Higgins. He feared that Mr de Valera's Government would make use of the physical force movement to suppress legitimate democratic opposition by Mr Cosgrave's Party. In actual fact, this matter was to work itself out. Mr de Valera allowed the I.R.A. latitude to harass the opposition, until he found that they had become a threat to his own party. Then he outlawed them. In the meantime, Cumann na nGaedheal had replied by forming an organization called the 'Blueshirts', which showed definite Fascist tendencies, until they, too, were outlawed in 1935.

Speaking on the Removal of the Oath Bill in May 1933, Gogarty voiced his fears on the consequences which the successful passage of this Bill through Parliament might have.

My view as regards the Oath is shortly this: I uphold it because I took it ...

I have not had sufficient evidence that would allow me to think that the Fianna Fail idea of freedom is sufficiently definite and liberal to justify this nation in separating itself from *five* other nations who have the Anglo-Saxon idea of freedom. In plain words, the Irish idea of freedom is not sufficiently generous or free. Until we arrive at a worthy idea

of liberty, let us not lose sight of the English criterion ...
The Oath means loyalty to the Commonwealth and that
really means that the Oath is the ticket to the world's best
Co-operative Store ...

I have been brought up in the ordinary traditions of
Nationality. I cannot flatter myself that posterity looking back
may say 'Why did those fellows betray their country? The
Oath was removed but why did they not vote to get rid of
it?' The reasonable answer is, we took the Oath and stand
for our country's honour. (However foolish we may yet
appear.) As a countryman of Shane the Proud, I do not want
to come sidling in here, unable to hold up my head because
of broken troths.

Mr de Valera's next step was to refuse to pay the land annuities
to the British Government. The payment of these annuities was
provided for in Clause 4 of the Treaty. Under the Wyndham Act
of 1904, Irish farmers could buy land outright from the Government which had been purchased by the Government from land-
lords; the farmers were to repay the purchase price over a period
of years. Mr de Valera's Government argued that, because the
Irish nation had been grossly overtaxed since the Act of Union,
these payments were not obligatory. The British Government replied by putting a tax on Irish export goods, one of the effects of
which was to ruin the Irish cattle trade with England, worth at
that time to the Irish agricultural community over £32,000,000
a year. The Irish Government rather weakly countered by putting
a similar tax on British imports. In order to do this, a Bill named
the Emergency Imposition of Duties Bill had to be introduced in
the Dail in 1932. Thus began the 'Economic War' between
England and Ireland, which was to last for six years. When the
Bill came before the Senate, introduced by Mr de Valera, Gogarty
unleashed the full force of his sarcasm on the Fianna Fail leader.

Never in my life have I heard such an utterance from any
responsible person as I have just listened to from the President. It was like a voice from a mathematical madhouse, from
some algebraical world of minus values where everything is
upside down and all the quantities are negatives. It would be
tolerable if it remained in its dimension, but it is terrible when
such dreams overflow into life.

246

He solemnly suggests that this country, with all its poverty, would be better if it were poorer still. He would cure its poverty and feed its hungry on other citizens' butter and beef and by the loss of a market worth £32,000,000 a year.

It is like the proposal to teach a crew swimming by scuttling the ship: or anticipating a ford by plunging into the morass.

By this Bill a man may be prevented from taking a holiday out of Ireland by this Mussolini of Miseries. This is a specimen of how a Republican interprets Freedom ...

I do not often make suggestions and up to this I have not been asked to advise His Holiness; but if he is ever thinking of giving titular honours to our President, he could call him not inappropriately 'The Prince of Denmark', for he is as hurling-worded and as overwhelmed as Hamlet, and he has done more for the Danish market and the prosperity of Denmark than the royal family thereof.

Instead of seizing the opportunity of plenty, he, like a fanatical edition of St Francis, is to wed his Lady Poverty – by proxy, of course – while we, who are hard set enough to live, are to tighten our belts. This sixpenny Savonarola, in a world of Woolworths, invites the nation deliberately to choose poverty, which he promised in his election confidence trick to prevent: there will be food for all from the unsaleable property of other Irishmen. Already they say in Clare that the blacksmiths are shoeing the cattle so that they may gallop round the fairs on the look out for a purchaser.

To be consistent the potato, introduced by Raleigh, should be extradited and smoking taxed as a foreign game ...

Therefore, I tell you to have a care, President de Valera, lest your silhouette may come to be regarded as the most sinister which ever darkened the light in genial Ireland and that it may not be without ominous significance that, during the election, your name was written on the dead walls and roofless ruins of this, our Country.

It is fair to say that, though the 'economic war' seriously disrupted the Irish economy, and is estimated to have cost the country £300,000,000, Mr de Valera secured an astonishingly good settlement in Ireland's favour in 1938 when he compounded the annuity debt for £10,000,000 and secured the evacuation of the three Irish ports still in the hands of the British navy. But it was impossible for anyone, in 1933, to have foreseen that imperial affairs would have fallen under such a benign administration as they did during Mr Chamberlain's premiership, from 1937 until 1940.

In 1934, Mr de Valera set about abolishing the university representation in the Dail. He could hardly claim that this was a legacy of British rule; there is a certain amount of strength in his opponents' argument, that it was simply a manœuvre to get rid of six seats, three from Trinity, three from the National University, which were unlikely to favour Fianna Fail when it came to voting on a Party issue. The argument in favour of abolition was that it gave a section of the electorate two votes and was, therefore, undemocratic. But in a parliament constructed as the Irish one was at that period, members with a university background were few and far between. The university members could make a real contribution to such a body. The Senate debate on the University Bill was on a particularly low level as the arguments in favour of abolition were generally weak and ill-considered. One Government nominee actually went so far as to suggest that the universities had contributed nothing to the movement for Irish freedom. Gogarty was able to counter this by citing the names of Wolfe Tone, Robert Emmet, Thomas Davis and Swift, all Trinity men, and then threw in, for good measure, the name of Hugh O'Neill, the rebel Earl of Tyrone, who had been at Oxford. He might have added, had he wished, the name of Padraic Pearse, the leader of the 1916 insurrection, who was a graduate of the Royal University. Gogarty regarded the motion as inspired by 'the worship of mud which is beginning to be popular in Ireland' and saw in it a mean attempt to conciliate the proletarian element among the electorate.

A new curse is come upon Ireland – one of the most sinister things that has ever happened to our country. When this country was handed its freedom, can it not be said that the only use it could make of it was to caricature the Irish character more than any stage Irishman caricatured him and to make idiotic mountebanks of the people? This is the real curse: that Irishmen should accept as their portrait or as

248

their image and likeness the poor specimen that the Government is only capable of creating. To every decent Irishman there comes a crisis in his life: there comes a moment of misgiving, a moment of self-contempt, and this is what engenders it, when he is casting out from himself that unworthy impression of an Irishman to which he has been forced subconsciously to submit.

We are all suffering from this most outrageous caricature, from the most infernal image of stage Irishman ever invented, a monstrosity left to a republican government to nourish. Since the outrage on Shakespeare caused by that bust in Stratford-on-Avon where you have him represented as a butcher-faced burgess, whereas he must have looked like Sir Philip Sidney, or Shelley, there has been no greater caricature than this caricature of the native so-called patriot raised up for worship by the native so-called republican government.

Let us examine the character and figure of this 'patriot' that the Government is endeavouring to erect. It is a figment of some vague indigenous idiot found in a bog like that 'old prophecy' imagined as perpetually aggrieved, perpetually pitiable, perpetually a pauper, and what is worse, full of self-pity.

The one detached vote that could be considered disinterested was the University vote. In the University, you do not get any slogans. You are taught not to lose your head, or to confuse emotions with arguments. You get a chance of seeing what has occurred, in given circumstances, in human history ... This is the last country in the world that should get rid of the vote in the Universities.

In March 1934, Mr de Valera introduced in the Dail his Bill for the abolition of the Senate. It had proved a stumbling block to him in his efforts to extricate the country from 'the paralysing dilemma of the Treaty'.

But its abolition would mean the disappearance from public life of men of authority and position in the community. The Senate was also a valuable life-line between the Unionist landowning class in Ulster and those who had accepted the Free State jurisdiction in the South; but Mr de Valera was implacable – the Senate must be abolished. It was during the last two years of the

Senate's existence that Gogarty really let himself go. Now that he knew the Upper House was doomed, he allowed all his talent for wit and irony to take control. Perhaps he felt that the dignity of the Senate was undermined by the insult offered to it and the only way of reaching the popular ear was by satire and jibe. He Mcame, during this period, according to General Richard beulcahy, a former Cumann na nGaedheal minister, 'a type of Jack Point, speaking the truth in mocking jests,' but with an element of sadness also.

On January 16th, 1936, Gogarty unleashed a ferocious attack on Mr de Valera, in the final stages of the Senate Abolition Bill, which left the Fianna Fail leader white with anger. In fact, the biographer learnt later from someone who was close to Mr de Valera on that day that he stumbled on a step as he left the Senate, so much had his concentration been upset by Gogarty's speech.

Spurred by the ridiculous nature of the proceedings, a Senate called upon to debate its own dissolution, Gogarty began after Senator Quirke, a Fianna Fail representative, had finished his speech.

DR GOGARTY. It is extraordinary that the last Senator thought it worth his while to join the House last December 12 months with a rope around his neck. I wondered why the President did not attend in the House when such a vital question was under discussion. I put it down to peevishness and megalomania, but I find now that he has got such an excellent subaltern in Senator Quirke, one of the few people who put into practice the unicameral or one-Chamber system of government, that there is no necessity for the President to attend while Senator Quirke is here as an exponent of one-Chamber Government, as this shows:

'*July* 11, 1935   *Seanad Eireann*
'To all whom it may concern:
'Those wishing to obtain interviews with me are hereby notified that no further interviews will be granted at Ballinard Castle. I will attend as usual for such purposes at the Denis Lacey Club, Clonmel, on the first Saturday of each month and at Leinster House in the mid-week. All other matters must be dealt with through the post.
'(signed) BILL QUIRKE'

Now we have not even a hope for a Second Chamber. Ballinard Castle is banged and bolted in the face of democracy and Senator Bill Quirke will only see them in the Seanad. He lamented that Senator MacLaughlin dealt with Omar Khayyam, talking about 'going out through the same door as in I went'. He took very good care to go out through another door in 1916, under Lord Wimborne's Lieutenancy, when he gave a pedigree bitch to a soldiers' and sailors' jumble sale, held March 21, 1916, the year of the Rising, when his patriotism was elastic enough to allow him to be on both sides:

' ... under the patronage of His Excellency the Lord Lieutenant of Ireland, in the Military Barracks, Fethard, in aid of the 18th R.I. Regiment Prisoners of War and Red Cross Association the donors of the miscellaneous gifts included William Quirke (now Senator); a greyhound bitch (pedigree at sale).'

I hope that for the jumble sale for the out-of-work Senators he will give us a pedigree dog. The President was stated to be busy, by his new lieutenant. I hope that new lieutenant will have as many rewards as Senator Connolly, now that he is in the Front Bench.

Senator Connolly described the President as the most loved statesman ever in the country, and Senator Quirke told us that hundreds of thousands of people were unanimous for him. What is the truth? What is the fact? He has got the biggest guard since Lynchehaun.

[Lynchehaun was a notorious criminal and escapee in Fenian times.]

MR QUIRKE. With regard to the pedigree bitch referred to by Senator Gogarty in my absence, I would like to explain that the progeny of that bitch turned out to be very illustrious. Some of them are not very far away from here and will be available for the jumble sale after the abolition of the Seanad.

DR GOGARTY. If you could cross your running dog with a calf, the progeny could sprint over the border for a fair with a

251

fair price. The popular President has the strongest body-guard that any man in this country had, except Lynche-haun, and I mention Lynchehaun because he turned on the hand that fed him and put his benefactor on a hot seat. History repeats itself and we are at a moment in Irish history.

PADRAIC O'MAILLE. Is it a proper illustration to give to compare the President of the State to a criminal?

DR GOGARTY. I have the greatest pleasure in withdrawing any comparison between the criminal Lynchehaun and President de Valera. I was only comparing the strength of their bodyguards, but I will alter it and say that the President is the greatest national fiasco since Jem Roche.

[Jem Roche was knocked out in 88 seconds in a world heavyweight title bout in Dublin in 1908.]

Ireland is again in the market place. It is again up for purchase. It was bought once by Castlereagh who cut his country's throat and then cut his own. I trust that when the President has abolished the warders from the mental home – in other words, when the Seanad is abolished – Senator Barniville and myself will render first aid in case of a repetition of any such lamentable attempt. Senator O'Neill is a charming person to interrupt. It reminds me that after 700 years of trying to break the fortress in which Dark Rosaleen was presumed to be imprisoned, it was opened in the year 1922 and what emerged? De Valera, an elongated Larry O'Neill.

President de Valera, who could not walk down Gloucester Street since coal became 2s. 6d. a sack, was raised into power on three betrayals. He betrayed the I.R.A., many of whom had assisted in putting him into power. Some of them are in Arbour Hill, where probably some of his supporters in this House will find themselves eventually.

President de Valera, as I say, rose into power on the betrayal of the I.R.A. and on the betrayal of the American ideal of democracy, which consists of a bicameral constitution.

Obstruction is the only tactics, and a thing to be thank-

ful for, when a nation is slipping down a precipice. I wish
to make no personal comments.

MR QUIRKE. You would not repeat it at any cross-roads in the
country, because if you did you would be torn to shreds.

DR GOGARTY. I do not go down to cross-roads.

MR QUIRKE. You go down to the gutter.

DR GOGARTY. You are speaking from a castle the door of which
you slapped in the face of democracy. I think it is largely
our own fault if the President is suffering from megalomania. We made so much of him. He was elected
Chancellor of the National University, he was hailed in
America as an avatar of Ireland, and it should come very
tardily from us before we begin disbelieving what we at
one time believed. As Chancellor of the National University, he had got such a hatred for the King's English
that he managed to crowd three mistakes into three words
which he spoke last week, when he said that dairying was
the 'most fundamental branch' of agriculture.

Now, that the six University members are going to be
put out, there will not be a single intelligent critic representing the Universities in the Dail, but all deputies will
be brought down to the intellectual level of President de
Valera. That is the fate of a country that once sent away
its sons to bring enlightenment to Europe. Since the
betrayal of Kinsale by Don Juan d'Aguila there had
never been a calamity comparable to the calamity that
our Spaniard has brought on the country, this month.

On March 19th, 1936, the Senate was finally dissolved by an
Act of the Lower House. It meant the disappearance from public
life of many who had a distinct contribution to make to the State.
They never returned to public life again, and it is one of the
anomalies of present-day Ireland that employers, without whose
support the finances of the state would collapse, have no more
standing as public figures than the men outside the unemployment
exchanges.

On March 19th, after a series of lengthy arguments (borrowed
without acknowledgment, as Mr Donal O'Sullivan has shown,
from an American work), Mr de Valera said:

I have never been able to get in anything I have read or

listened, a suggestion that would satisfy me that it is worth while spending money on the second chamber.

Two years later, it was Mr de Valera who reintroduced a Second Chamber but this time it was one of his own making, formed on a vocational basis. It has, with a few exceptions, evolved into a stamping ground for Party hacks and does, indeed, provide a strong argument in favour of not spending money on a second chamber, if such a body is to be established on the impractical basis that Mr de Valera's second chamber has shown itself to be.

EIGHTEEN

In the decade before the war, a gradual change can be observed in Gogarty's outlook. Though he continued his practice as a surgeon, his interest in his profession grew less and less, while his preoccupation with literature increased.

Between 1928 and 1939, he published three books of verse and three prose works.

Wild Apples (forty-eight poems) was published in Ireland in 1928 by the Cuala Press and in America, a year later, by Jonathan Cape and Harrison Smith. This was followed by a volume of collected verse in 1938, *Others to Adorn*, and a slim volume, *Elbow Room*, twelve poems published by Cuala in 1939.

In 1936, his first book of memoirs, *As I Was Going Down Sackville Street*, appeared, published by Rich and Cowan. The same firm brought out *I Follow Saint Patrick* two years later, but Constable published *Tumbling in the Hay*, a memoir of his student days, in 1939.

Quiller-Couch had included 'The Image Maker' and 'The Plum Tree by the House' in a revised edition of *The Oxford Book of English Verse* which appeared in 1927. As comparatively few contemporary poets received mention in this collection, which covered English poetry from 1250 to 1918, this was encouraging recognition for Gogarty.

The Oxford Book of Modern Verse, when it appeared in 1936, edited by Yeats, caused something of a sensation. There were seventeen poems of Gogarty's included, almost twice as many as any other poet in the book. It was felt at the time that Yeats had perhaps selected rather too many of Gogarty's poems and it may have reacted on his reputation as a poet and given it a temporary set-back: but it was heartening to find himself referred to in the preface as 'one of the great lyric poets of our age'.

His increasing fame as a literary figure tended to diminish Gogarty's list of private patients. People became reluctant to have their noses and throats examined by one whom they imagined might be searching for a spondee, as his fingers explored their antrums. Consequently, he tended to take less interest in his medical practice. Though he never failed to turn up at the Meath Hospital for his morning operating sessions, in the afternoons he was to be found less frequently at his house in Ely Place.

Renvyle, reopened as an hotel in 1930, kept him out of town some of the time. Then, as a literary personage, he felt free to spend more time in the Bohemian company of the city bars. Besides The Bailey, he frequented Fanning's of Lincoln Place and the Dolphin Hotel. He could drink large quantities of lager at this time without interfering with his health or his equilibrium. After an evening of talking and drinking, it became his custom to finish off the night eating pigs' feet in a night-house in Harcourt Place. The following morning, he would be up at seven for his 'cure': a quick drive to Tara Street Baths with his young friend, Robert O'Doherty, than a breath-taking plunge off the balustrade to commence eight lengths of the baths, before going up to O'Meara's pub in Rathmines for a glass of buttermilk.

As he found his political and medical career on the wane, Gogarty gave his flair for gesture full rein. In August 1932, he issued a challenge to a Fianna Fail minister to a duel on land, sea and air. The minister, Mr Frank Aiken, had referred to Gogarty in the Dail as 'a lazy body'. Gogarty replied by sending a letter to the newspapers, challenging him to a competition in running, swimming and in an aeroplane. Mr Aiken did not take up the offer.

As each new book of verse appeared, Gogarty's reputation as a poet increased. In 1928, he won another Taillteann gold medal for verse, with his volume *Wild Apples*. According to the poet F. R. Higgins his book tied with Monk Gibbon's *The Branch of Hawthorn Tree*. The judges referred the matter to Yeats and asked him to give a casting vote. He gave the award to Gogarty for the second time and the younger man received the silver medal. A.E. said at the presentation ceremony:

This work contains verses which would make us think Herrick was reborn with a more delicate sense of the loveliness of girlhood, beauty and wit, creatures which rarely co-exist in poetry for beauty shrivels before wit, and wit loses its aim when it looks on beauty.

James Stephens wrote to Gogarty after the publication of *The Oxford Book of Modern Verse*:

I think that after Yeats himself, you are the best poet of our land: and that, outside your land, and in the English-speaking mode, you are the sole example of the classical poet writing anywhere today. It may be that, perhaps, you will not be praised as you should be until about fifty years after you are dead: but I write now to you, secretly as it were, for every letter is a secret, to assert, all in your own ear, that no poet whatever writing at this moment is so good as Oliver St John Gogarty.

When *Others to Adorn* appeared in 1938, the notices, which varied, on the whole endorsed Yeats's view, expressed in the preface to *The Oxford Book of Modern Verse*.

The *Times Literary Supplement* noted 'the pure and chiselled form' of Gogarty's best poems. Basil de Selincourt, in the *Manchester Guardian*, had no doubt about the quality of the poems.

In their sharp realism and quick brainwork, they often recall Meredith, but against that, they have an aromatic largesse and monumental splendour of allusiveness that recall Herrick as often. 'Exuberance is Beauty,' said Blake. Mr Gogarty's poetry has poured out of him, gallant and generous, because in a world as lovely as this he would have been ashamed to be silent. In its texture rich as earth, in its grace and swiftness of music and motion, in its lightning-flash of wit, its subtler beam of penetrative meditation, this volume is not easily matchable. But on many a page, one is astounded to think on how many, the authentic voice is heard which, heard once, can never be forgotten.

Yeats had stressed the classical element in Gogarty's poems in making his selection for *The Oxford Book of Modern Verse*. The majority of classical poems in *Others to Adorn* had appeared already in *Wild Apples* or *An Offering of Swans*; poems like 'With a Coin from Syracuse', 'Portrait with a Background', 'Nymphis et Fontibus', 'After Galen'. But 'Marcus Curtius' was new, and so was 'Portrait' (*Diana clothed*).

Two metaphysical poems based on the Platonic conception of the origins of Beauty are included: 'The Phoenix' and 'The Emperor's Dream'. But the distinctive element to emerge in *Others to Adorn* is the development of the mock-heroic form which Gogarty had used earlier in poems like 'The Old Goose' and 'The Cock'. Now, he applied this form to classical themes, 'Leda and the Swan', and 'Europa and the Bull'. The mock-heroic was the ideal mood to express myth to an age which did not believe in myth, but which paradoxically recognized that myth had its origins in universal human instincts, and therefore a special validity of its own. A. J. Stobart, the Greek historian, wrote that Ovid 'drew the ancient tales, the loves of the gods out into the light again: gilded them with his wit, and made them altogether charming for the Roman drawing-room.'

Gogarty made myth palatable for the post-Freudian drawing-rooms. Who but he would have thought of using the metre of 'Goosey-Goosey Gander' to tell the tale of Leda in verse. Mrs Desmond Williams, Gogarty's daughter, has suggested that there may have been a link between the rhythm of 'Leda' and Meredith's 'Love in the Valley', which her father used to quote to her. Gogarty has split Meredith's longer line into pairs. Meredith writes,

> When her mother tends her before the lighted mirror,
> Loosening her laces, combing down her curls,
> Often she thinks, were this wild thing wedded,
> I should miss but one for many boys and girls.

The diaeresis in the fourth line, however, shifts the metre into different gear, and while Meredith's poem must have been in Gogarty's memory when writing 'Leda', it was the rhythmic scheme of the nursery rhyme that predominated.

> Though her Mother told her
>   Not to go a-bathing,
> Leda loved the river
>   And she could not keep away:
> Wading in its freshets
>   When the noon was heavy;
> Walking by the water
>   At the close of day.

When the Swan appears, Leda hails him:

> What was it she called him:
>   Goosey-goosey gander?
> For she knew no better
>   Way to call a swan;

And the bird responding,
Seemed to understand her,
For he left his sailing
For the bank to waddle on.

The legendary coupling is described in three-dimensional form:
the landscape that the unclothed girl sees as she sinks beneath the
swan's weight, fades, to use a cinematic term, to the image of the
girl, as the swan sees her beneath his outspread wings.

Apple blossoms under
Hills of Lacedaemon,
With the snow beyond them
In the still blue air,
To the swan who hid them
With his wings asunder,
Than the breasts of Leda,
Were not lovelier!

Gogarty's depiction of Leda telling her mother what happened,
is superb. We can see the old woman as she hears the news, standing with arms akimbo, an incredulous look on her face.

Of the tales that daughters
Tell their poor old mothers,
Which by all accounts are
Often very odd;
Leda's was a story
Stranger than all others.
What was there to say but:
Glory be to God?

Only in the last verse are the classical allusions mentioned,
exquisitely strung on the difficult framework of nursery rhyme
metre.

When the hyacinthine
Eggs were in the basket,
Blue as at the whiteness
Where a cloud begins;
Who would dream there lay there
All that Trojan brightness;
Agamemnon murdered;
And the mighty Twins?

259

Gogarty once remarked to Shane Leslie that, 'It was necessary to put a little petrol in the poetry nowadays,' and the description of the God-bull in the companion piece, 'Europa and the Bull', careering across the waves, has, like 'Leda', a cinematic quality about it.

> Gambolling and charging,
> Low head shaken sideways,
> Swerving as though guided
> By his tassel rudder tail,
> Snorting more than stamping
> A ripple on the tideways,
> A Bull, where nothing ever
> Drew a furrow but a sail!

But though he is modern in his approach, Gogarty still adheres to the old maxim of the Attic School, that truth is found in beauty before it is revealed by science.

> Because I hold an Age of Faith
> Whose dogma is emphatic
> Is happier than such as this
> When, if there's faith about,
> 'Tis not in gods by girls transformed,
> But Jewish mathematic,
> I go for Truth to Beauty
> Which is subject to less doubt.

Gogarty adapted an ancient Irish theme to the modern mood in his poem 'The Old Woman of Beare' with the same success that he had transformed 'Leda' and 'Europa'. For some curious reason, this poem does not appear in *Others to Adorn* but is included in the collected edition of Gogarty's verse published in 1952. That it was written before 1938 is evident from a letter of F. R. Higgins, written in 1936, in which he says that it was hearing Yeats chant this poem which first made him recognize that Gogarty's poems 'were peaks starred with gold, and ranges illuminated by fastidious craft.'

Gogarty's version is based on an old Gaelic poem of the eighth century, 'The Hag of Beare'. Kuno Meyer had given it its first English translation. It is the lament of an aged lover for the adventures of her youth. The same theme appears in Villon's

'Lament for the Belle Healmauire' and Alan Ramsay's 'Last Advice of Lucky Spense'. But Ramsay and Villon rely on an element of pathos for their effect, the aged bawd's regret for the excesses of her past, and the fading of her beauty. In Gogarty's poem, following the mood of the Gaelic original, there is a quality of defiance, which recalls Don Giovanni's descent to Hell, unrepentant of his unnumbered loves.

Gogarty contributes his own introduction to the poem, comparing the eighth-century figure with the untrammelled personalities he had known in the brothel area in the Dublin of his student days.

THE OLD WOMAN OF BEARE
(From the Irish)

This today had been Fresh Nellie,
For she had as wild a belly
Or a kind of Mrs Mack,
For she had a bonny back;
Or the Honourable Mrs Lepple,
Nipple to a kingly nipple
For she never took advantage
Of the favours of her frontage;
Therefore she was held in honour
By the warty boys who won her.
Therefore some old Abbey's shelf
Kept the record of herself,
Telling to men who disapprove
Of Love, the long regrets of Love.

Now my tide of youth is gone
And my ebb of age comes on;
Though the sonsie may be happy,
I'm no longer soft and sappy.

Age is causing all my woes:
I who had new underclothes
As I queened it every day
Now have no-one's castaway.

O the times that I had then!
You have money, I had men
Who could give their horse the reins
Yet not leave their own demesnes.

Of the men for whom I stript
None was weaker when we clipt,
But the fury of my flame
Magnified the man in him.

Now each bargain-driving clown
Wants two ups for one go down;
God, if I reciprocated,
They would think themselves castrated! ...

The lads I loved are all abroad,
And strain through Alma's reedy ford;
No logs of oak will break and glow
To warn the beds where they are now! ...

Glory be! I'm half content
Just to think of all I spent.
Passion never waned in me
For the want of ... Glory be! ...

Cups of whey at night and morn
For the crescent drinking horn;
But the nuns and all their whey
Have not washed my rage away!

Of another poem in this genre, Yeats wrote:

I have not been able to forget these two years, that Ringsend
whore's drunken lament, that little red lamp before some
holy picture, that music at the end.

RINGSEND
(After reading Tolstoy)
I will live in Ringsend
With a red-headed whore,
And the fanlight gone in
Where it lights the hall-door;
And listen each night
For her querulous shout,
As at last she streels in
And the pubs empty out.
To soothe that wild breast
With my old-fangled songs,
Till she feels it redressed

From inordinate wrongs,
Imagined, outrageous,
Preposterous wrongs,
Till peace at last comes,
Shall be all I will do,
Where the little lamp blooms
Like a rose in the stew;
And up the back garden
The sound comes to me
Of the lapsing, unsoilable,
Whispering sea.

In March 1933, George Moore died. His funeral like his life was unique. He had directed that his ashes be put in an urn and placed in a crypt on Castle Island in the centre of Lough Carra. The pagan nature of the ceremony necessitated a police guard on the island for some nights before in case of interference with the crypt by local people. This led Gogarty to remark:

Men have been burned for heresy. Here was a man turned into a heretic because he had ordered his body to be burned.

The local boatmen refused to row the mourners to the island so Gogarty undertook to row one of the boats himself. As he rowed Mrs Kilkelly, Mrs Virginia Crawford, the original of the heroine in *Evelyn Innes* and *Sister Teresa*, and L. T. Fleming, a newspaperman, away from the shore, he was able to observe the changing contour of Moore's family house, Moore Hall.

'Lough Carra is the only green lake in Ireland,' he noted the next day. 'It is the colour of a yellow-green wine, a unique lake which in another country would be as famous for its colour as the Grotto d'Azzura of Capri. As our boat drew away from its lime-white shore, Moore Hall gradually rose over its lawn, cut like a wedge in the woods which spring was renewing. Higher and higher it arose, until I could see the lower storey, and now the pillars of the hall-door appear.'

By the time they reached the island, an argument was in progress about the inscription to be placed on the crypt. It was to read:

GEORGE A. MOORE
Moore Hall. Died 1933 London
He deserted country and friends for his art

Gogarty and Dr Richard Best thought that the word 'forsook' should be substituted for 'deserted'. But the proposed inscription was retained. Dr Best, the Director of the National Library and a close friend of Moore, read the funeral oration which had been written by A.E. Only a short while before, A.E. had drawn a ferocious vignette of Moore in his novel *The Avatars*. But in death he saw him plain:

> However Moore warred on the ideals of his nation he knew it was his Irish ancestry which gave him the faculties which made him one of the most talented and unfilial of Ireland's children. His enmities even made his nation to be admired and loved, as the praise of its patriots. He had the speech of the artist which men remember while they forget the indiscriminating voices which had nothing but love. If any would condemn him for creed of theirs he had assailed, let them be certain first that they laboured for their ideals as faithfully as he did for his.

After the funeral Colonel Moore, a pious Catholic, who was somewhat scandalized by the nature of the ceremony he had taken part in, explained to newspapermen that the rite which had preceded his brother's burial went back to 'the early years of Ireland's civilization, to the Bronze Age, when Ireland was the richest and most cultured country in Western Europe, and traded even as far as Palestine before the time of Solomon.'

This was a prize piece of blatherskite that would have turned Moore's gorge had he been alive. Gogarty struck a more authentic note on his way back from the island: 'Half way across', L. T. Fleming recalls, 'Gogarty dropped the oars and looked sadly at his blistered hands. "Ah well," he said, "they call poor George a pagan, and yet he has already worked one miracle – the stigmata."'

Yeats and Gogarty were by now boon companions. One day Yeats, reading Lawrence's *Seven Pillars of Wisdom*, had come across the description of his bodyguard:

> Young Arabs, men proud of themselves and without families, dressed like a bed of tulips,

and recognized an Elizabethan quality:

> that sense of hardship born out of pride and joy,

which he had noted in Gogarty. This was the opposite to his own mood. He had been a public man, but not a man of action in the physical sense. To him Gogarty's poetry was 'a gay, stoical, heroic song'. As he grew older, all that mattered to him was the heroic. But the mood of his age was anti-heroic.

> We, Irish, born into that ancient sect,
> But thrown upon the filthy modern tide,
> And by its formless spawning fury wrecked,
> Climb to our proper dark, that we may trace
> The lineaments of a plummet-measured face.

He turned to Gogarty as a ladder by which he might raise himself once more to the heroic image, before age bade him turn for theme to and lie down in the foul rag-and-bone shop of the heart.

He was his schoolmaster too, when Yeats wanted to embody classical themes in his poems. Gogarty had helped him with his final version of *Oedipus*, which was first performed in 1928, chanting the lines in Greek in Yeats's ear, so that the poet could capture their euphony in English, though he admitted to Lady Wellesley, in a letter, that here and there, occasionally, an Elizabethan line steals in.

Yeats, as we have seen, perceived in Gogarty's personality a link between the two Irelands.

> Out of old Gaelic stock had come a figure with the qualities
> of the 'swift, indifferent men', the swashbuckling, Anglo-Irish of the hunting fields, who were heroes of Yeats' youth.

One of Yeats's last poems reiterates this theme, that the new Ireland will be formed from a fusion of these elements in the nation.

> Sing the peasantry, and then
> Hard-riding country gentlemen,
> The holiness of monks, and after
> Porter-drinkers' randy laughter;
> That we in coming days may be
> Still the indomitable Irishry.

Gogarty admired Yeats as the greatest living poet and thought him the finest talker he had ever heard. He admired also his public courage. This did not prevent him from parading tales and witty remarks about the poet's eccentricities, in the taverns and eating-houses of the city. 'Yeats is becoming so aristocratic, he's evicting imaginary tenants,' he quipped to J. B. Priestley. On another occasion, he told a medical acquaintance of Yeats's reaction to the Steinach operation, which he had undergone to improve his sexual powers. The acquaintance was shocked that Gogarty should speak of a friend in this way. But, as Denis Johnston points out, this sort of amusing malice on Gogarty's part was conditioned by a desire to please his listener, not just to talk for his own satisfaction. Yeats knew quite well that Gogarty made him the centre of many a tale, behind his back, but he knew the nature of such tales – carefully embroidered fantasies, thought out as Oscar Wilde might have invented them, only with an individual touch of Gogartian derision. It made no difference to his friendship with Gogarty. In their daily meetings, he knew that Gogarty could stoke the fire-born moods of his mind, which was all that mattered when art and imagination were primary concerns. Most days, Gogarty snatched time to run out in his car to Riverdale in Rathfarnham, for a chat with Yeats. One day he had to bring with him what amounted to a death sentence. A Spanish doctor had written a report on Yeats couched in quaint medical jargon: 'We have here an antique cardiosclerotic of advanced years.' Gogarty tried to withhold the news from him at first, but Yeats insisted on hearing the truth. 'It is my letter, Gogarty. I must see it.' As he read it he rolled the word 'cardiosclerotic' lovingly on his tongue. He looked up, his great shock of white hair tumbling over his bronzed features: 'You know, Gogarty, I'd rather be called cardiosclerotic, than Lord of Lower Egypt.'

In 1932, Yeats had the idea of forming an Irish Academy of Letters. Its main purpose was to protect Irish writers against the Censorship Board. In a public letter to the newspapers, signed by Yeats and Shaw, they stated their intention of forming an Academy 'so that we may have an organ through which we can address the public, or appeal collectively to the Government.'

T. E. Lawrence and James Joyce were invited to join. Joyce refused, but Lawrence became an associate member. Gogarty, to his surprise, found himself elected. His friends, Shane Leslie and Lord Dunsany, had not been invited to full membership, presumably because they were out of favour with Yeats. In an early novel, *Doomsland*, Leslie had parodied Yeats, and the poet, Dublin-like, did not forget it. Gogarty prophesied Dunsany's rejection, in an amusing letter written to Shane Leslie on April 19th, 1932.

Prophecy

On Friday 29th, I shall hear Yeats to this effect:

'Gogarty, you may have seen the account of an interview with me, last week, no, this year, last year, maybe, well, no matter ... My memory ... but the thing that is important is that I want you to attach no import to ... it must not be read to the latter. I asked for an Irish Academy of Jetters, a truculent Academy and I left you out because I feared that it might injure you as a doctor. You are a wild man but you have not injured yourself by your writing. I have no knowledge of these things but here in Ireland not to be single-minded is to invite suspicion. I would not injure you in your profession.'

'Thanks, Yeats. Is it because Dunsany had an Uncle who was interested in modern medicine that you refrained from including him? He has been practising as a prophylactic precautioner if not a practitioner, by discouraging the sale of saline bone-dust and by being an heresiarch as far as some advertisements go.'

'I included Du ... let me see ... Could I? ... There was Shaw, McKenna, Joyce ... '

'Really, Yeats, if you include Joyce in anything but an isolation camp, please exclude me. Joyce is the opposite to everything Academical, to all ordered thought, to all style in literature. He is the anarchist who came before Lenin. A scrambler of the Ledaean eggs ... '

'Ledaean eggs ... eggs. I must ask George what I did with Dunsany.'

Some years later Dunsany was elected a full member of the Academy. Gogarty spoke at a dinner to welcome him and though Yeats was present it did not prevent him from saying in the course of his speech, 'Since this Academy was founded to keep Dunsany out we ought to dissolve it, now that he's admitted.'

In fact, though Gogarty felt himself honoured to be a member of an Academy which included Shaw, Yeats and A.E., he looked on it as a mixed blessing. He did not want to become a cock-shy for the extreme Catholic papers which were calling for increased censorship, and regarded the Academy as a libertine institution. Privately, he regarded the censorship as baleful. In a letter to Shane Leslie, he writes:

> The Censorship will end in our having to import a Pandemian Venus (not her of the notes!) to engender interest enough to make us procreate. Think of the Synod Meeting at Maynooth when in view of a falling birth-rate, they will have reluctantly to give their imprimatur to the importation of a Venus! An English one, no! French – worse! German less alluring, but Luther was a German – No; if we have a pagan, a Saracen such as Nicolette, and get a lady from Mustapha Kemal who rules over Cnidos, if I mistake not, and who may send the genuine thing!

He consoled Leslie for not being elected a member, by reminding him of an incident in which Mahaffy and Yeats clashed.

> If only Mahaffy were alive! He sent the quantities marked to Yeats when it was necessary for him to take the oath in Latin before permission could be obtained to read in T.C.D. library: 'My ear is warther sensitive.'
>
> I prepared a tornado of a letter to Mahaffy to avenge the poet, but Yeats took the insult lying down, and refused to let me send it. And now he avoids the classics though he calls his institution an Academy. However, it is more thinkable than a Lyceum in Erin, though a Colosseum would have suited us better. I am rather an ass to stay in. It is more important to select one's readers than books; and yet 'he took me in'.

> There was a kind poet called Yeats
> Who put me with those whom he rates –
>   Don't think it bad of me –
>   In his Academy;
> Off which of our heads are the slates?

Renvyle had been opened as an hotel when it was rebuilt in 1930. Perhaps the best picture we can get of the hotel and its host, is from the pen of the Italian scholar, Dr Rossi, an authority on Swift and Berkeley, who visited Renvyle with Yeats and Gogarty in 1932.

This region is animated by the presence of a man who recalls the great Italians of the Quattrocento. For me at least, to know Gogarty was to realise the enthusiasm of the man who lives with full consciousness for that admirable phenomenon which is called life.

In the chaos of activity, Gogarty combines the sharp precise manner of an American with the benevolent simple spirit of his own country, Ireland. Surgeon, conversationalist, politician, airman, poet, he has sufficient humanity for all that he does, and he is equally at his ease whether he laughs at his neighbour or scans a poem, like a natural force which adapts itself at once to a thousand manifestations. He sums up Ireland.

The Irishman is exactly this ironical and assiduous type, pervaded with such a vitality that verse flows from him as the normal expression of his passion and emotion.

Renvyle House is the kingdom of Gogarty; the most westerly hotel in Europe, beaten by all the Atlantic winds, crowded with guests, a peculiar combination of the great Alpine hotel and the hospitable home. It is not easy to say who is there as Gogarty's guest and who is there as the guest of the hotel. You fail to understand how so many people have arrived there across eighteen miles of an impossible road; nevertheless you find there, a sort of mundane tone which couples insensibly with the wildest nature.

On the way down to Renvyle, Rossi had sat in the back, while Gogarty drove with Yeats in the front. From Galway to Renvyle, the two poets were absorbed in the construction of an epigram and Rossi was terrified as the car took corners at seventy miles an hour, while Gogarty took his hands off the wheel to scan the metre, his left hand raised, his first finger stretched, his second, half bent. When they reached the Connemara hills, Rossi felt that behind them lay some primordial sea.

I have reached the West. I can never be further off from the world in which I have lived because that world ends here. The vague and empty word 'Europe' acquires in my imagination a perfect sense. Completed. For here, I truly feel the boundary. A foreseen boundary which I have attained, across hills so violet as to be unreal, across a mist which thickens with the miles – towards an ever more pervasive, an ever more looming desolation.

To the hotel, many distinguished visitors came during the next nine years. It was all excellent entertainment for Gogarty, who liked company that was intelligent and handsome. We find him writing to Shane Leslie in 1931, asking him to lead a retinue of beauty to Renvyle, as Augustus John had done the year before. A.E. has said that Gogarty cast a glamour over women, in the way that Gainsborough did in painting, but which Reynolds did not.

I doubt if Oliver was in love with any of the women he praises, but as we read we feel that we could easily fall in love with the women he depicts. His cool eye has noted that second of illumination when the light on limb and dress become one with the light in the heart, and he can have no peace until he can give that transience permanence.

When Helen Wills-Moody, whom he called 'his best and only fan', invited him to see her play at Wimbledon, he went over, enthusiastically, to watch this modern Diana in action.
Had he not written :

> When she takes the ball, left-handed,
> Speed and sweetness are so blended,
> Nothing awkward can she do.

He liked to bring handsome young men and women together and watch their friendships develop. Once, he consoled an envious youth, watching a fragile pair, man and girl, holding hands, beautiful in the evening glow.

Don't worry; they're like fireflies; all light and no heat.

Augustus John stayed at Renvyle for most of the summer of 1930. Gogarty had suggested that a portrait should be done of Yeats, in old age, to complement the two John had painted of the poet as a young man. It was at Renvyle in this year, that John painted his last portrait of Yeats. He painted also, that year, Gogarty's daughter, Brenda. On the ridge overlooking Tully

Lake, he spent long hours painting landscapes on panels of sycamore wood, which he sold later to a Japanese battleship-builder.

With his Viking hair, yellow beard, and piercing blue eyes, John seemed a figure from another age. John shared with Gogarty and another friend of his, Sir Compton Mackenzie, an unashamed delight in the joy of living. When one thinks of any one of the three, Welshman, Irishman and Scot, it is the luminous laughter in their eyes, lit by a passing reference or image, that immediately comes to mind; that joyous gaiety of the Celt which generates delight in those around like a dynamo. Some northern strain also has mingled with the Celt in them which shows itself in their blue eyes, long heads and passion for action and adventure.

The fascination which John held for Gogarty did not diminish with the years. During the Second World War, Gogarty never forgot his friend and constantly bombarded him with presents of food from America. In a tiny, fragile verse, he has set down how much Augustus's friendship meant to him:

> When my hawk's soul shall be
> With little talk in her,
> Trembling, about to flee,
> And Father Falconer
> Touches her off for me,
> And I am gone –
> All shall forgotten be
> Save for you, John!

Though Arthur Griffith and Tom Kettle were dead, and James Stephens was in exile, Gogarty, Jimmy Montgomery, Seamus O'Sullivan, Valentine Nolan-Whelan, Joe Boyd Barrett, George Redding and Seamus Burke, continued to meet in The Bailey during the 'thirties. Gogarty, Boyd Barrett and O'Sullivan bestowed their patronage at this period upon another licensed premises in Lincoln Place, owned by Senator Fanning. Brinsley McNamara, the playwright and novelist, R. M. S. Smyllie, the Editor of the *Irish Times*, and a mixed group of airmen, journalists, 'characters' and businessmen, with a common interest in the wit and scandal of the town, used to meet there, about six o'clock in the evening. Fanning's was known as 'Indignation House'. Its title derived from the owner's habit of emitting an apoplectic roar, if he happened to hear the name of De Valera mentioned in conversation. Whether he was down a trap-door, bottling beer, or washing glasses under the counter, he would always appear somehow, at the sound of the name. Unfolding his long, elegant body over the counter, his face turning from wine-red to puce, he would deliver a diatribe usually finishing up with his favourite ejaculation, 'Abso-bloody-lutely.' A noted phrase of his was: 'De Valera is about as good a Nation builder as an advocate of birth-control.'

From 'Indignation House' and The Bailey, a constant stream of satirical verse poured out, directed against the antics of the new Government. In 1932, the Fianna Fail Cabinet rejected the top hat and morning suit, as symbols of imperialism, and declined to wear either at formal gatherings, even to greet the Papal Nuncio, when he arrived in Dublin for the Eucharistic Congress that summer. Previously, at an Imperial Conference in Ottawa, Fianna Fail Ministers, despite their self-imposed sartorial restrictions, had appeared in formal attire. This manœuvre evoked a bright quatrain from Jimmy Montgomery, who managed to slip in as well a reference to the economic war which had destroyed Ireland's export trade in cattle with England.

> We'll have the best of everything,
> On meat and milk we'll gorge,
> With cloth caps for Christ the King,
> And toppers for King George.

George Redding lamented the passing of the old Dublin and attributed the current mood of gloom to the leader of the Fianna Fail Party.

> But God be with the days when we
> Wrote of such rogues so feelingly;
> There's hardly left (and more's the pity),
> A decent rogue in this dull city.
> Still less a single man of mettle
> To rank with Markiewicz or Kettle.
> The brave are dead, or half-alive,
> Like Seamus, driven home at five.
> My grief! The votes of corner-boys
> Have banished mirth and chilled our joys,
> Withdrawn, we watch each twist and trick

Of that gaunt Spanish fanatic,
And wonder will he last forever,
Or hamstrung, fall from his endeavour,
While Ireland, worn to bones and marrow,
Like Joyce's sow, eats up her farrow.

In 1933, A.E. had left Ireland, disgusted with De Valera's 'obtuseness', and relieved to get away from the country in its 'present mood of smugness' and the 'half-crazy Gaeldom growing about him'. Yeats was flirting with Fascism about this time, in the form of an organization called the Blueshirts, a body who had adopted a number of the more undesirable characteristics of their continental equivalents in Germany and Italy, including an attempted *coup d'état* in August 1934, which was only forestalled by placing police with machine-guns on top of government buildings. For this body, with its Hitler salute, Yeats had composed a hymn, and summoned its leaders to his presence that he might talk his 'anti-democratic philosophy' to them. A verse of Gogarty's suggests that he, too, favoured government by the few, if it would provide an alternative to the current version of democracy. There is no evidence, however, that Gogarty had any connection with the Blueshirts.

Why should there have been such resentment in intellectual circles in Ireland at this time, against the new regime? One cause was the civil war: the Party who had defied the law were now administering it. A malaise seemed to have settled on the country – a feeling of helplessness. It was the Left wing of a Left-wing Party that was in control and they played down to what Yeats called 'the ignorance that had in part, put them in power'. Once elected to government, the Fianna Fail Party, with expert organization throughout the country-side, had seen to it that local administration was conducted on lines likely to favour the Party machine. Certain Government actions at the time seemed to conciliate revolutionary elements which were still a powerful force in the country. For instance, as soon as the Cabinet was formed, the Minister for Defence walked into Arbour Hill and extended a cordial welcome to Republican prisoners, as he released them from their cells.

Mr Cosgrave's Party must share some responsibility for the general decline. Cumann na nGaedheal disintegrated into splinter

273

groups. Mr Cosgrave resigned from the leadership of his fractured Party. A roaring Fascist, General O'Duffy, was elected in his place. It was not until 1934, when Mr de Valera at last outlawed the I.R.A., and later, when he secured a settlement of the economic war, and new housing schemes initiated by his Party showed signs of ending the shame of Dublin's slums, that confidence in native government began to be restored.

On July 16th, 1935, Gogarty received a telegram to say that A.E. was seriously ill in Bournemouth. He immediately caught the night boat and arrived at the poet's bedside a short while before he died. He was rewarded by the deepening of the great blue light in A.E.'s eyes as he recognized his friend's face. As he leant over the bed, Gogarty heard A.E. murmur, 'I have realized all my ambitions. I have had an astonishing interest in life. I have had great friends. What more can a man want?' The surgeon in attendance turned away for a moment in tears.

'The hero in the man looked out,' Gogarty wrote in an obituary in the *Irish Times* next day, 'and it was his friends who had to brace themselves against life with its loss.'

A.E. was one of three friends (Arthur Griffith and Tom Kettle were the others) whom Gogarty regarded as beyond criticism. A.E. he thought of almost as a saint.

A.E.'s death, following within two years of Moore's, made Gogarty realize that the great figures he had known as a young man were passing away. One by one the lights were going out which had brightened the story of his youth.

In 1928, Jonathan Cape had suggested to Gogarty that he write his memoirs in a volume, but Gogarty replied that this would bring on his last end. 'If you forget, shall I remember? What a unique position; a resident Memoir writer.'

But he remembered that his Norman tower, Dungorey, which he bought in 1926, was not yet roofed, and he thought he might pay for its restoration out of the proceeds of a book of memoirs. He began the work in the early 'thirties and, writing it in intervals, finished it in 1935. It was published in 1936. The reviews were favourable. Desmond Shawe-Taylor, in *The New Statesman*, wrote: '*Sackville Street* remains a fine rich Irish stew, compounded of the same juicy ingredients that gave us *Ulysses* and *Hail and Farewell*,

274

but Joyce and Moore, though the pride of rival kitchens, both learnt their cooking in France.'

There is this in common between the early Joyce, Moore and Gogarty, that their prose works are written out of their own experience with real, and not imaginary, characters in them. *The Times Literary Supplement* puts its finger on the reason for this. 'With so many vivid personalities to choose from, Irish writers were tempted to abandon imaginary characters, and invent imaginary conversations.'

The writer in *The Times Literary Supplement*, alas, anonymous, noted an instance of how Gogarty uses real figures to epitomize national moods.

As characteristic and symbolic of a period in which extravagance of spirit too often signified an inner frustration, Dr Gogarty chooses 'Endymion', a well-known public figure of the time. Wearing a tail-coat over his cricket trousers, two sabres in shining scabbards of patent leather under his left arm, his right hand grasping a hunting-crop such as whippers-in use for hounds, 'Endymion' paced the sunny streets of vice-regal Dublin. Among these memories he appears warningly or in mockery at critical moments with a nice disregard for common sense and chronology.

In *Sackville Street* Gogarty has 'eschewed perspective, like the Chinese' and allowed his imagination to body forth ideas, spontaneously, without regard to chronology, as he would do if he were in conversation. He never allows himself to be manacled by the tyranny of relevance and his mind darts off in speculative excursions on which the reader accompanies him with pleasure, because of the spontaneity of prose which has the quality of conversational utterance. Thus, on page after page, in lightning changes from description to narrative, from narrative to anecdote, we get a glimpse of what the talk of the great Irishmen of the past may have been like. That special Irish characteristic is present on every page, the power of quick analogy which gave rise to the first joke in modern Europe when Charles the Bald asked the Irish philosopher, Eriugena, what is the difference between a Scot and a sot? The Irish at that time were known as Scots. They were opposite each other at dinner, and the Irishman promptly replied: 'The width of the table.'

275

NINETEEN

I n February 1937, Henry Morris Sinclair commenced proceedings for libel against Gogarty. He alleged that two passages in *As I Was Going Down Sackville Street* were defamatory of him. The passage which appeared on page 71 referred to an old usurer whose habit was to entice small girls into his office for the purposes of sexual entertainment; it also referred to his grandchildren who were supposed to have inherited their grandfather's predilection for the immature. Sinclair claimed that he could show that his grandfather had been accused of procuring small girls and interfering with them and that, therefore, he was identified by the passage in the book as one of the grandchildren who, it was suggested, indulged in similar practices.

The passage on page 71 was set out in the statement of claim.

'This what?' asked Mrs Shillington.

'Orgy,' I repeated. 'When there is any pleasant and private feast from which a few, who think they should have been invited, are excluded, they invariably call it an orgy. I have always regretted that I was never at an orgy; I am trying to repair that shortcoming now. As I say, I will produce George ... '

'Well, until you do, just recite his latest.'

'Very well,' said I. 'You must know that George is not only the arbiter elegantiae of Dublin, but a critic of the grosser forms of licence. Now, there was an old usurer who had eyes like a pair of periwinkles on which somebody had been experimenting with a pin, and a nose like a shrunken tomato, one side of which swung independently of the other. The older he grew the more he pursued the immature, and enticed little girls into his office. That was bad enough; but he had grandsons, and these directed the steps of their youth to follow in grandfather's footsteps, with more zeal than discrimination. I explained the position to George, who, after due fermentation produced the following pronunciamento:

> It is a thing to wonder at, but hardly
>   to admire,
> How they who do desire the most,

guard most against desire:
They chose their friend or mistress
so that none may yearn to touch her,
Thus did the twin grandchildren of the
ancient Chicken Butcher …

'I like the roll and oracular sound of "Thus did," etc., and the play on the meanings of wonder and admire – Nil admirari! – And the organ-note in that "Twin grandchildren" which endows their infamy with grandeur until it almost equals the fame of the Great Twin Brethren, Castor and beneficent Pollux. "Verse calls them forth" from vulgar obloquy.'

'Another laurel or burden for "George" to bear,' said Mrs Shillington. 'Who are the Great Twin Brethren?'

'Consummations of the poet's dream. Shadows invoked by sound. Men who do not exist. I thought I made that clear.'

The statement of claim also set out verses which appeared on page 65, which the plaintiff alleged libelled him.

'And one thing more – where can we buy antiques?'

'Nassau Street, Sackville Street, Liffey Street, where Naylor's is, and all along the quays. Have you not heard?

"Two Jews grew in Sackville Street
And not in Piccadilly,
One was gaitered on the feet,
The other one was Willie.

"And if you took your pick of them,
Whichever one you chose,
You'd like the other one more than him,
So wistful were these Jews.

"They kept a shop for objects wrought
By Masters famed of old,
Where you, no matter what you bought
Were genuinely sold.

"But Willie spent the sesterces
And brought on strange disasters
Because he sought new mistresses
More keenly than old Masters.

"Two Jews grew in Sackville Street
And not in Piccadilly,
One was gaitered on the feet,
The other one was Willie.

"And if you took the pick of them,
Whichever one you choose,
You'd like the other one more than him,
So wistful were these Jews." '

The third and fourth verses appeared only in the American edition.

The case created a sensation in Dublin. There is an illusion common among Dubliners, that they are potential writers or barristers. The opportunity of seeing both professions simultaneously on display was not to be missed. There were queues for seats in the gallery of the court. The action was tried in Court No. 4 of the High Court, which is one of four court rooms forming a circle under the copper dome in the front of the Four Courts. This building, designed by Richard Gandon in 1781, is only a road's width from the Liffey's edge, where a graceful curving balustrade sets it off against the brown tide with its drifting swans.

Both the English and Irish press gave the case full coverage. The *Daily Mail* and *Daily Express* featured it in their headlines. Charles Graves, who wrote a popular column in the *Daily Express*, was sent over to give the case special coverage.

Counsel for the plaintiff were Albert Wood, K.C., Joseph McCarthy, K.C., and Ernest Wood. The Leader of the Irish Bar J. M. Fitzgerald, K.C., Ralph Brereton Barry, K.C., and Oliver Gogarty appeared for Gogarty. Oliver was Gogarty's barrister son.

Charles Graves noted the contrast between the leading Counsel on both sides.

Wood, born at Norwich, is benign, gentle, serious. In cross-examination, he has a persistence and a cooing, wooing approach which I should have found more alarming than the savage pounce to which it usually led.

Fitzgerald is sharp-looking and rosy with thin lips that purse in a sardonic semicircle, and glasses over which he stares with incredulous scorn. He conducts cross-examinations with pyrotechnical daring.

Fitzgerald, educated at Clongowes and Trinity, had read a brilliant academic course in classics and law. He was a fine orator in the grandiose style, and could get away, even in front of hard-boiled juries, with sentences like 'When the summer evenings were still long, and summer was just dying on the lap of autumn', simply by the compelling intonation and timbre of his speaking voice.

Wood, largely self-educated, was polemical, aggressive and a master of corrosive invective in a jury speech. He had had two alternative ambitions, to be Primate or Lord Chancellor of England. He abandoned the first after a year's Divinity in Trinity, and almost brought off the second when he stood for Norwich in the 1925 general election, and when his party lost probably through the publication of the forged Zinoviev letter. Had Labour won, Wood, as the only lawyer of note in the party, might have become Solicitor-General for England. He cultivated carefully waxed moustaches, and was known as 'The Thunderer'.

Fashionable Dublin filled the court on the first day of the court. Charles Graves counted '85 briefless barristers' in the front of the court. 'Only the Pickwick Papers rewritten by James Joyce', he wrote, 'could really recapture the atmosphere of this trial.'

As Mr Justice O'Byrne entered the Court, Fitzgerald pushed the decanter of water towards Wood and said, 'This will last us the morning.' Graves noted that it didn't outlast counsels' amiability. As Fitzgerald was examining a witness who found difficulty in understanding what was being said to him, Wood said: 'It's the Cork accent.' Fitzgerald was from Cork. While Wood was addressing the jury, with his back turned to the judge and facing the gallery, a typical pose of his, Fitzgerald raised his eyes to the jury and murmured audibly: 'Deafening.' Finally the judge said that these exchanges between counsel must cease.

Wood opened the case to the jury in vivid fashion:

Dr Gogarty has vilified the living and the dead in a pen dipped in the scourgings of a putrid and amoral mind. He has pursued the plaintiff with savagery and ghoulishness which could only fit in with the aberrations of an amoral mind in a pot-boiling scurrility run for the private gain of the author.

He ended with a dramatic plea to the jury:

Is there a hope that a Jew will not receive justice from a Dublin jury? Is it the gambler's throw? Throughout all our chequered history one of the great traditions of our city is that it has never persecuted the Jews, and I know, members of the jury, that you will preserve that tradition.

The first witness was the plaintiff. He told the court that he had a twin brother, William Sinclair, who had died some years before; they were grandsons of Morris Sinclair who kept an antique shop in Nassau Street. Their father was a member of the Church of Ireland, but their grandfather had brought them up in the Jewish religion. He described his grandfather's nose as bulbous. He then put into evidence documents which showed that his grandfather had been accused of enticing newspaper girls under the age of twelve into his shop, and interfering with them, after paying them small sums such as twopence and threepence.

He and his brother had inherited the antique shop from their grandfather.

Fitzgerald's cross-examination was short. He put it to Sinclair that his name which derived from St Clair of Assisi was an inappropriate one for a Jew to bear. His comment on Sinclair's mode of identifying himself as one of the 'twin grandchildren' was: 'You have dug up your grandfather!'

When he had finished with Sinclair, he pitched into Samuel Beckett, the playwright and novelist, author of *Waiting for Godot*, etc., who had told the court that he identified the plaintiff from the two passages in the book.

Beckett admitted in cross-examination that Mr William Sinclair's wife was his aunt; but he said he would 'leave it to counsel to work out the relationship'.

'A little more kind than kin,' Fitzgerald flashed back, but his Hamlet allusion was lost on the jury and there was hardly a murmur in court. Beckett added that he had been asked to buy the book by Sinclair, before he identified him in it. He made no reply when it was suggested that he had made an affidavit at a previous hearing in the High Court, implying that he was an impartial witness, but had not referred to his relationship with the plaintiff.

Counsel then asked Beckett had he written a book on 'Marcel Prowst'. Fitzgerald, who spoke perfect French, deliberately mispronounced Proust's name. As he had hoped, Beckett corrected him acidly, creating a bad effect on the jury:

Q. Was Proust a man who indulged in the psychology of sex?
A. I have not been aware of that.
Q. But you have written about him. How long did it take before your book was banned by the censorship of Ireland?
A. About six months.
Q. I suggest it was banned because it was a blasphemous and obscene book?
A. I have never discovered why it was banned.

Fitzgerald then read an extract from the book describing a conversation in a bus between 'The Polar Bear' and a member of the Jesuit Order, and asked the witness if that conversation was not a blasphemous caricature of Our Redeemer. Beckett said the characters were fictitious and that he could put words in the mouths of characters which he did not share.

Q. Do you call yourself a Christian, Jew or Atheist?
A. None of the three.

In further cross-examination, witness admitted that he had written another book called *Horoscope* with the letter 'W' prefixed, and had it printed privately and circulated for the enjoyment of his friends. He said it was likely that his two uncles-in-law were among the small circle of friends for whom the book was printed.

Fitzgerald sat down well satisfied. Beckett had not made the sort of impression likely to appeal to Dublin jurymen who usually have a streak of piety in their make-up.

Then followed a number of publication witnesses. In actions for defamation, it is necessary to prove publication of the libel: that is, that it has come within the knowledge of persons other than the plaintiff and that these persons can identify the plaintiff from the words complained of.

A feature of the Sinclair case was that all the publication witnesses produced by the plaintiff were either relatives or employees of his, or had purchased the book at his suggestion before identifying him in it. Normally this should have had the effect of reducing the damages to nominal ones if the jury found a libel at all. Recognizing this, Fitzgerald ran his defence along lines calculated to discredit the publication witnesses in the minds of the jury.

The last witness was Mr Seamus Fenning, a swarthy bookseller from Dawson Street. In cross-examination, he denied that he was a Jew who had become a Catholic.

FITZGERALD. Where did you get that accent of yours, you didn't get it in the Gaeltacht. Have you been in England?

FENNING. No.

Further questioned, the witness said that he had done business, from time to time, with Mr Sinclair for the past five years. He lived in Newcastle-on-Tyne for a few months.

FITZGERALD. Newcastle-on-Tyne must have a very strong influence on phonetics.

MR WOOD, K.C. Are you a well-known billiard player to the extent that you won a billiard championship?

FENNING. I have won about ten championships in this city.

His Lordship observed that he did not see any relevance in this.

MR WOOD. It is suggested that he came from nowhere, out of the clouds, and that he is an apostate as regards religion.

This ended the plaintiff's case.

On the second day of the trial, a sensation occurred.

The judge asked counsel for the plaintiff had he any further submissions to make. When he received a negative reply, he said he proposed to withdraw the case from the jury as authorship of the book had not been proved. Albert Wood was thunderstruck. Speechless for a second, he suddenly thought of the solution and, turning round, called Gogarty to the witness-box. By this manœuvre, he saved the day. Had Gogarty not been in court, the case might have been withdrawn from the jury. It is debatable whether or not, on appeal, the superior court would have upheld the judge's decision – there had been references to Gogarty's authorship at the preliminary proceedings – but, at the very least, a new trial might have been directed, which would have been to Gogarty's benefit.

Gogarty was now Wood's witness. 'The Thunderer' had to confine himself to direct examination. As he loved to lacerate in cross-examination, the effort must have nearly strangled him. Gogarty admitted he knew Morris Sinclair; that he knew William Sinclair, but added that William Sinclair was known to everyone as 'Boss'. Gogarty had been a friend of 'Boss' Sinclair, who was on close terms with Orpen in pre-war days. The name 'Willie' was used in the verse because it rhymed with 'Piccadilly'; the poems did not refer to the Sinclairs but were a composite photograph. He was not aware that the Sinclairs were twins. He explained the reference to the 'Twin grandchildren' by allusions to Celtic and Greek mythology. The composite photograph was to throw discredit on usury and money-lending generally.

After Gogarty had finished his evidence, Fitzgerald opened the defence to the jury. His speech went along the lines disclosed in his cross-examination, that the libel – if there was one – was so obscure as to be obvious only to intimate associates of the plaintiff.

The Jury [he said] were entitled to the assistance of witnesses who had not been cajoled into giving evidence as partisans as had happened in this case. It was unfortunate that Mr Wood had whittled boomerangs which, when he threw them, came back and struck his own case. One example was when he likened Gogarty to one of those men who would dive into an ashbin for garbage. There were poor but respectable people who had to do that but it could equally apply to Mr Sinclair, who was searching dustbins in the form of Gogarty's book but not looking for garbage but money. Mr Wood had referred to the coterie of 'bawds and blasphemers'. This was another boomerang. He did not know where Mr Wood got the phrase, but it fitted the gentleman who was put forward as the principal witness, Mr Samuel Beckett, the nephew-in-law of Mr Henry Morris Sinclair. Certainly, if anybody could be said to belong to a coterie of bawds and blasphemers, it was Mr Beckett. He might well have stayed in Paris. Could they imagine that wretched creature making representation to the High Court as an ordinary reasonable man?

The evidence of Mr Murray, the optician, was remarkable. His spectacles were perhaps useful in finding libels. Mr Geraghty, another witness, for some reason best known to himself had ceased to be in business for twenty years. Not a single one of the witnesses had ever looked at the book until they had been approached by Mr Sinclair to find libel or had seen the report of the court proceedings.

W. R. Fearon, professor of Biochemistry in Trinity and the author of a play on Parnell, then gave evidence that he had heard similar rhymes to those complained of, in his student days, and that as a Dublin person he couldn't connect them with the plaintiff.* R. M. Smyllie, Editor of the *Irish Times,* said he regarded the poems as folk-lore and could not identify the plaintiff from them. In evidence taken on commission and read in court, F. R. Higgins, the poet, stated that he considered the verses 'folk songs' and that he had heard Gogarty recite them to the plaintiff in the Dolphin Hotel when no objection had been taken.

Fitzgerald did not address the jury a second time, but Wood took the opportunity to deliver a *balaclava.*

> The most serious aspect of the case was the raking in the ashes of the dead as if it were necessary in order to tickle the literary palates of the world with the description of that dead old man. The book provided lightning flashes for those who lived in its period: they were not only identification, they were brands, and they burned into the flesh of Mr Sinclair. The book spoke of the 'streamy-eyed solicitor', the politician described as the 'Yellow leprechaun who stole power through a confidence trick on the ignorance and illusions of an electorate that was narrow', and referred to that solicitor as 'that coffin worm devouring widows and orphans'. Who was the 'coffin worm'? Was the solicitor or the doctor the coffin worm?

Mr Justice O'Byrne then summed up and the jury retired. Fitzgerald seems to have been optimistic about the result. He hadn't chosen to exercise his right to address the jury a second time or to make use of the rare privilege of cross-examining his own client. Though the judge had failed to stress salient features of the case in his summing-up, the absence for instance of impartial publication witnesses, there had been no objections from the defence or request for the recall of the jury. After an hour and a half's absence, the jury announced they had found in favour of the plaintiff awarding him £900 damages plus costs. The amount of the damages surprised the legal profession: it was considered a brilliant coup for Wood.

Gogarty knew the case would cost him in the neighbourhood of £2,000. He was angry and embittered that his fellow citizens should have treated him in this way.

---

* 'I will', said Gogarty later to Fearon, 'be grateful to you for the rest of my puff, until my head collides with the stars.'

'The Jew sold his stinking past, dug up a skeleton! Ah well', he wrote a few days later to Montgomery Hyde. But he told Charles Graves, with typical flippancy, that he didn't care about the result as long as it made Dublin verse-conscious.

That a fellow writer like Beckett should have given evidence against him hurt him deeply. He never forgot it. In 1956, he wrote to the biographer, referring to a talk given on the Third Programme of the B.B.C.:

I am sorry you praised Beckett's play [*Waiting for Godot*]. It's nothing but a long wail.

By a curious piece of irony, it seems that the actual verses may not have been written by Gogarty at all. A reporter in the *Irish Times* of that period, Mr L. T. Fleming, has written to the biographer as follows: 'Redding told me that the verses which caused the famous libel action, "Two Jews lived in Sackville Street" were written by himself.' Redding wrote many verses on similar themes which are in the biographer's possession. Their style resembles closely that of the verses which appear in *Sackville Street*.

Gogarty lost more by the libel action than the £2,000 he had to pay in costs and damages. The sale of the book was affected and his expectancy of a sizeable sum from that source was not fulfilled.

A month after the action he had made up his mind to leave Dublin. He took rooms in Upper Wimpole Street, London, and recommenced practice as an ear, nose and throat specialist. As before in the 'twenties, there were numerous medical friends who were glad to send him patients. But though he took his medical work seriously enough for a while, the Bohemian habits of his last years in Dublin were not entirely eradicated. He soon became a well-known figure in Fleet Street. He contributed articles under his own name to Lord Beaverbrook's *Evening Standard*. He appeared on radio and television.

He liked to picture himself as a dilettante unhampered by a conventional background. When his daughter, Brenda, who was studying at a London art school at the time, went to call for him once at a dinner, she got the impression that he was slightly annoyed that it should be known he had a family.

'At his suggestion I called for Father around 10.30 p.m. where he was dining with friends,' Mrs Desmond Williams writes. 'We were to go on to a dance at Lord Beaverbrook's together. When I arrived, the butler said, "They are still in the drawing-room but I will tell Mrs —— you are here." He showed me up to the drawing-room where the hostess joined me a few minutes later. When I introduced myself, she said, "Good gracious, I never knew Dr Gogarty was married." Afterwards in the taxi, I thought I would tease him about this, so I said, "You would never guess what your hostess said to me." "No? What did she say?" "Good gracious, I never knew Dr Gogarty was married!" He did not think it at all funny, and replied rather irritably, "She must be a very stupid woman to say a thing like that." '

Meanwhile, he had two new books on the stocks. The first was a study of St Patrick, which was published in 1938. Gogarty had visited the various places associated in legend and history with Ireland's patron saint. He had flown over Downpatrick with the Marquis of Londonderry in the cockpit, to photograph the scene of the saint's landing place in Ireland at Strangford Lough. He climbed Croagh Patrick, the Pilgrim's mountain in the West dedicated to the saint, where thousands of Irish men and women still make the ascent barefooted in penance for their sins. He had visited St Patrick's Purgatory, the grim Retreat House in Lough Derg, also used today as a place of penance in memory of a saint whose name conjures up light-heartedness and mirth. In Belfast he stayed with Montgomery Hyde and his sister Diana and the latter arranged for him to witness an Orange procession. This evoked a fine piece of prose assonance from Gogarty's pen.

Whack! The Flagellants scourged the drums as they punished themselves in their frenzy. Blood flowed and splashed from bleeding wrists and stained a hand's breadth of the drum where the tendons of the adept came in contact with the rim. Boom! And the jailed giants roared and erupted sound like a volcano. Outside, the careless notes of the fifes and flutes led on. But the Typhonic thunder of the drums drowned all. The fifes wailed like panic-stricken furies from all this Congo of the drums. Boom! Boom! Boom! The crowd cheers. The waggonettes respond with Druidical dignity. No hats are raised. A halt. Time marked. A whistle. Silence. The kilted pipers come into view, cheeks distended, eyes bulging. Boom! On it moves. For two hours the procession passes.

'No surrender.' It is written on the drum. 'The Ballymena Boys' Brigade.' Boom! 'The Protestants of Portadown', a particular stronghold. Boom! Portadown! Doon! Boom!

My heart goes out in an undercurrent to the poor Orangemen, curt, monosyllabic, honest, reliable and free from humbug, who have for their portion not the joys, but the noise of life. May they never be merged with the South, or driven drumming up the Capitol in Rome. Athens might as well attempt to bring in Sparta – leave them alone. We want no drums in Dreamland.

I Follow St Patrick is a blend of light scholarship and Gogartian discursiveness. It was re-published in 1950. His other work, *Tumbling in the Hay*, was published in 1939. It contained his student memoirs written in the conversational mode of *Sackville Street*, with chapters which, for their delineation of character, recall the style of the great essayists – Leigh Hunt, Lamb and Hazlitt. The war interfered with its sales; but Harold Nicolson, writing in the *Daily Telegraph*, warned the reader not to mistake for entertainment what was obviously a work of art.

Gogarty had arranged to go to America on a lecture tour in September 1939. When the war broke out he volunteered instantly for the R.A.M.C. Turned down because of his age, which was sixty, he volunteered for the R.A.F. as a doctor but, though the Marquis of Londonderry used influence on his behalf, he was again turned down. In September, he set off to fulfil his engagements in America. He was not to return to the British Isles for five years.

America captivated him. He found he could make a pleasant living there writing articles and lecturing. His fame soon spread and he was in demand once again, as he had been in London in the 'twenties, at fashionable gatherings and house parties, as a conversationalist and story-teller. He made one last attempt to enter the armed forces: he volunteered for the Canadian R.A.M.C. but was turned down once more on age grounds.

He intended to practise as a doctor in New York, but a State examination was compulsory before he could do so. He felt too old to sit for an examination at his age. And so he continued his profitable journalism and lecturing, and in the intervals writing novels and poetry.

TWENTY

I<small>N</small> America he wrote a considerable amount of journalism for magazines like *Vogue, Harper's Magazine, Esquire,* and *The Atlantic Monthly.* He also found a market for his poetry in magazines which catered to widely differing tastes, such as *Contemporary Poetry* and *Colliers.* In a letter written to Shane Leslie, shortly after he had begun to settle down in America, Gogarty gives an account of his literary activities, as well as adducing the reasons why he was unable to return to England as he had wished.

I shall try to cross to England as a medico with some Canadian contingent. Already I have sent in my name. I owe my present inactivity and my absence from Europe to that shrimp Kingsley Wood for he referred me back to the B.M.A. when I tried through Londonderry, ex-Air-Minister, to cash in on my experience of flying and join up as a doctor to some flying squadron and so get in front of a long waiting list which the B.M.A. had already said they had.

As all the news I get from home is by cablegrams, I cannot say what the position is in Ireland. I read that the Germans have been bombing dairymaids and destroying a creamery: a hint to the long-memoried Irish that there is no use crying over spilt milk?

This country, with the exception of the Middle West which, unfortunately, is too much this country, is overwhelming pro-English in sympathy, but averse to War, sentiments which Hoover (ex-Pres.) tells me will soon clash. However, seeing that here they are almost unarmed and distracted with anxieties about their S. American Markets and Japan's strength, they are doing all in their power to help.

I preceded Duff Cooper on his extensive tour last Autumn. We were 'put on the air' – Lord Marley, D.C. and I – by a fellow who is said to be a renegade Englishman, an American edition of Lord Haw Haw; as 'spies', that is, as propagandists. This led to the picketing of Duff Cooper's first lecture but he carried on unintimidated. If we were spies I am glad to say so were and still are, all the decent editors of the daily newspapers on the East Coast.

Have you read *Letters on Poetry From W. B. Yeats to Dorothy Wellesley*? It is full of interest and shows how dearly Yeats could love a lady even if he disliked a lord in the person of Dunsany.

Saddened by the drabness, misery and meanness of my natal city under the exclusive commune, I, finding myself the only householder left, sold Ely Pl., to that treble contradiction in terms The Royal Hibernian Academy. The Constitution is to turn my garden into a non-Platonic Academy and build its picture gallery thereon.

Thanks for writing to me. I got your letter within 3 weeks uncensored which shows what fine work the navy is doing. I hope Winston bears up under the Atlas weight of his responsibilities.

The reference at the end of the letter to the sale of his Dublin house, shows how Gogarty had persevered in his intention of making a clean break with Ireland. Another letter to his old friend, Jim Montgomery, finishes on the same note.

I wish you could just for an experience see the United States. I don't mean that you should see seventy cities as I had to do for an Oriental called Colston Leigh in '39; but to see the vast country with rivers which dwarf anything we have, mountains and endless forests with quick-growing oaks. And then the clarified atmosphere which makes the days skip by with alarming haste. They say that the impression one gets here of time being faster than in Europe is due to the amount of distractions which are at everyone's disposal; but I think without being mystical or Fourth Dimensionary that Time here is actually accelerated. A week goes like a week-end and there is a dint in the moon the day after she is full. My 3 years here have gone like one. Maybe it was the relief from petty dislikes and frustrations that made me for the first time in my life experience freedom.

> We rose to bring about Eutopia,
> But all we got was Dev's myopia.

In between writing articles and lecturing, Gogarty had begun writing novels. *Mr Petunia* and *Mad Grandeur* were published between 1940 and 1944. *Mr Petunia*, a rather attenuated novel, is a clever study of a schizophrenic Virginian watchmaker in the eighteenth century, but *Mad Grandeur*, a tale of eighteenth-century Ireland, has little cohesion, and was probably written with an eye to selling it as a Hollywood film script.

From time to time letters arrived from home, with news of those who had formed the group who met for evening conversations in Indignation House. Some of the letters brought melancholy news of the passing away of old friends and the plaints of men who had outlived the excited atmosphere which had enlivened their youth. Others like those of Seamus Burke, the ex-Minister for Home Affairs, whose Norman origins Gogarty prized so much, were full of amusing and informative gossip of the 'town', of the sort with which Gogarty and his friends would regale themselves in Fanning's circle at five-thirty each evening. Burke would write,

Kevin Smith showed me your letter, so I took your address. Glad to learn you have been able to ride the whirl wind all who go to America must do or be hurled into oblivion.

I am living within a bowshot of Wyckham, the old Man's home, Dundrum. I cast contour eyes on it occasionally as I pass. I am looking ahead. Its most distinguished resident during the last few years was Spud Murphy. He had a talent for the 'Mot Juste' but was a little tedious. He had founded his style on Sterne, who could ruminate through a hundred pages under the inspiration of a motionless hansom-cab in France. What would he have written under the inspiration of a Dublin cab, jolting over the cobble stones round Stephen's Green, with a two-backed beast inside? Murphy thought a lot of you, particularly since you removed that carbuncle from his forehead. I saw a great deal of him as you may imagine. He repudiated with scorn the soft impeachment in the lines. 'He will not know, He will not care; they will not run before him there – when he goes down.' He went down for the last time around Xmas – had his breakfast, went up to his room, leaned over to tie his shoe, went out on the top of his head and was dead. It was lucky for the poor old fellow he went so quick.

Fanning nearly emulated the death of Cœur-de-Lion recently, who as you know died from gangrene caused by an arrow wound. Fanning, while rusticating in the ancestral home in Tipperary, scratched his hand on a broken branch. The abrasion went septic and it was feared the whole arm would have to be amputated. That goose must not have been properly inoculated* after all. However, he is out again as fresh as a daisy.

The Major, who, when you were here, had an Emu brand Burgundy complexion, has now turned the colour of dark purple ink. Otherwise he is doing nicely.

Joe B.B. I regret to say is in hospital – heart. He has not been looking well for a long time. It would be better for Joe if there was a little walk between himself and the bar.

Charlie R. has sought sanctuary in Grangegorman† from his creditors, but is available for a chat on the phone at any time.

Excuse pen. I can't type which is now a form of illiteracy.

By the way, Smyllie of the *Irish Times* is also laid up for repairs – too close to the Palace Bar, but I understand he will come alright.

I am keeping very quiet up here in the mountains – The Lamb-Doyle's, the local. My nearest neighbour is Jo Hone whom I see now and again. I suppose you read his biography of Yeats. He told me Yeats had been given monkey-glands. I did not know that before. It gives additional emphasis to 'Come.'

The last time I saw Jimmy Montgomery was on Grafton St. Opposite us, Sir Val Grace came puffing and blowing out of Jackson's Antique Shop with a small grandfather clock in his arms. Jimmy gave him a quick glance, then the merry eye and roguish smile flashed at me 'More grease than Grace.'

George Bonass, one of the circle, wrote in September 1941, in a less carefree strain.

I have written you half a dozen times – but have not seen your pretty hand for many moons. I get no word of you or your books – can't get any volumes of you – and since I can't have

---

* This is probably a reference to a fabled goose in the T.C.D. Medical School when Gogarty was a student. The goose had been experimented on until it was literally a walking arsenal of bacteria. Gogarty and friends kidnapped the animal, and from its liver made a *pâté* which they generously fed to Fanning as a prophylactic against future disease.

† Grangegorman is Dublin's mental hospital.

volumes perchance you'd post me even a card to prove you are still in the land of the living. I see Joe very often and he makes the same plaint. Have you deserted all your old friends and really gone native? Charlie is just a name to me of mixed memories – Never see him. The Round Corner is I understand still alive in spots – Have been unlucky in my visits – Never found anyone. Gerry, Harper, and the Dentist visit there occasionally. Fanning as you are probably aware got over six thousand for it and now spends all his days feeding the ducks in the Green. I find rest, refreshment and solitude in the House of Kennedy – at the Corner. The solitude is seldom broken except by request. But then, Oliver, I live up to your dictums and you always stated that you could not suffer fools gladly. Neither can I. Did I tell you that my delightful Doris has drawn a winner in the Marriage Stakes? You know I'm the luckiest trainer of fillies in Ireland. Practically every one of them, both on the flat and over the sticks has landed some pretty useful prize. It is most interesting to meet them afterwards as brood mares. Technique of course counts for a lot these days, and as we know experience counts a lot even in the selling platers. I hope to see Joe to-morrow evening when possibly I may have some original views if not news for you.

I live such a very quiet life. However, it might be that there's a good time coming, Oliver, when all the world grows sane lad and all the Janes are Queens. God love you, Oliver. Write to me soon.

Two years later in 1943, Joseph Boyd Barrett, his old school friend, and companion of the Bailey days, was writing to tell Gogarty of Bonass's death:

I hope all goes well with you. I miss you *very* much. 'Perdere amicum est damnorum maximum' as the old Romans truly said.

The 'strong, unmerciful tyrant' has been very busy here in Dublin. Dear old George Bonass has left us and also Jim Montgomery. I started a letter to you about George; but did not finish it. It was too sad. His last words to me were 'Give my love to Oliver.' Poor Jim died with a jest on his lips, as you might expect. 'I am hovering between wife and death.'

I wrote to you after the death of F. R. Higgins and after your wonderful poem about Yeats. 'The best thing written for many years,' as Fitzgerald Kenny said to me.

Nolan Whelan was asking for you last night. He has not one grey hair yet. He still lives in his round room in Cliff Hotel. 'The captain closeted in his tour.'

The round corner is still going strong. Harpur, Kevin Smyth, Paddy O'Callaghan, Arthur McDonald, and Colbert. Jerry O'Carroll has a job in England. Russell is in a doubtful business – 'charcoal'. McDonald still makes his exits and entrances. 'Still thro the ivy flits the bee, O singer of Persephone.' Did you hear Colbert's joke about Fanning? He is the first merchant who made a success on the principle that the customer was always wrong.

I saw Fanning lately. He is as straight when standing and as quick when walking as ever. He lent us your little gem about Croker of Ballinagarde. You ought to send it to Smyllie for the *Irish Times*. I am settled in Dunleary at Gresham House, a private Hotel next the Royal Marine Hotel and have joined a Yacht Club (or pub). Gresham House occupies a charming position with lovely gardens and a view of Dublin Bay. 'Neptunem spectare furentem. Oblitus meorum oblivescendus et illis.'

I feel fine although I had a touch of blood pressure some months ago. I can still get my ration of the 'dull opiate' with ease.

I have much more to tell you in another letter. It is dreadful to count the years. 'Dieu que le temps passe vite.'

Good bye for the present 'Primus sodalium meorum'.

Yours, JOE

Though Gogarty was happy and elated in America, there is evidence that deep down he still felt the pull of the Irish scene, and was disappointed that the circumstances of Irish politics prevented him from retiring to, and being in the congenial company of his own countrymen. A letter, written to Niall Montgomery on the death of his father, Gogarty's old friend, James Montgomery, in 1944, shows how virulent Gogarty's antagonisms against the land that bred him, had become.

293

Dear Niall,

I heartily sympathise with you in the double loss of a father and brother. You need not blame the light coat that your father wore for causing his bronchial pneumonia. Lying in bed could cause that – hypostatic pneumonia. Had he been told of your brother's death, this and the shock which must have followed his operation were enough. As for the treatment the Government dealt him: he surely was philosopher enough to expect but rudeness from a knot of boors. That Government has won the tolerant contempt of those who were lately Ireland's friends.

I wish that you would, for the prime of your life, avail yourself of wider horizons than that bounded by bureaucrats. Ireland presents, now before it goes down the ruinous way France went, the interesting example of a Government of a Katostocracy! Now that the soul of the city died with your father to what would one go back?

I hope you get this letter. In deep sympathy.

Sincerely yours,

OLIVER ST J. GOGARTY

Yeats had died in January 1939, just before Gogarty set out for America. In an obituary article, which was published next day in the *Evening Standard*, Gogarty had written:

Yeats was the greatest conversationalist I ever met. Ireland's greatest most powerful voice is silent. He lived at the risk of being misunderstood against the political propaganda that passed for poetry in the Ireland of his time. He has written somewhere that he never wrote bad verse so that he might have a heavier purse.

I shall always remember him one morning when he stayed with me, how he walked up and down a passage with his hands behind his back while the house vibrated as he hummed, his mind like a swarm of bees distilling the golden honey of his song.

The fire-borne moods of his mind will live on everlastingly and undiminished past that death, which men have invented, and be for us a glory and a joy.

Now in America, he worked on the draft of what was to be one of his finest poems, the 'Elegy on the Death of the Archpoet'. He reiterates in it his belief that with Yeats had died the last figure of the revival which had illuminated the days of his youth. The bell in the Trinity Campanile had tolled for the going out of his old professors, and now his tutor in the art of song had been gathered into the womb of the universe.

> Chiefly the loss of friends:
> Tyrrell, Mahaffy and Macran,
> The last the gentlest gentleman,
> And golden Russell – all were gone,
> Still I could turn to you alone.
> Now you have turned away
> Into the land of sleep or dreams
> (If dreams, you rule them yet meseems).

And he remembered how his native city had treated the greatest figure in the arts that Ireland had produced, by refusing him the freedom of the city, and granting it to Boss Croker whose horse had won the Derby.

> To think its mounted-beggar race
> Makes Dublin the most famous place
> For famous men to leave:
> Where City Fathers stage a farce
> And honoured one who owned a horse;
> They win right well our sneers,
> Who of their son took no account
> Though he had Pegasus to mount
> And rode two hemispheres.
> Return Dean Swift, and elevate
> Our townsmen to the equine state!

He is reminded too how the coming seasons will bring back the memory of his friend.

> Now you are gone beyond the glow
> As muted as a world of snow;
> And I am left amid the scene
> Where April comes new-drenched in green,
> To watch the budding trees that grow
> And cast, where quiet waters flow,
> Their hueless patterns below;

And think upon the clear bright rill
That lulled your garden on the hill;
And wonder when shall I be made
Like you, beyond the stream, a shade.

Earlier in the poem he remembers the great years of fabulous talk, when he and the poet met each day to range their minds over subjects from Adam to the atom.

O happy were your days on earth
When we sat by the household hearth
And, as the Autumn glow went out,
Bandied the whole bright world about,
Making Reality betray
The edges of sincerer day;
Or in that orchard house of mine, –
The firelight glancing in the wine
Or on your ring that Dulac made –
How merrily your fancy played
With the lost egg that Leda laid,
The lost, third egg, Herodotus
In Sparta said he came across ...

Gogarty found himself enchanted by the speed and enthusiasms of American life. When he went on his lecture tours, he always flew if there was an opportunity, and sometimes piloted his own plane. Once climbing into his machine to fly off from the University of Virginia, Padraic Colum asked him if he wasn't afraid of crashing; and Gogarty replied, 'It's not death we're afraid of but dying.' He had many friends in America whom he knew of old: Major Eugene Kincaid, James Healy, Joseph Campbell, John Ford and Robert Flaherty, of the film world. There were others whom he met after his arrival in the States and who extended to him the hospitality of their homes and estates. He who had found the country houses in decline at home, found himself a welcome visitor in American country houses, in Virginia, the Carolinas and New England. He had become by 1940 a well-known figure round Broadway. Hostesses were always glad to have him at dinners and parties. Lord Beaverbrook, who had met him in earlier years in Dublin, met him again in New York. He found him as brilliant as ever.

He told me many stories, some of which I remember in substance. But to set them down on paper would be to slaughter them. They were stories that require to be told, and they require Gogarty to tell them. He was a brilliant raconteur. His style of speech was highly individual. In New York he would join me at my hotel. We would talk a great deal and drink a little.

Irishmen are naturally vain and the prospect of finding himself the centre of attention, and with a ready audience for whom to display his talents, was never unpleasing to Gogarty. Nearing seventy he was in the happy position of finding himself a celebrated figure and celebrated for the one pastime above all he liked to indulge himself in, conversation. But there were moments when the dream broke, and he saw that he was using the excitement and vitality of America like a drug, to drown his bitterness and disappointment that the Ireland he had helped to build was no longer a fit place for him to live in. Richard Aherne remembers him in a bar in New York in the 'forties.

There were five or six of us sitting in a booth and Gogarty was telling many of his wonderful stories and we were about to move off, but before we did so he said 'Now I want to tell you this, a delightful story.' So he proceeded to tell this story and, when he was about to come to the point of the story, a young man who was sitting by the bar got up off the stool, went over, placed a coin in the juke box, and all hell broke loose. The expression on Gogarty's face changed, and became very sad, a combination of sadness and anger; he said: 'Oh dear God in heaven, that I should find myself thousands of miles from home, at the mercy of every retarded son of a bitch, who has a nickel to drop in that bloody illuminated coal-scuttle.'

TWENTY-ONE

IN 1945, Gogarty returned to Dublin, his 'unfriendly bitter Ithaca'. It was his first visit in six years. The first thing that struck him was how clean Dublin was.

I had to travel half way round the world to realise this. Dirty Dublin indeed!

Merrion Square still seemed to him to have the air of the eighteenth century with 'blue plumes of turf smoke staining the sky', and its crystal clear atmosphere. He had forgotten how leisurely Dublin was. After the turmoil of New York, it was curious to see forty yards between groups of people and no one in a hurry.

It was as gossipy a town as ever. Gogarty had just got into his bath in the Shelbourne after arriving, when the 'Pope' Flanagan stuck his head through the steam, 'I heard you got back,' he said. He gave Gogarty the latest news. 'The Spanish Grandee is dead [Joe Boyd Barrett]. The Major still comes into a Tavern by a different door each time; the Colonel is under restraint, the Marquis died on his honeymoon.' They discussed the latest scandal about De Valera, that 'laugh in mourning' as Gogarty called him.

When he stepped out into the streets, Gogarty noted with nostalgia that the taverns in which the 'famous company' used to meet had changed hands. 'Indignation House' and the 'One-eyed Man's' were no more. People stopped to greet him in the streets, glad that he was back. No man had more fame in his native town from surgeon to sailor, from parson to pedlar than Gogarty had. And his fame since he had left had grown even more, for the Irish prefer to weave dreams about a legend than to have to add embellishment to reality. A visit to Trinity brought him many memories. He had slipped away from the crowded streets one afternoon and was soon enveloped in the atmosphere of the tall classical buildings, whose grey stone somehow manages to appear friendly, and the great wide sweep of the cobbled squares, silent now for him, for the great men of his youth were gone: Tyrrell, Mahaffy, Macran, the whole of that singular band, eminent in social as well as intellectual prowess. Immersed in the greenery of the College Park, with only a distant din in his ears to remind him

298

of the traffic outside, he thought of the youth who had skimmed round the grass circumference on his bicycle, and passed the finishing line in front of his challengers.

But Gogarty was too much of an optimist to sink back into nostalgic yearnings for a past that could never be revived. Dublin had changed, or the part of it that he knew had changed, and it would have been a Herculean task to invert himself into its daily life again. Apart from anything else, it offered him no means of earning his living. A professional man cannot leave his practice for eight years and expect to find it there when he returns.

In America, on the other hand, he had an adequate income from the proceeds of his journalism and poetry. In January 1952, he wrote gleefully to his son, Noll, to say he had just sold thirty-two lines of verse for 200 dollars. On December 7th, 1954, he wrote: 'I have been awarded 5,000 dollars (by the Poetry Society of America) for my "genius" in writing poetry, so I am in the chips.' This was one reason for returning to America. Anyway he found it a wonderfully vital place to live in for a man who was growing old in body, but who remained gay in spirit, and who retained the energy of a man half his age.

'Their mode of living is a profusion,' he told those who asked him why he liked America. 'And they want you to share it with them.'

On his visits home, he kept in close touch with his family. Usually he stayed at 22 Earlsfort Terrace with his son, Noll. Occasionally he moved round the corner to the Hatch Hotel near by.

On Sundays, either Noll or Frank Flanagan would take him on motor drives through the country-side. Observant as of old, Gogarty would recollect with his flawless memory details about each place they passed, public house, mansion or church, noting the changes which had taken place since he had last been there. Some of the time he spent with his daughter, Brenda, at Tulla-more, or at the house on the island in Tully Lake, Renvyle, which his son-in-law had purchased. He took a keen interest in his small grandson, Guy, and his letters to Mrs Williams contain constant advice as to the boy's health, diet and the necessity for teaching him to swim at an early age. He wrote regularly to Noll up to the week of his death on September 22nd, 1957, his letters often containing amusing comments on current affairs and persons in high places in Ireland.

He made two return visits between 1945 and 1948. On both occasions, he stayed only a few months. His second visit was in 1948. These visits seem to have revived something of his old exuberance in words. In 1948, he began a new volume of auto-biography. It didn't come out till six years later. *It isn't this time of year at all* is an uneven work, but here and there, there are flashes of genuine Gogartiana in it.

In 1952, his collected poems appeared in a limited edition of 500 copies with prefaces by Yeats and A.E. This volume contained almost all the poems which had already appeared in *An Offering of Swans* (1924), *Wild Apples* (1928) and *Others to Adorn* (1939), with the addition of the Yeats Elegy and one or two other poems he had written after he had gone to America. Among curious omissions in the *Collected Poems* are some early lyrics, the most notable being 'My Love is Dark' and 'Folia Caduca'.

Iain Hamilton, reviewing the edition in the *Manchester Guardian*, wrote that the poems at their best showed 'how close Gogarty comes to justifying Yeats' opinion of him as "one of the great lyric poets of our age".' The reviewer continued:

> Yeats himself had something to learn from Gogarty whose love of the natural world is a rare frenzy and who seldom succumbs to the English curse 'of mixing philosophy up with verse'.
>
> Gogarty is a classical poet, not merely in the lesser sense, that he moves with sufficient ease between Praxiteles and Petronius Arbiter, but that he has the unmistakeable air of bringing a vastness of passion under control subjecting it to strict proportion working down as it were from the surface of the rough matrix towards the potential perfection at the core.

In 1954, Gogarty returned again to Ireland. When the bio-grapher met him on this occasion he was well-preserved, lean and hawk-like handsome. At this period, he neither smoked nor drank alcohol. He was fit enough to lie down on the carpet, and demon-strate his cycling exercises from an upside-down position. He stayed in an old-fashioned hotel in Hatch Street, where I used to find him in the sitting-room reading detective novels when I called. His eyes were strikingly blue, set in a face that was rather white, and which seemed as carved and ascetic as a monk's, except when laughter broke over it and it became lit by humour.

At dinner, one could observe his conversational technique, which now was limited to some extent by the failing of what once had been a unique gift of memory. He still told his anecdotes as brilliantly as ever and quoted with flawless precision, but now one got the impression that there were certain set pieces which he brought in, as if it was expected that he must fulfil his reputation as a master of conversation. Perhaps this was the influence of his sojourn in America, where living up to his reputation had become to a great extent his mode of living. He gave two sparkling impersonations now, standing up for these, of Osbert Sitwell and Edith Sitwell on their American tours. He disliked them because of what he regarded as their pretentious attitude to poetry. For a man of seventy-four, he had phenomenal vitality and he looked no older than his mid fifties.

He returned again in 1956; full of energy and verve, and fulminating against De Valera. His figure at 76 was erect and slim. His step was fast and spry. One day I walked from Hatch Street down Grafton Street over to Kildare Street and up through Stephen's Green with him, while he talked the whole time, except when he stopped to meet old acquaintances whom he greeted with exceptional charm. It was as if he had never been away. There was none whom he did not seem glad to see and to talk with for a minute over some memory of the old days. I said goodbye to him one day in Kildare Street and handed him a photograph taken of him in his cycling days, showing a slim, handsome, boyish figure. He took it with interest, put it in his wallet, and then was gone. It was as if for a moment I had revived a past which he did not wish to think about too much if he was returning to America.

Yet it was this visit which seemed to have decided him about retiring to Ireland. He had made up his mind to return for good in October 1957. But on September 19th, he was taken ill with a heart attack in a street in New York and removed to the Beth David Hospital there.* Gogarty was placed immediately in an oxygen tent; even in these straitened circumstances, he never forgot his medical professor Sir Thomas Myles's advice 'Be

* The previous day Ringling North, the famous circus-proprietor and an admirer of Gogarty's writings, had called him on the telephone, inviting him to the circus as his guest and to supper afterwards. Gogarty replied typically, 'I'll come tonight.' North was unable to be present himself that evening, but he booked a box for Gogarty and arranged a date for a dinner that never took place.

merrie, Laddie.' And he constantly joked with those in neighbouring beds and the visitors who came to see him.

Earlier in the year, President Cosgrave, his friend in Ireland, had written to him reminding him in friendly Irish fashion that his age warranted doing something about the state of his soul. For some months before his illness a tactful Jesuit, Father Richards, had been doing patchwork on what Gogarty regarded as a slightly tattered part of his metaphysical self, and this priest gave him the rites of the Church before he died on the 22nd. It is curious that John Butler Yeats, the poet's father, who also spent his closing years in New York, had made a similar resolution to return to Ireland, but died just before fulfilling it. (A Mass for Gogarty was celebrated in St Patrick's Cathedral: the ceremony was attended by a number of his friends, including Montgomery Hyde.) Gogarty's body was flown back from America for the funeral. At Shannon, the coffin was met by his son Oliver, his daughter-in-law, his daughter Brenda and her husband, and driven from there to a chapel near Renvyle in Connemara. Gogarty had asked to be buried near Renvyle.

* * *

At the funeral we stood on a hill over a small lake, with the Connemara mountains green and blue in the distance, the long incredible distance of the West, where the eye can see for many miles, yet there are never clear outlines, but forms blurred by bright colours. To the left of the grave a white ash tree stretched crooked and bent, silver against the lake's blue. A priest said the Latin prayers as the coffin was lowered into the grave. William Cosgrave, first President of the Irish Free State, stood near by. Lennox Robinson swaying in the breeze, vague as the hills behind him, bore a wreath from the Irish Academy of Letters. Standing at the graveside beside me was Monsignor Patrick Browne, who had earlier sung the Requiem Mass at Letterfrack chapel; unbent by age, straight as a lance at six foot three, his carved aquiline features looked more than ever like a Florentine from a painting by del Sarto. 'Paddy' Browne had been very much a part of the pre-first war Gogarty set and his elephantine memory for verse had enabled him to compete conversation-wise with them.

The priest at the graveside began sprinkling the holy water, I'm glad to say, out of a naggin bottle, and to chant the De Profundis:

'*De profundis clamavi ad te domine ...*'

Presently Monsignor Paddy began to recite a Gogarty Limerick in my ear, his voice alternating with the Latin chant:

'Then out spoke the king of Siam
For women I don't give a damn ...'

The priest at the graveside continued:

'*Fiant aures tua intendente et vocem deprecationem meam ...*'

The Monsignor lowered his voice:

'You may think it odd of me
I prefer sodomy
They say I'm a bugger, I am.'

He looked for approval, then said:

'Oliver wrote marvellous parodies. He parodied Keats's *Silent upon a Peak in Darien* with "Potent behind a cart with Mary Ann".'

As he bent to my ear, I saw in the distance, on Shanbollard Lake below, a swan move towards the centre. Where had it come from? No one saw it leave the bank. As it floated away till it became a silver point, I heard the Monsignor chant in a low voice:

Mein lieber Schwan – ach diese letzte traurige Fahrt
(My beloved swan. Now for this last sad journey.)

He saw Oliver's soul borne to Paradise by the graceful bird, as the swan in German legend drew Lohengrin's barque to Montsalvat. I thought of a spring day thirty-three years before when the Liffey received her swans, how Gogarty and Yeats had celebrated in their poems the swan-god's passionate swoop.

303

Whitest of all earthly
Things, the white that's rarest
Is the snow on mountains
Standing in the sun.
Next the clouds above them.
Then the down is fairest
On the breast and pinions
Of a proudly sailing swan.

Above Shanbollard Lake that day, one realised why he had written once that here was his proper home:

Where there was neither time nor tide, nor any change of all, something friendly and akin and full of all that might be needed if need were to arise; but it never did, for you felt that nothing was lacking. And you did not want to speak.

When King Edward VII made a royal visit to Dublin in 1907, Gogarty wrote a commemorative ballad of a reputed encounter between the monarch and one of Mrs Mack's girls in a brothel in Nighttown. Appropriately, it is written in the François Villon *ballade* form (see page 55).

THE OLD PIANIST

There was a time I was not found
Outside the pubs in slants of light
Forgotten as the drink goes round
Unwelcomed as a drizzling night,
Insulted by each half-bred shite,
Who drinks, as if 'twas drink he feared –
I who played up to wild delight,
In days before the Kips were cleared.

It was not with a whistle then
I kept the insteps off the floor,
And oh by God I played for men,
Lovers alike of horse and whore;
When Life was like a long encore
Of 'Here's the Best' and 'What is yours?'
You could not drown my playful score
Now matter how you laughed with whores.

I played the night the Prince of Wales
Up from the Curragh came disguised,
We got the tip to reef our sails,
And yet let on we were surprised;
Poor Mrs Mack was paralysed,
She grew so lady-like and stately,
And got herself so bowdlerised
She lost her grip of things completely.

The Prince was not for bed that night
Had it not been for our Fresh Nelly
Who got herself so yelping tight

That in she came and slapped her belly
'Ye're all so damn stuck up, I tell ye.'
That no one thinks of sticking up
His bollocks where there's quaking jelly;
''Twould be the making of that pup!'

'Excuse me gloves!' sez Mrs Mack,
Then whispered 'Christ, when I get after
That mouldy whore, I'll break her back!'
The Prince, he simply roared with laughter,
And said, 'I hope you have not chaft her
On my account. It would be grand
To take, although I bump the rafter,
A bird with such a bush in hand.'

Mack muttered 'O the bloody bitch
To burst into a lady's parlour
With no respect for Kings and sich!
You'd think Yerself was Nosey Barlow!
Enough to bring my lucky star low
And make you think me common stuff.'
The Prince said 'Who in Monte Carlo
Has such a belly, bubs or buff.'

The slavey we send to hear
Said Nelly said 'Your Royal Highness,
I only took a sup of beer
To cure my modesty and shyness;'
Then Mother Mack put on such fineness
She almost made me want to puke,
You'd think she only let to line us
An odd Archbishop or a Duke.

'Don't mind me Kiddie, if I'm shy
Beat me to death, and then I'm mastered;
There's not a hair on either thigh
This belly never bore a bastard;
My bubs are round and alabastered
And firm enough to crack a flea,

306

And when I come, the sheets are plastered
Like Europe with the Zuyder Zee.'

I played to drown the chandelier
That chattered on the parlour ceiling.
'Be Gob, he's making Nelly roar,
An' all the better for good feeling.'
'But soon the plaster will be peeling'
Sez Mack, 'before he rings her bell.'
I said as one romance revealing:
'What Nellie peels, she plasters well.'

While this short time was going on,
Then up and spoke a bold equerry,
'Be kind enough to send me one
Well quartered lass to make me merry
I'd like to offer you a sherry
But since His Nibs is on a beano,
All drinks would be derogatory
Below a Pommery and Greno.'

'Send up Piano Mary here'
Sez Mack, 'and then send up a bottle;
She is a dreamy little dear
But she can bend the strongest wattle.
Your spine will know what tunes that mott'll
Strum on it like a piano player's
She is the best thing in the brothel
Since Nelly's cooling down upstairs.'

'Be Christ' sez Mack, 'the Kip's in luck
When even them on guard gets randy;
Go out and say I'll stand a fuck
To that plain clothes man choked with brandy,
How are you standing Napper Dandy?
I used to think, it sounds a farce
The Sun of Heaven shone from your bandy,
Shone from, by Heaven, your bandy arse!'

307

BIBLIOGRAPHY

Bailey, Kenneth C., *Trinity College, Dublin, 1892–1945*
Barrington, Sir Jonah, *Barrington's Personal Recollections*
Barry, Tom, *Guerilla Days in Ireland*
Beaslai, Piaras, *Michael Collins and the Making of a New Ireland*
Bennett, Richard, *The Black and Tans*
Birkenhead, Second Earl of, *F.E. By his Son*
Bowen, Elizabeth, *Collected Impressions*
        Seven Winters (A Dublin Girlhood)
Boyd, Ernest, *The Irish Literary Renaissance*
Bramsback, Birgit, *James Stephens*
Breen, Dan, *My Fight for Irish Freedom*
Bromage, Mary C., *De Valera and the March of a Nation*
Burckhardt, Jakob, *The Civilization of the Renaissance in Italy*
Buxton, E. M. Wilmot, *Old Celtic Tales*
Callwell, Maj.-Gen. Sir C. E., *Field-Marshal Sir Henry Wilson*,
    vols I and II
Chamberlain, Sir Austen, *Down the Years*
Chart, D. A., *Dublin*
Churchill, Sir Winston, *Thoughts and Adventures*
Clery, Arthur, *Dublin Essays*
Clifton, Violet, *The Book of Talbot*
        The Clongownian, 1895–1900, 1902–7
Cohen, J. M., *Rabelais : Gargantua, Pantagruel*
Colby Library Quarterly, A. E. Memorial Edition, November 1958
Colum, Mary and Padraic, *Our Friend James Joyce*
Colum, Padraic, *Arthur Griffith*
Connolly, James, *Labour in Ireland*
Cooper-Prichard, A. H., *Conversation with Oscar Wilde*
Corkery, Daniel, *J. M. Synge and the Irish Dramatic Movement*
Cousins, J. H. and M. E., *We Two Together*
Coxhead, Elizabeth, *Lady Gregory*
Craig, Maurice, *Dublin, 1600–1860*
Crozier, Brig.-Gen. F. P., *Ireland for Ever*
Curtis, Edmund, *A History of Ireland*

Dáil Eireann Nollaig 1921–Eanair 1922 (Treaty debates)
Dalton, Charles, *With the Dublin Brigade*
Dana, 1905 (Hodges Figgis & Co.)
Desmond, Shaw, *The Drama of Sinn Fein*
De Valera, Eamon, *Ireland's Case Against Conscription* (pamphlet, 1919)
Dickinson, P. L., *The Dublin of Yesterday*
Donochue, Florence P., *No Other Law*
Doolin, William, *Wayfarers in Medicine*
Drury, T. W. E., *Unforgotten*
Dublin Civic Week 1927
Dunsany, Lord, *My Ireland*
           Patches of Sunlight
Dwane, David T., *The Life of Eamon de Valera*
The Early Joyce (book reviews, 1902–3)
Echoes from Kottabos, edited by R. Y. Tyrrell
Eglinton, John, *A Memoir of A.E.*
           Irish Literary Portraits
Ellman, Richard, *James Joyce, A Biography*
English Wits, edited by Leonard Russell
Essays of William Hazlitt
Ewart, W., *A Journey in Ireland, 1921*
Fay, W. G., *The Fays of the Abbey Theatre*
Fianna Fail. An Chead Treimhse
Figgis, Darrell, *Irishmen of Today. A.E. and George W. Russell*
Files of *'An Saorstat'*
Fitzpatrick, W. J., *The Life of Charles Lever*
Fitz-Patrick, W. F., *The Sham Squire and Informers of 1798*
Flower, Robin, *The Western Island*
Francis, A. L. and Tatum, H. F., *Martial's Epigrams*
Fraser, G. S., *W. B. Yeats*
Gallagher, Frank, *Days Without Fear*
Gibbon, Monk, *The Masterpiece and the Man. Yeats as I Knew Him*
Glover, T. R., *The Ancient World*
Gogarty, Oliver St John and O'Connor, Joseph (Alpha and Omega), *Blight*
Gogarty, Oliver St John, *An Offering of Swans and Other Poems*
           As I Was Walking Down Sackville Street
           Collected Poems
           Elbow Room

Gogarty, Oliver St John, *I Follow St Patrick*
It Isn't This Time of Year at All
Mad Grandeur
Mr Petunia
Tumbling in the Hay
Gorman, Herbert, *James Joyce*
Golding, Douglas, *A Stranger in Ireland*
Grant, Michael, *Roman Literature*
Roman Readings
Gregory, Lady, *Journals, 1916–1930*
Gwynn, Denis, *Edward Martyn and the Irish Revival*
The Life of John Redmond
Gwynn, Stephen, *The Life and Friendships of Dean Swift*
Saints and Scholars
Hall, J. B., *Random Records of a Reporter*
Harris, Frank, *Oscar Wilde. His Life and Confessions*, vols I and II
Harrison, Capt. Henry, *The Neutrality of Ireland*
Harrison, Wilmot, *Memorable Dublin Houses*
Headlam, Maurice, *Irish Reminiscences*
Healy, Maurice, *The Old Munster Circuit*
Healy, T. M., *Letters and Leaders of My Day*
Hegarty, P. S. P., *History of Ireland Under the Union, 1801–1922*
Hogan, David, *The Four Glorious Years*
Holt, Edgar, *Protest in Arms. The Irish Troubles, 1916–1923*
Hone, Joseph, *The Life of George Moore*
W. B. Yeats
Hull, Eleanor, *Cuchulain – The Hound of Ulster*
Hudson, William Henry, *The Story of the Renaissance*
Hutchins, Patricia, *James Joyce's Dublin*
James Joyce's World
Hyde, Douglas, *The Story of Early Gaelic Literature*
Hyde, H. Montgomery, *Carson*
Inglis, Brian, *The Story of Ireland*
Ireland, Denis, *Patriot Adventurer*
Irish Book, The, vol I, no. I
Ireton, Victor, *James Connolly*
Jeffares, A. Norman, *Oliver St John Gogarty* (Chatterton Lecture, 1960)
W. B. Yeats, Man and Poet
Jerrold, Walter, *A Book of Famous Wits*

Johnston, Charles, *From the Upanishads*
Joyce, James, *A Portrait of the Artist as a Young Man*
   Chamber Music
Joyce, Stanislaus, *Diaries*
   My Brother's Keeper
Kelly, W. J., *Ireland 60 Years Ago*
Kettle, T. M., *An Irishman's Calendar*
   The Day's Burden
   The Ways of War
Kitto, H. D. F., *The Greeks*
Lang, A., *Theocritus, Bion and Moschus*
Laver, James, *Whistler*
Lavery, Sir John, *The Life of a Painter*
Lawrence, T. E., *Seven Pillars of Wisdom*
Lazenby, Elizabeth, *Ireland – A Catspaw*
Lecky, William Edward Hartpole, *A History of Ireland in the Eighteenth Century*
Leslie, Shane, *A Film of Memory*
Lever, Charles, *Charles O'Malley*
Lewis, D. B. Wyndham, *François Villon*
Longford, Christine, *A Biography of Dublin*
Lyons, George, *Some Recollections of Griffith and His Times*
Macardle, Dorothy, *The Irish Republic*
   Tragedies of Kerry (1922–3)
Macmanus, M. J., *Adventures of an Irish Bookman*
Martin, Hugh, *Ireland in Insurrection*
Martin and Oliver, *The Works of Allan Ramsay*, vols I and II
Maurois, André, *Aspects of Biography*
Maxwell, M. H., *Wild Sports of the West*
McCarthy, Desmond, *Experience*
   The Crock of Gold
McCready, Sir Nevil, *Annals of an Active Life*, vols I and II
Memoirs of Benvenuto Cellini
Memories of Father Healy of Little Bray
Midleton, Earl of, *Records and Reactions, 1856–1937*
Mitchell, Susan L., *George Moore*
Monteith, Robert, *Casement's Last Adventure*
Moore, George, *Ave, Salve and Vale* (Hail and Farewell)
   Confessions of a Young Man
   Collected Works

Moore, George, *Esther Waters*
            Muslin
            Memoirs of the Life of the Right Honourable Richard Brinsley Sheridan
Murry, Rev. Robert H., *Archbishop Bernard*
O'Brien, William, *The Irish Revolution and How It Came About*
O'Connor, Batt, *With Michael Collins*
O'Connor, Frank, *The Big Fellow* (A Life of Michael Collins)
O'Connor, Sir James, *History of Ireland, 1798–1924*, vols I and II
O'Connor, Joseph and Gogarty, Oliver St John (Alpha and Omega), *Blight*
O'Faolain, Sean, *De Valera*
O'Hegarty, P. S., *The Victory of Sinn Fein*
Oireachtas Companion and Saorstat Guide for 1928
O'Malley, Ernie, *On Another Man's Wound*
O'Sullivan, Donal, *The Irish Free State and Its Senate*
O'Sullivan, Seamus, *Essays and Recollections*
            Mud and Purple
Oxford Book of English Verse, 1250–1918, edited by Sir Arthur Quiller-Couch
Oxford Book of Modern Verse, edited by W. B. Yeats
Pakenham, Lord, *Peace by Ordeal*
Pearson, Hesketh, *The Man Whistler*
            The Smith of Smiths
Peter, A., *Dublin Fragments, Social and Historic*
Pollard, Capt. H. B. C., *The Secret Societies of Ireland*
Pollock, J. H., *Noted Irish Lives. William Butler Yeats*
Rabelais, *Complete Works*, translated by Urquhart
Ransome, Arthur, *Oscar Wilde*
Rebel Cork's Fighting Story
Redmond, Maj. William, *Trench Pictures from France*
Riddell, Lord, *More Pages from My Diary, 1908–1914*
Robinson, Lennox, Bryan Cooper (A Life of Wolfe Tone)
            Ireland's Abbey Theatre. A History, 1899–1951
            Palette and Plough (A life of Desmond O'Brien)
Ryan, A. P., *Mutiny at the Curragh*
Ryan, Desmond, *Remembering Sion*
            Sean Treacy and the Third Tipperary Brigade
            Unique Dictator (A life of Eamon de Valera)
Salute to the Soldiers of 1922 (Brian O'Higgins)

Secret Springs of Dublin Song (Talbot Press Ltd, 1918)
Seventy Years Young. Memories of the Countess of Fingall, edited
    by Pamela Hinkson
Sherard, R. D., *Life of Oscar Wilde*
Sheridan, Clare, *To the Four Winds*
Sheridan, John D., *Mangan*
Song of Roland, The, translated by Dorothy L. Sayers
Stanford, W. B., *The Ulysses Theme*
Stephens, James, *Essay on Arthur Griffith*
                 The Insurrection in Dublin
Street, C. J. C., *The Administration of Ireland*
Strong, L. A. G., *Personal Remarks*
            The Minstrel Boy
Studies. An Irish quarterly review. 1935
Sullivan, A. M., *The Last Serjeant*
Swinburne's Poems. Collected Volumes
Swinnerton, Frank, *The Georgian Literary Scene*
Tayor, Rex, *Michael Collins*
Téry, Simon, *En Irlande*
Unificus, *Ireland's Opportunity.* Introduction by W. F. Trench
Wade, Allan, *The Letters of W. B. Yeats*
What's Past is Prologue (A history of Dublin medicine), edited by
    William Doolin and Oliver Fitzgerald
White, Capt. J. R., *Misfit*
White, N. J. D., *Some Recollections of Trinity College, Dublin*
White, Terence de Vere, *Kevin O'Higgins*
Wilde, Oscar, *A Critic in Pall Mall*
Wilson, T. G., *Victorian Doctor* (A life of Sir William Wilde)
Wolfe, Humbert, *The Life of George Moore*
Wright, Arnold, *Disturbed Dublin* (A history of the 1913 strike)
Yeats, W. B., *Autobiographies*
        Images of a Poet
        On the Boiler

INDEX